A CENTURY
OF OUTBOARD RACING

A CENTURY

KEVIN DESMOND

OF OUTBOARD RACING

This edition first published in 2001
by MBI Publishing Company,
729 Prospect Avenue, PO Box 1, Osceola,
WI 54020-0001, USA

Edited by Gérald Guétat

Previously published in 2000,
copyright © Editions Van de Velde Maritime,
37230 Fondettes, France, under the title :
Un siècle de Hors-Bord - Courses et records.

The information in this book is true and complete
to the best of our knowledge. All recommenda-
tions are made without any guarantee on the part
of the author or publisher, who also disclaim any
liability incurred in connection with the use
of this data or specific details.

We recognize that some words, model names
and designations, for example, mentioned herein
are the property of the trademark holder. We use
them for identification purposes only. This is not
an official publication.

MBI Publishing Company books are also available
at discounts in bulk quantity for industrial or
sales-promotional use. For details write to Special
Sales Manager at Motorbooks International
Wholesalers & Distributors, 729 Propect Avenue,
PO Box 1, Osceola, WI 54020-0001, USA.

Library of Congress Cataloging-in-Publication
Data Available.
ISBN 0-7603-1047-5

Printed in Spain by Artes Gráficas Toledo S.A.U.
D.L. TO: 317-2001

Ackowledgments

I am indebted to Charles D. Strang (alias RO115) for his sustained advice and support throughout a challenging international project. Also to my editor and fellow powerboating historian, Gérald Guétat, without forgetting the careful reviewing of this edition by Peter Hunn.

Many thanks also go
to the following :
Russell Ackley
Peter Allen
The Antique Outboard Club Inc.
Ray Bulman
Mike Beard
Dr. Armando Boscolo
Dave Burgess
Guido Cappellini (DAC)
Julie Canavan (National Motor
Boat Museum, England)
Rod Champkin
Clive Curtis
" Wild Bill " Cantrell
Burmah-Castrol Trading Ltd.
Cougar Holdings
E.T. Bedford Davie
L.J. Derrington
J.-V. Deguisne
Alan Darby
Chris Davies (Formula
Photographic)
Brian Dewey (Photocall)
Peter Dredge (R.Y.A.)
Colin D. Fair
François Fouger

Federazione Italiana
Motonautica (Luciano Cucchia)
the Earl of Granard
Bart and Gary Garbrecht
Gérald Guétat
Fred Hauenstein and Rick
Mackie (Mercury Marine)
John Hill
Chris Hodges
Peter Hunn
Jon Jones
Count J.E.Johnston-Noad
Teruo Kaneko (Marine Sports
Foundation of Japan)
Dieter König
Renato Levi
Ocke Mannerfelt
John Merryfield
Len Melly
Anthony Meyer
Giorgio Molinari
David Moore
Roger Moreau
Bob and John May
Anthony Needell
Rosalind Nott
OMC

David Parkinson
Tom Percival
Carlo Leto di Priolo
Roland Prout
Guido Romani
Michel Rousse
Bob Spalding
Bill Seebold Jr.
Dieter Schulze
Eric See
Bert Savidge
Charlie Sheppard
Oivind Sivertsen
Richard K. Stoff
Bob Switzer
Regine Vandekerckove (UIM)
Angelo Vassena
John Walker
Jackie Wilson
Giovanni Alberto Zanoletti
di Rozzano
Special thanks also
to Catherine Chaboisson
and Line Sionneau
for their patience and warmth.

BENINI, Aroldo and CORTI, Marco : « Pietro Vassena et il suo C3 ; storia di un inventore » progetto di Angelo Vassena. (Cattaneo Editore 1999)

BOSCOLO, Armando : « 75 anni di F.I.M» (Federazione Italiana Motonautica 1998)

DESMOND, Kevin : « The Guinness Book of Motorboating Facts & Feats & Origins & Development of Motor Craft » (Guinness Superlatives Ltd. 1979)

DESMOND, Kevin : « Bud's Brilliant Career » (« Boat International » N°6 1985)

DESMOND, Kevin : « Power Boat Speed - Racing and Record Breaking 1897 to the present » (Conway Maritime Press 1988)

FJARLIE, Craig : « The Offspring of Cameron Beach Waterman : A History of Outboard racing in the Northwest »

HUNN, Peter : « The Old Outboard Book » (International Marine, 1994)

RODENGEN, Jeffrey L : « Iron Fist : the lives of Carl Kiekhaefer, industrial Caesar of a marine industry empire.» (Write Stuff Syndicate, Inc. 1991)

RODENGEN, Jeffrey L : « Evinrude - Johnson and the Legend of OMC (Write Stuff Syndicate, Inc. 1993)

STRANG, Charles D : « With the Outboarders » (« Motorboating » 1950-1963)

SPELTZ, Bob : « A Real Runabouts Review of Outboard Motors » (1991)

WEBB, W. J. with CARRICK, Robert W : « The Pictorial History of Outboard Motors » (Renaissance Editions Inc. NY 1967)

UIM Yearbooks

Contents

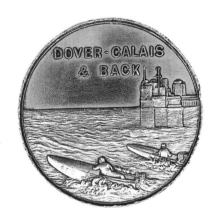

Foreword

As the 19th century segued into the 20th, innovators everywhere were seeking to apply the new and exciting internal combustion engine to all forms of transportation - on land, in the air and on the water. Thus it was that the automobile, the airplane and the outboard motorboat all appeared on the scene within a decade or so of each other.

Since that time, roughly 100 years ago, all three vehicles have been widely used in races and other contests of speed - to improve the breed technically, to promote sales to the public and to provide a challenge for daring men and women bored with everyday life. The histories of automobile and airplane racing since that beginning have been well documented, but until Kevin Desmond took up the gauntlet, nobody had brought forth a definitive history of outboard motorboat racing from its very inception to the present day.

Covering the evolution of the sport in its many forms and in its many arenas - Europe, North America and Asia - the story is presented in incredible detail. Clearly this is the result of intense library research, bolstered by interviews with people fortunate enough to have participated in creating many of the products and events which comprise much of that history. Well described are many of the technical innovations which led to the sport as we know it today. The changes have been sweeping. When I drove in my first outboard race in 1937, having just turned sixteen, the most powerful racing motor that one could buy delivered about 60 horsepower. Today racing outboards of over 300 horsepower are common, while outboards of 400-plus horsepower are not unknown. Similarly, the single-step Century Cyclone hydroplane in which I knelt for that first race would be unthinkable in today's racing. Again, the book follows the transition from the single-step hydro, as well as its predecessors, to the three-point picklefork hydros and the tunnel boats of today - all of which are now more airborne than waterborne. The result? In 1937 most of us only dreamed of ever seeing 60 mph. Now the record for an outboard raceboat stands at 176 mph! Appearing, most appropriately, just as we enter a new century, this book serves to commemorate the pioneering innovators who led the evolution of the sport through the 20th century. In

the process it provides fascinating reading for the layman and the enthusiast alike. Now we have the history of outboard racing at our fingertips. But whither the sport in the 21st century? With speeds as high as they now are - and slated to go even higher - safety has become paramount. Rule-making bodies and technical types alike are actively working to protect the race driver from his own courage. And, as outboard motors for the non-racing public undergo major technical changes to meet ever stiffer exhaust-emission goals, it is inevitable that some of this new technology will find its way into outboard racing motors.

Thus we will see a more complex and costlier sport, perhaps with fewer participants able to afford racing than was the case in the 20th century.

Yet, somehow, when the history of outboard racing in the 21st century is written, I'm sure that the sport will have continued to prosper, its appeal to the daring and competitive being as powerful as it is!

Charles D. Strang :

Mercury Marine 1951-1964, Executive Vice-President and Engineering Vice-President.

Outboard Marine Corporation 1966-1990, Chairman of the Board and Chief Executive Officer.

- Hall of Fame of the National Marine Manufacturers Association, Recipient.

- President's American Vocation Success Award (from President George Bush).

- American Power Boat Association 1937 to now, former President and currently life member of the Board of Directors.

- Union for International Motorboating 1964 to now, Vice-President.

- National Association for Stock Car Automobile Racing (NASCAR), The National Commissioner.

- Society of Automotive Engineers, Life Member.

Charles D. Strang

Preface

This book is not merely the saga of an extraordinary sport. Nor is it simply a record of one hundred years of corporate bravery, mostly based on experience, but occasionally wrecklessness. It is a tribute to engineering ingenuity and innovative logic.

It began quite innocently with a Parisian inventor overcoming the challenge of lifting his experimental electric motor on and off a boat. Twenty years later, an internal combustion-engined version was described as "detachable" and encouraged users to throw away the oars of their rowing boat. But made in cumbersome steel and bronze, the next challenge was to make it lighter. Once achieved, improved horsepower-to-weight ratio enabled those of a sportive nature to go weekend racing against each other. Thus began the never-ending challenge of seeing just how fast it could push a boat. It came to be known "the poor man's racing motorboat". But because the poor man's outboard raceboat was smaller than the rich man's inboard plaything, it became possible to innovate more frequently, and less expensively. So much so that ingenious, less expensive, lower horsepower outboards sometimes shamed cost-absorbing multiple-horsepower inboards.

When outboard horsepower began to grow in leaps and bounds, the ingenuity of the raceboat-builders was taxed to the limit. The challenge became to keep the ever-faster boat on the water, to prevent it from taking off. As monstrous horsepower threatened to turn a sport into a lethal bloodsport, the challenge was to develop a safer boat. Tomorrow, with the appearance of worldwide environmental concern, comes a new challenge - to make a cleaner, less polluting engine. This book is also a magnificent celebration of great photography, often achieved in challenging if not impossible conditions. How ironic, therefore, that the very components which seem to make up that unique lure of outboard speed are noticeably lacking from this tribute: those hypnotic, constantly changing moods of the water, coupled with the speed of colourful hulls both through and over it and that, deafening, chest-pounding roar of stern-mounted engines.

But perhaps most timeless of all, no matter when or where an outboard race took place - on Lake Pewaukee in 1911, on the Seine in 1936, or in Abu Dhabi in 1999 - those qualities which have hallmarked the great outboard drivers, have always remained the same and involve the ability to corner at the highest possible speeds commensurate with still having stability on the boat, whilst also taking advantage of other people's washes, or missing them as the case may be. You have to judge your tactics from minute to minute as you go along. You can't plan because water conditions might alter so much within seconds that you have to take instant decisions as to whether to overtake in rough water or give him a little more leeway and take a longer course round, go a bit near to the bank to get calm water. It's a feel, a touch, a care for boat and machinery. He doesn't let the seat of his pants overrule his brain when he's out on the course. He may be balls-out in the lead, then he will take it easy for a couple of laps, to cool off his motor, for he will go as fast as is necessary to win and no more. He is the driver who, when he sees the front of the boat lift, has enough brains to back off on the throttle, instead of flipping over. He is the driver able to bring his outboard boat back to the dock in one piece and say: " the bottom end is sticky on that one. I don't believe it will last much longer". This may even be in the early stages of the race. And when they pull it out, the gears may have picked up but haven't quite broken, an engine mount is coming loose, a prop-blade is out of true. So they tighten or replace it, and he gets back in that race. And even if he has slipped down to fifteenth position, he can now get back on course, and maybe win.

Such sentiments have now been hurtling round the buoys long enough for as many as four generations to both win their spurs and, on the other side of the ladder, to hang up their helmets. But enough said. Let our saga begin.

1880 : The world's first outboard-engined boat, le Telephone, *during trials on the Seine in Paris. Her mechanic bravely uses her cables to control both her power and her direction. The motor's inventor, Gustave Trouvé serves as both observer and ballast.*

A Detachable Sport

Although this book celebrates one hundred years of outboard racing, our story begins even earlier. In May 1880, a Parisian electrical precision instrument maker, Gustave Trouvé, patented a small 11 lbs electric motor and described its possible applications in the French patent n° 136,560. At first this concerned the propulsion of boats, where Trouvé envisaged two such motors each directly driving a paddle wheel on either side of the hull. After this he progressed to a multi-bladed propeller. Modifications to this master patent date from August 1880, then March, July, November and December 1881. To quote: "It is the rudder containing the propeller and its motor, the whole of which is removable and easily lifted off the boat...." With this invention, not only can Trouvé lay claim to the world's first marine outboard engine, but in taking the same motor and adapting it as the drive mechanism of a Coventry-Rotary pedal tricycle, Trouvé also pioneered the world's first electric vehicle.

On August 1st, 1881, Trouvé made his benchmark report to the French Academy of Sciences in these words: "I had the honour to submit to this Academy, in the session of July 7th, 1880, a new electric motor based on the eccentricity of the Siemens coil flange. By successive studies, which have allowed me to reduce the weight of all the components of the motor, I have succeeded in obtaining an output which to me appears quite remarkable. A motor weighing 11 lbs producing an effective work of 7 kgm per second, was placed, on April 8th, on a tricycle whose weight, including the rider and the batteries rose to 360 lbs and recorded a speed of 7.5 mph. The same motor, placed on May 26th in a boat of 18 ft long by 4 ft beam, carrying three people, gave it a speed of 2.7 yards per second in going down the Seine at Pont-Royal and 1.6 yards per second in going back up the river. The motor was driven by two bichromate of potassium batteries and with a three-bladed propeller. On June 26th, 1881, I repeated this experiment on the calm waters of the upper lake of the Bois de Boulogne, with a four-bladed propeller 11 in. in diameter and 12 elements of Ruhmkorff-type Bunsen plates,

Trouvé's revolutionary little motor is today conserved at the Musée des Arts et Métiers in Paris. Weighing only 11 lbs, the inventor designed this unit around the eccentricity of the coil flange as developed by Sir William Siemens.

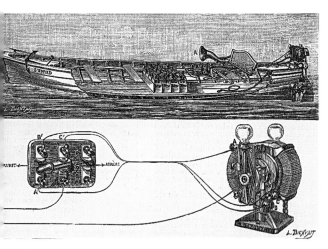

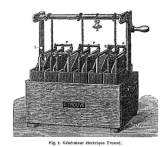

Fig. 1. Générateur électrique Trouvé;

*Trouvé simple
"Forward/Reverse"
controller.*

*A "Motogodille" produced
around 1910
with the propshaft aligned
to the crankshaft.*

*Trouvé's "electric generator"
was made up of 12 elements
of Ruhmkorff-type Bunsen
plates. One bichromate
battery, enclosed in a 1 ft 8
inches long case, would give
a constant current during
7 to 8 hours.*

charged with one part hydrochloric acid, one part nitric acid and two parts water in the porous vase so as to lessen the emission of nitrous fumes. The speed at the start, measured by an ordinary log, reached 164 yards in 48 seconds–or little more than 3.2 yards per second; but after three hours of functioning, this had fallen to 164 yards in 55 seconds and after five hours, this had further fallen to the same distance in 65 seconds."

Thus Gustave Trouvé made the first unofficial outboard speed record of 6.7 mph. He called his boat *Le Téléphone*, after an invention patented only five years before by Alexander Graham Bell.

During the fifteen years that followed, it is estimated that well over one hundred Trouvé electric motors were installed in pleasure-launches. Some of these were fitted with his new electric head-lights and electric horns. There is no record of a race, but given the number of Trouvé units sold, one feels sure that on more than one occasion enthusiastic French boatmen said "the first to reach the jetty buys the champagne!"

To show the speed with which an electric boat could move in a race situation, on October 8th, 1882, a Trouvé launched onto the River Aube was steered onto a regatta course only five minutes before the start. It left at gunfire and spectators noticed, not without astonishment that the electric boat covered more than 2 miles in 17 minutes, averaging 6.8 mph and slowing down to make four turns around the buoys.

The world's first internal combustion-engined outboard motor was the "Moto-Godille" tested in 1892 by Alfred Seguin at the Geneva Nautical Club in Switzerland. We do not know the exact configuration of this motor (it was probably a straight-shaft design) but can be certain it was not raced. As for the "portable electric boat propeller" manufactured some three years later by Frank Allen's Electric Boat Company of New York, nor was this powerful enough to be used for anything beyond fishing and duck-shooting. But as the century drew to a close, back in France, a novel marine sport was discovered. Under the aegis of the French Yachting Union, in the summer of 1898 the Meulan Sailing Club–and three weeks later the Asnières Sailing Club–both based on the River Seine, had organized some very successful races for launches powered by either steam, naptha or petrol engines, mounted inboard.

The following year, at a competition organized on the Seine by the Hélice Club de France, among the entrants was the 20 ft Paul as helmed by M. Ducassou, administrator of the Universal Detachable Engine Company. Its motor can only have been one of this company's "Autonautiles", a prototype inboard engine/outboard drive, first produced the year before. Hence we have the first time that a semi-outboard-engined boat took part in a race.

It was the following year that a 9 hp Autonautile established, perhaps, the first internal combustion outboard-engined speed record. This motor was mounted inboard but with an outboard leg. On June 16th, 1901, at the races of the Nogent-Joinville Sailing Club, the 26 ft *Albert* owned by M. Ducassou, covered 18 miles at 12.2 mph. He was also among the entries in the speed boats category for the autumn meeting of 1902 organized at

Suresnes by the Hélice-Club de France. During the next meeting in 1903, the Autonautile-engined *Propulseur II* had covered 20 miles at an average 16.7 mph.

In the USA, Cameron B. Waterman, a Yale University Law graduate with back-breaking recollections of being on the famous campus rowing team -"We never lost to Harvard"- returned to Detroit, Michigan. He started thinking about a portable gasoline propulsion system for small boats. Together with engine designer Oliver Barthel, Waterman produced a single-cylinder detachable marine motor with its flywheel enclosed in the crank case, and called it the Waterman "Outboard Porto".

Following an initial batch of 25 engines in 1906, the design was revamped with a water-cooled cylinder and no less than 3,000 outboards were built in 1907, a number of them exported to Denmark. With such a production output, the sporting attitude was bound to embrace at least a couple of Waterman "Porto" owners.

From 1904, there was an annual international powerboat racing regatta in the Mediterranean Principality of Monaco. At first, whilst most of the competitors piloted large inboard displacement hulls, a handful of designers believed that

The first Waterman "Outboard Porto" engine.

An early english Watermota engine, "Sectional model" of 1923

The Anzani-engined Motogodille "glisseur" on show here at the 1906 Monaco Exhibition. Here is one of the world's first outboard-engined hydroplanes.

One of the first Evinrude manufactured around 1910.

In an age where businesswomen were rare, Bess Evinrude made a great success of her husband's invention.

An early model of Swedish engine Archimedes. Note the rudder fin attached to the lower unit.

they could obtain the same speeds by fitting smaller engines into smaller boats whose stepped hull bottoms enabled them to skim across the water like a flat stone. On April 9th, 1907, there was a 6.2 miles pioneer race off Monaco harbour for three such "hydroplanes": Count de Lambert's *Glisseur*; then the Le Las brothers, Maurice and Claude, with their Bonnemaison-patented *Obus-Ricochet-Nautilus*, its Mutel engine driving an aerial propeller; and finally the 36-year-old Gabriel Trouche who had mounted one of his 8 hp alternate-firing twin Anzani-engined "Motogodilles" on the back of a Boisford hydroplane fitted with windshield, bucket seat and spray rails. The Le Las brothers' boat maintained a winning speed of 20 mph.

Back in the USA, in 1908, 31-year-old, Norwegian-born, pattern maker and engineer, Ole Evinrude, was persuaded by his wife Bess that it would be a shrewd move to market the single-cylinder iron and brass detachable rowboat motor, which he had taken a couple of years to quietly develop and now successfully test on the local Kinnikinnic River near Milwaukee, Wisconsin. Having cleaned up its ugly "coffee-grinder" appearance, Evinrude now bought and made parts for 25 engines. After a friend's demonstration of the motor on Pewaukee Lake, Evinrude received orders for ten motors, which he hand-built himself and sold for $62 each. These were single-cylinder, water-cooled units, developing 1.5 hp at 1,000 rpm and weighing 60 lbs. Following many orders promoted by Bess Evinrude's publicity campaigning and business acumen, in 1911 Chris Meyer, President of Meyer Tug Boat Lines, put up $5,000 and became a 50 % partner in the Evinrude Motor Company.

It so happened that Chris Meyer was a keen yachtsman. As a charter member of the Pewaukee Yacht Club, Meyer sailed a 38 ft "A" Class Scow, sloop rigged with light canvas sails. So it was perhaps quite logical that the first outboard race for Evinrude owners took place during a club regatta in 1911 on Lake Pewaukee. There was a panel of judges, course buoys, starting cannon, a chequered flag, a gun for the finish and cups for prizes. Of this pioneer field of contestants piloting bulky, flat-bottomed rowboats and skiffs, we do not know the name of the winner.

By this time, the family firm of Evinrude was employing 300 people and working furiously in a specially built factory to satisfy orders for the domestic market and abroad. Oluf Mikkelsen of the New York export firm of Melchior, Armstrong & Dessau, was responsible for the arrival of the Evinrude detachable in Scandinavia. Following an initial shipment of two motors, then six, then fifty units to Denmark, cabled orders very quickly arrived from Norway and Sweden. Through Bess Evinrude's cleverness, the company soon received an order for one thousand units.

Naturally, this soon led to outboard racing on the nordic fjords. Indeed in a 1912 advert, Evinrude stated: "... Awarded special prize for Endurance and Reliability at Stockholm, Sweden Motor Boat Races 1911..."

Also, in 1912, the Swedish engineering brothers, Carl Alrik and Oskar Alfrid Hult, built and internationally patented the world's first two-cylinder production detachable motor, employing the so-called "balance" system with one cylinder on each side of the crankshaft. It was also the first outboard motor in the world that could be tilted up. This first 2.5 hp "Archimedes" engine was soon followed by a 5 hp unit, primarily intended to propel barges and workboats.

*The Evinrude was
a single-cylinder,
two-stroke, water-cooled
unit, developing 1.5 hp
at 1.000 rpm
and weighing 60 lbs.*

Don't Row
use the
Evinrude
Detachable
ROW BOAT MOTOR

Clamped on any square stern boat
in 2 minutes. Simple and Compact.
Clean. Reliable and Lasting. Easily
carried by hand. Engine weighs
only 32 lbs.

EVINRUDE MOTOR CO.
220 Lake Street, Milwaukee, U.S.A.

*Dreamed up one evening
by Bess as she sat
at the kitchen table,
this slogan made an
irresistable appeal to folk
who liked to go pleasure-
boating in a lazy way.*

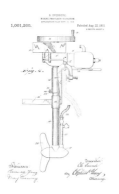

*Evinrude US Patent
drawing dated 1911.*

Cover of the 1917 Evinrude Motors Catalogue. Ready for a picnic, but hardly dressed for racing !

Evinrude's workforce grew rapidly. Here is a team photo outside the factory. Ole is on the bottom row, seventh from the left.

Archimedes soon became the largest–but not the only–manufacturer of outboards motors in Europe.

Whilst the Evinrude was already on sale in Great Britain, by May 1912, in France, the mail-order firm of Manufrance began to import the Evinrude from Milwaukee and offered it in their catalogue under the name of "Propulsor" for 425 FF. Two years later, Marcel Echard, based on the Seine near Paris, had begun to manufacture a "moteur amovible" very similar to the Evinrude, but whose small steering wheel enabled it to be steered into reverse. Inevitably Evinrude owners were soon racing against Archimedes in Sweden and against Echards in France to see who has the most powerful.

In Italy, a young man by name of Serafino Riva succeeded in travelling at over 14 mph in an outboard raceboat on Lake Iseo in Northern Italy. This was the beginning of a line of Riva motorboats, climaxing in a range of increasingly deluxe inboard mahogany runabouts developped by his son Carlo who would make Riva of Sarnico world famous.

Back in the States, to further promote their outboard, Bess Evinrude ordered a specially engraved "Evinrude Cup" and staged their own race. Unfortunately the April 1914 four-mile event did not provide the firm with any usable publicity. Some entrants from California showed up with a "hot" Waterman outboard motor and won the Evinrude Trophy! As Waterman sold off his company the following year and soon disappeared from outboard history, this defeat was largely ignored.

Unofficial rowboat-motor-racing continued between brands. Against Evinrude competition, Koban of Milwaukee and Ferro of Cleveland, Ohio, were both producing "portable" rowboat motors developing all of 3 hp at 900 rpm and, made of iron and bronze, weighing in at a cumbersome 85 lbs, some 35 lbs heavier–hence slower–than the Evinrude.

Most of these detachable motors were started by turning a wooden knob on the flywheel with sufficient vigour to crank up the engine. Beware, for, once started, that same knob could come round and crack you on the knuckles. So, these engines were often nicknamed "knuckle-busters". Soon after the Caille brothers of Detroit came up with a more painless system of a self-winding starter rope. The best choice of boats for racing during this period was the square-stern canoe, its slim hull displacing less water than beamier rowboats.

In France, on June 28th, 1914, at a regatta at Lagny-sur-Marne, there were two races for detachable motors of single-cylinder and multi-cylinder output. Six competitors took part in the second event, won by M. Desvignes in an Echard-engined boat. Unknown to him, this race took place on the very day that Gabriel Princzip assassinated the Archduke Franz Ferdinand and the Duchess of Hohenberg at Sarajevo, which event was the fatal spark which set off World War I. Not unnaturally, another event organized by the French Motor Yacht Club for "motocanots" scheduled to start on the Seine at Herblay that July, never took place. That same year, the overworked, exhausted Evinrudes sold out to co-director Meyer for $140,000 and went on an extended vacation, on the understanding that Ole would not re-enter the outboard market for five years.

Seven years later, in 1921, the Evinrude family team was back in business with the first outboard motor to make extensive use of aluminium alloy as developed for the aircraft industry during the War. Called by Bess the "Evinrude Light Twin Outboard" or ELTO, it weighed only 48 lbs. This was a horizontally-opposed unit developing 3 hp, with its underwater exhaust through the pro-

In 1912, Marcel Echard, based near Paris began begun to manufacture a "moteur amovible" very similar to the Evinrude, but whose small steering wheel enabled it to be helmed into reverse.

In 1911, Chris Meyer became a 50% partner in the Evinrude Motor Co. In this rare family photo, Meyer shows a cleverly mounted Evinrude on a double-ender canoe for cruising on Lake Pewaukee.

peller hub as another innovation. As Evinrude President Chris Meyer showed lit-tle interest in this innovation, Ole and Bess decided to create a new company, called of course Elto Outboard Motor Company. Their new outboard's lightness was soon pushing square-stern canoes to 10 mph - fast in outboarding circles. Some 1,051 units were sold in their first year of business, followed by 3,549 units in 1922. Over in South Bend, Indiana State, on the banks of the St Joe River, the Johnson brothers–Clarence, Harry and Julius "Lou"–had been work-ing with a Norwegian-born, Purdue University engineering graduate called Finn T. Irgens on the development of a 2 hp twin cylinder alloy outboard, with full-pivot steering and reverse, weighing only 35 lbs. It bore little resemblance to other outboards on the market at that time when more than 30 companies crowd-ed the field.

A friend of the Johnson brothers, Warren Conover built a very lightweight boat, known as *The Scooter* or *The Shingle*, 9 ft long and weighing only 40 lbs, in order to test the prototype engine: "I could not for the life of me get the boat to plane, as the propeller would cavitate, so I put a short drive shaft through the bottom of the hull and I was in the fast boat business at 14 mph. It really planed beautifully, but not with me and my 180 lbs. My son Clay was then eleven years old, so I put him in the boat, and that was the first time I know of that a boat was planed by an outboard motor." Introduced at the 1922 New York Boat Show, the Johnson "Light Twin" soon gained the nickname of "The Waterbug". Over 3,000 motors were sold that first year at $140 each.

Ole Evinrude tests his latest innovation —the Elto—the first outboard motor to make extensive use of aluminium alloy as developed for the aircraft industry during WWI. Called by Bess the "Evinrude Light Twin Outboard", it weighed only 48 lbs.

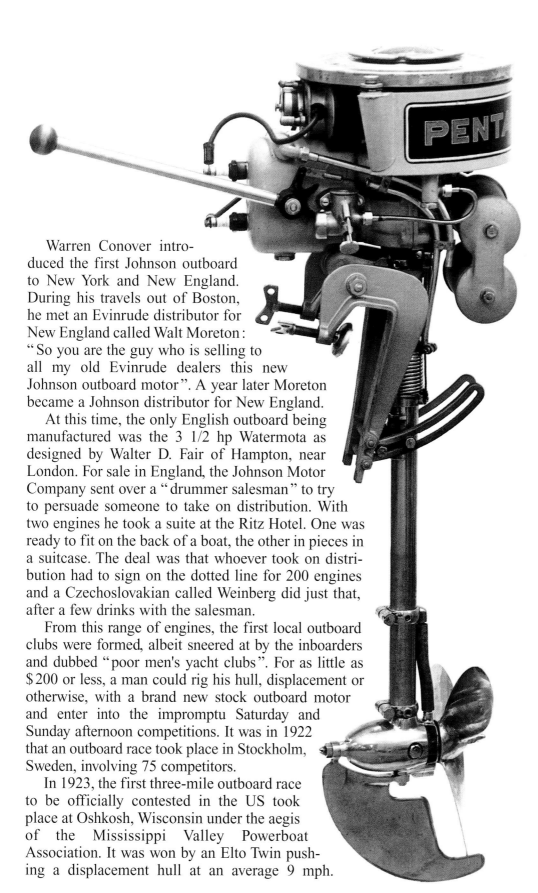

The renowned Penta U2 outboard first appeared in 1922. It remained in production in a practically unchanged form up to 1953.

Warren Conover introduced the first Johnson outboard to New York and New England. During his travels out of Boston, he met an Evinrude distributor for New England called Walt Moreton: "So you are the guy who is selling to all my old Evinrude dealers this new Johnson outboard motor". A year later Moreton became a Johnson distributor for New England.

At this time, the only English outboard being manufactured was the 3 1/2 hp Watermota as designed by Walter D. Fair of Hampton, near London. For sale in England, the Johnson Motor Company sent over a "drummer salesman" to try to persuade someone to take on distribution. With two engines he took a suite at the Ritz Hotel. One was ready to fit on the back of a boat, the other in pieces in a suitcase. The deal was that whoever took on distribution had to sign on the dotted line for 200 engines and a Czechoslovakian called Weinberg did just that, after a few drinks with the salesman.

From this range of engines, the first local outboard clubs were formed, albeit sneered at by the inboarders and dubbed "poor men's yacht clubs". For as little as $200 or less, a man could rig his hull, displacement or otherwise, with a brand new stock outboard motor and enter into the impromptu Saturday and Sunday afternoon competitions. It was in 1922 that an outboard race took place in Stockholm, Sweden, involving 75 competitors.

In 1923, the first three-mile outboard race to be officially contested in the US took place at Oshkosh, Wisconsin under the aegis of the Mississippi Valley Powerboat Association. It was won by an Elto Twin pushing a displacement hull at an average 9 mph.

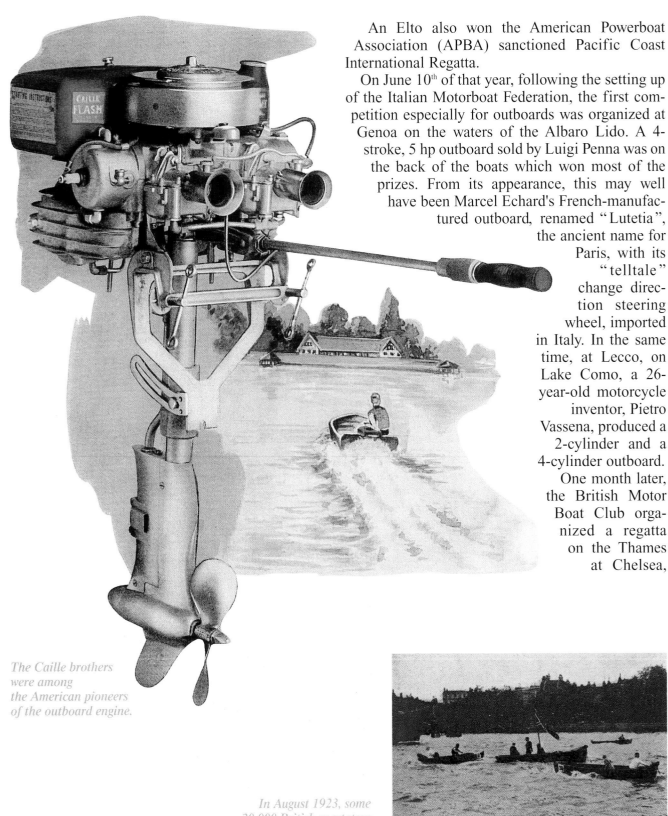

An Elto also won the American Powerboat Association (APBA) sanctioned Pacific Coast International Regatta.

On June 10th of that year, following the setting up of the Italian Motorboat Federation, the first competition especially for outboards was organized at Genoa on the waters of the Albaro Lido. A 4-stroke, 5 hp outboard sold by Luigi Penna was on the back of the boats which won most of the prizes. From its appearance, this may well have been Marcel Echard's French-manufactured outboard, renamed "Lutetia", the ancient name for Paris, with its "telltale" change direction steering wheel, imported in Italy. In the same time, at Lecco, on Lake Como, a 26-year-old motorcycle inventor, Pietro Vassena, produced a 2-cylinder and a 4-cylinder outboard. One month later, the British Motor Boat Club organized a regatta on the Thames at Chelsea,

The Caille brothers were among the American pioneers of the outboard engine.

In August 1923, some 20,000 British spectators watched an outboard regatta on the Thames.

An early, friendly outboard race, circa 1923. One at the helm, the other to keep the bows low.

London. Almost 20,000 people watched from riverbanks. Although the program was largely for inboard boats, event n° 4 on the program was a handicap race for outboard motor dinghies not exceeding 18 ft. It was won by Frank Snoxell in his Elto-engined 16 ft narrow river skiff, *Alicia* at 6.7 mph. Second and third places were taken by 2.5 hp Knight-engined boats.

Such was the acceleration of interest in the US that in 1924, the APBA hurriedly worked out a set of rules to apply to boats powered by detachable motors :
Class A : under 12 cubic inches (200 cc)
Class B : 12 to 17 cubic inches (200 cc to 280 cc)
Class C : 17 to 30 cubic inches (280 cc to 500 cc)
Class D : 30 and over (500 cc to...)

But despite their light weight, at only 2 or 3 hp neither the Elto nor the Johnson was powerful enough to make a boat plane with an adult on board. What was needed was a doubling in horsepower and this is exactly the step that the red-haired Johnson brothers took.

The First Horsepower Race

They called it, quite simply, the Johnson "Big Twin". With a capacity of 22.73 cubic inches, it developed 6 horsepower, weighed just 80 lbs and was priced at $190. It was the first outboard to incorporate die-castings. The Big Twin was first tested on the St Joe River in the summer of 1925. A couple of weeks later, on July 4th, it made its first public appearance at White Lake, Michigan. Every race at that regatta was won with Johnson Big Twins. Warren Conover, now the Johnson factory manager, used it to clock 16.68 mph so breaking the existing speed record by 11 mph. During the rest of that year, the Johnson new engine progressively increased the record up to 23.32 mph - some 4 to 5 miles faster than most had considered an outboard capable of. The Johnson engine arrived in Europe. On Sunday May 24th, 1925, a baton-carrying relay race for outboards of 250 cc and 500 cc took place in France on the Seine at Maisons-Lafitte. Of the five boats which took part, three of them were Motogodilles, although the Allied Machinery Company entered an imported Johnson. Indeed the outboard race was now becoming sufficiently entertaining for several to be staged between heats of the 1925 Gold Cup Regatta at Long Island Sound.

To go with their engines, Johnson Motors sponsored the 14 ft "Baby Buzz" hydroplane with its stepless planing bottom. By the end of 1926 the Johnson-engined Baby Buzz was everywhere.

Such outboard speeds were bound to catch the public's fancy. Other motor makers and boat builders took note. Hull shapes were modified to make the best of the power available and new outboard speeds were racked up almost daily. One of those who enjoyed the family sport then was driver Bill Cantrell: "You cranked the motor with the throttle wide open, sometimes it fired, then you laid on hull and steered with a tiller. One day in a race on the Ohio River, my hands were greasy and they started slipping, then I started wobbling all over and ran over a couple of canoes and an anchor line, finishing up on the bank".

Here is the revolutionary Elsinore hull. Notice its side wings, which enabled it to use a slight tunnel-hull to ride on three points.

Higher speeds were achieved with more sophisticated hulls, for the "poor men's yacht clubs" had a distinct advantage over the "big buck inboarders" in that it cost them far less to experiment. H.G. Ferguson, nicknamed "The Californian Blue Streak", was one of these. He began to develop and test-drive outboard-engined hydroplanes that used a slight tunnel-hull to ride on three points. For the next four years, Ferguson, one of the first drivers to get brand new factory engines, was virtually unbeatable. One of the first outboard marathon races also took place in1926. The course, from New York to Bear Mountain and back to New York, covered 71 miles. It was won by Vic Withstandly in four hours, 46 minutes using a 6 hp Johnson Big on the back of a 16 ft hydroplane. It was also in 1926 that the three-year-old, Brussels-based Union Internationale de Yachting Automobile (UIYA) decided to rule outboard-racing with cubic capacities such as 250 cc, 350 cc, and 500 cc. Over in England, 24-year-old Colin Fair of the Walter D. Fair engine-manufacturing company in Teddington, was persuaded by the company draughtsman, Walter Lunn, that getting their Watermota engine involved with racing might boost sales. Colin asked his friend, brilliant Japanese engine designer Shingi Yano, to design a cylinder to give their current outboard greater power. The result was the Watermota "Speed Model", built in only six weeks. It had a bore and stroke of 3 inches, developing 11 hp at 4,000 rpm with a cubic capacity of 345 cc and weighing only 65 lbs. Meanwhile, Colin Fair had a pattern-maker build him a 10 ft racing hydroplane to plans of Bruno Beckhardt's successful *Nize Baby* as published in an American boating magazine. Fair called the boat *British Maid I*: "The great day came when I tested out a brand new racing engine on the boat. At first I ploughed along at 4.5 mph, leaving a terrific wash behind. There must have been sufficient vibration from the vortex to break off our standard rudder, because as I started to climb up forward to see if I could get the bows down, suddenly, without warning at all, she accelerated to 25 mph! I rolled from the bow to the stern and to my amazement, *British Maid*

By using Elsinore hulls and supplied with brand new factory engines, H.G. Ferguson was virtually unbeatable.

remained on a straight course". *British Maid* became the most successful British outboard-engined hydro of 1927. Her first significant race was run in presence of Major Henry Segrave. Not long before, the Major had created a new World Land Speed Record of 203.7 mph on Daytona Beach, Florida. Soon after, Gar Wood gave Segrave a further thrill by taking him as passenger on a high-speed run in his twin aero-engined *Miss America V* hydroplane. For Wood was now desperate that someone make a serious challenge for the Harmsworth Trophy. Before they parted Wood bought an English Sunbeam car and Segrave took two 14 ft Johnson "Baby Stepper" hydroplanes back to England. Although unsuccessful against Colin Fair's *British Maid*, not long after Segrave drove his *Meteorite* to his first outboard race victory, albeit at only 20 mph. By which time, others had seen the potential of the outboard sport. Percy See, running a boat building yard at Fareham, Hampshire, found that the square after edge of his prototype outboard hydroplane caused the water flow to hinder the after planing surface and prevent maximum speed. He therefore gave his second boat, 12 ft long and called *See II*, a step with a V-shaped after edge. On See's local measured quarter mile at Fareham Creek, this boat, powered by only an 8 hp Evinrude was timed at over 30 mph on its first run out. Very soon after it was bought by the Evinrude concessionaire in London, Mr George Spicer, who re-named it *Flash I*. Whilst a Johnson-engined 12 ft dinghy made the first - albeit four-and-a-half-hour - one way crossing of the Channel, over in Germany a prototype, gearless longshaft outboard was clamped to the side of his boat by an engineer called König.

Back in the States, the latest Johnson P-35 Big Twin was stepped up to 8 hp for the 1927 season, enabling new records to be notched up almost weekly. On Labor Day, a skiff called *No Foolin* used Big Twin power to set up a new record of

Colin Fair (right) asked the brilliant engineer Shingi Yano (left), to boost the power of the Watermota engine manufactured by his father Walter D. Fair. Knowing that a pretty girl always attracted more interest, they also invited Miss Zoe Livesey to race with them.

Colin Fair tests out the new Watermota on the back of a hull built from plans published in an American boating magazine.

The name British Maid was a pun on "Made in Britain" and "young woman".

32.142 mph. Soon afterwards, Julius Herbst of Wilmington, North Carolina, piloted his *Kayo II* again with a Big Twin on the stern, to 32.32 mph.

During this time Johnson outboards were selling so well that the brothers invested in a brand new factory at Waukegan, Illinois.

Although Evinrude had taken the powerhead of his "Light Twin" and by fitting it to a more advanced leg and lower unit, created the 7 hp Elto "Speedster" in 1927, this was not enough. So Ole, working with his 21-year-old son Ralph, created America's first four-cylinder, two-cycle outboard motor. In 1928, they simply mounted one powerhead on top of another and christened it the Elto "Quad". With a cubic capacity of 40 cubic inches, the super-tuned Quad's 18 hp now enabled boats to approached 40 mph. That summer, for example, Charles Holt of Los Angeles drove his Quad-powered *Firefly II* to a new mark of 38.43 mph.

It was at this point that the APBA's Contest Board refined their racing rules for outboard including revised engine class limits, divisions for amateur (I) and free-for-all (II) classes, stock motor definition, approved course lengths and methods for starting and timing.

Engines classes were now divided as follows:
Lightweights: 5-10 cu/in = 1-3 hp
Class A: < 14 cu/in = < 250 cc = 6-10 hp
Class B: < 20 cu/in = < 350 cc = 12-15 hp
Class C: < 30 cu/in = < 500 cc = 18-22 hp
Class D: < 40 cu/in = < 650 cc = 25-30 hp
Class E: < 50 cu/in = < 850 cc = 30-35 hp
Class F: < 60 cu/in = < 1,000 cc = 36-40 hp

Under these rules, better organized races and mile trials took place from Lake Elsinore on the West Coast to Lake Quinsigamond on the East Coast. Speeds increased in Classes A to F. It was during the Midwest regatta at Peoria, on September 29th and 30th, 1928 that, according to the magazine *Rudder*: "Several hundred speed boat fans watched new world's records hung up in quick succession

Old Town was one of the first competitors to pioneer offshore racing from Boston to New York on June 16th, 1928.

of events. A number of marks made by the outboard racers are so remarkable that they are likely to stand unbroken for some time to come." One of these was the Class D record average of 41.748 mph, based on six runs, created by a home-town Peoria boy called Eldon Travers in *Spirit of Peoria*, a 12 ft Boyd-Martin "Bullet Jr" hull designed by Frederick Martin and built by Jack Boyd of Delphi, Indiana. Her power came from - obviously - an Elto Quad engine.

The Quad was becoming legendary taking the industry by storm and beating everything in sight. By the end of the season, Elto held the top time trial records in racing. That year Elto sold over 10,000 units, although Johnson still remained the most popular manufacturer with more than double this volume.

Proving an outboard's reliability through marathon racing also caught on. Half a dozen such "back-breakers" were held across the States. It began in April with a 125-mile haul on the Hudson River from Albany to New York. Out of 100 entries, the twenty-one participants could select any one of four days, these being the Saturday and Sunday of two successive weekends. Before its first running, atrocious weather made the race committee estimate that the 15 competing boats would take at least 12 hours to reach New York. Fortunately, some of the commit-

tee disagreed with this opinion and travelled direct to the finish in time to welcome the winner - 4 hours 44 minutes later - Kirk Amos in the Evinrude-engined *Baby Whale*, averaging 29.7 mph.

A 250-mile race from Boston to New York, staged by the New England Outboard Motor Boat Association saw 34 outboarders shepherded by no less than three Coast Guard destroyers and twenty 75 ft cutters. To win, C.P. Stevens piloted his Class C Evinrude/Sea Sled *Corker* for a gruelling 14 hours.

Perhaps most challenging of all was a 203-mile grind from Peoria to St. Louis along the Mississippi River where people threw gasoline cans to the boats. Some 47 outboards started and of the 20 which reached St. Louis, speed record holder Eldon Travers of Peoria averaged a winning 33 mph over six hours in his Elto/Hooton skiff.

American outboards also did well abroad. Following a trip to America where he had personally watched the growing popularity of outboard racing, wealthy English sportsman Count John Edward Johnston-Noad returned home convinced that a mass-start race could be staged by the outboard section of the British Motor Boat Club of which he was vice-commodore. Winning the Duke of York's Trophy for the second time in his 1.5-litre inboard-engined hydroplane at a speed only just superior to the fastest outboard motivated the energetic monocled Count to campaign for a really successful regatta.

As a fitting sequel to her husband's Trophy, the Duchess of York consented to present a trophy for Class C (350 to 500 cc) outboards, whilst *The Motor Boat* magazine put up a parallel trophy for Class B (250 to 350 cc).

In July 1928, thousands lined the banks of the Welsh Harp Lake at Hendon, North London to watch both these contests and a stunt where a Puss Moth bi-plane bombarded a circling Chris-Craft runabout with sacks of flour. An impressive 77

Slightly choppy waters help the boat reach planing speed.

C.P. Stevens drove his Evinrude Classe C Corker to victory at the Boston to New York race.

John Edward Johnston-Noad organised a very popular outboard meeting near London in 1928.

outboard-engined boats competed, nine of them built by See of Fareham, powered by Evinrude 486 cc units. *Sea Hopper* driven by Harry J. Bomford, a stock-broker who had never raced before, won the Duchess of York's Trophy, averaging 30.71 mph for the nine miles. Colin Fair won *The Motor Boat* Trophy in his Watermota-engined *British Maid*. Another of those dedicated to racing See hulls was Jack S. Holroyd, an ex pre-1914 Isle of Man T.T. motorcycle rider with a great experience in engine tuning. When Holroyd turned up at the Hendon meeting with his boat called *See I*, officials refused such blatant advertising. Changing the name to *Sea Bee* then and there, he had placed third at 29.1 mph in the Duchess's race.

The success of the Hendon meeting led to Count Johnston-Noad's founding the British Outboard Racing Club, with a handful of motorsporting British aristocrats heading its committee, planning to landscape the Welsh Harp Lake into a regular outboard race circuit for subsequent seasons. Meanwhile, Holroyd and the Hon. Victor Bruce approached Percy See for a hull with which Mrs Bruce could attempt a double crossing of the English Channel. Percy built one of his standard "Type IV" hulls, using a partially flexible canvas bonding, sandwiched between its planks. Fitted with an Elto Quad as supplied by Jack W. Shillan, that September the red-coloured *Mosquito* only took one hour 40 minutes to make the crossing. By that time the ever-industrious Fareham Creek yard had produced the See "Type V", a stretched-out version of the IV. Around a skeleton of steamed timbers there was a double skin of inner silver spruce and outer mahogany and a double-skinned spruce bottom. Beside a seven-gallon gas tank in the bows, there was both a sliding cockpit cover and a sliding steering wheel, otherwise

known as the See "Patent Telescopic Steering System". This enabled a driver to lean forward along the foredeck to get his hydroplane over the hump and then lean back whilst still in control of his steering. A Captain Bilby was the first to acquire a Type V, which he called *Caillach,* and with a four-cylinder Johnson Utility model, clocked a healthy 34 mph. That summer Harry Bomford and his *Seahopper* cleaned up in races at Shoreham, Ostend for the King of the Belgians Trophy and Glasgow for the Scottish Championships. With a new and modified *Seahopper II,* Bomford came second at 38.55 mph at the Sussex Motor Yacht Club's outboard race, Jack Holroyd third in *Sea Bee* at 35.7 mph, George Newman fourth in *Queenie* and See's test-driver Arthur Browning fifth in *Tiny Tim,* all of them being See hulls. Then in the first running of a 100-mile race on the River Bann, Northern Ireland, *Seahopper II* led for 25 out of the 30 laps and took second place, averaging 26.46 mph, only 3 mph slower than the winner. Holroyd had George Spikins to time him on the measured mile at Poole. With an Elto Quad, *Sea Bee* clocked an unofficial 41 mph - equivalent to the World record homologated across the Atlantic by the APBA.

American hulls were also improved. Mr. Sechermann founded the Century Boat Company at Milwaukee, Wisconsin, where he employed the experienced design abilities of John L. Hacker and George Eddy. Before long Century's "Cyclone", "Kid" and "Hurricane" hulls were competing against Al Buffington's "Cute Craft" designs right across America. Other builders included Penn Yan, Ludington and Hooten. There was the Bossert "Pirate", built by an early and large producer of prefabricated houses in the New York area. Most of these were long, slender single step hydroplanes with hard chines that made them prone to barrel roll in the turns. J. Lewis Chapman of Albert Hickman's Sea Sled Corporation of West Mystic, Connecticut, entered several outboard-engined sea-sleds in races and found them fully capable of over 25 mph. This was the beginning of the outboard-engined tunnel hull.

To lesser extent, small outboard-engined hydrofoils began to appear on the race circuits, designed by Casey Baldwin, colleague of the late Alexander Graham Bell. From their record-breaking Liberty aero-engined *Hydrodome IV*, Baldwin, now working with an established New York naval architect called Philip L. Rhodes, produced *HD-9* and *HD-13* for the outboard fraternity. Although only a few of these were built for the more enterprising, they were reasonably successful.

But such racing hulls were soon to be eclipsed by the ingenious productions of a family boatyard in North Bergen, New Jersey. The latter was run by a sexagenarian of Bavarian origins by name of Jacoby. Fred Jacoby Sr., recently retired from the US Navy Yard, had begun building small dinghies at his home when his son Fred Jr. decided to go outboard racing. Jacoby Sr. built Jr. a boat. Following his first race at nearby Lake Hopatcong, New Jersey, with hands-on feedback from his son, Fred Sr. began to modify raceboats for better acceleration and cornering. As Fred Jr. began to score an increasing number of race victories, an increasing number of orders started to come in for identical hydroplanes. Naming these hulls "Flyaway", from now on "Pop" Jacoby and sons would be building an almost endless sequence of 8 to 12 footers. One of the Jacobys' earliest customers was E. T. Bedford "Bud" Davie of Tuxedo, New York, 15 years old, but not without means, thanks to his family's great wealth from corn products and the oil industry. In the decade to come, Davie and Jacoby began to develop outboard raceboats into more sophisticated machines, beginning by replacing tiller-throttle control with an automobile steering wheel. Perhaps their greatest and fiercest rival was driver-boatbuilder Dick Neal, whose hulls became the standard in middle America. To put it very mildly, Jacoby and Neal disliked each other and whenever they raced in the same event, things got rough! During one regatta in the Midwest, Neal and a number of his customers are reported to have ganged up on Jacoby, bumping and

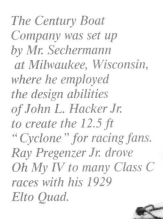

The Century Boat Company was set up by Mr. Sechermann at Milwaukee, Wisconsin, where he employed the design abilities of John L. Hacker Jr. to create the 12.5 ft "Cyclone" for racing fans. Ray Pregenzer Jr. drove Oh My IV to many Class C races with his 1929 Elto Quad.

banging him around the course. Fred swore that the next time he would race out there he would encircle his boat with projecting steel spikes.

Among the diverse races for outboard competition was the Albany-New York marathon, for which the Haynes-Griffin Trophy had been donated. In the years which followed, this marathon, in Bud Davie's opinion: "Became possibly the funniest race in the world. One hundred and twenty-five miles on your knees in a scrap of a boat. Of course, none of us knew how to read the waters of the Hudson River, so you'd run into fishermen's shard nets, mud flats, floating carcasses and God knows

what kind of garbage. The control center was at Poughkeepsie, halfway along the course. You had aeroplanes flying overhead, circling round, following you and reporting back by radio. If something happened to you, you'd wave up at the nearest aeroplane and they'd organize a trailer to come and get you out. Nobody got hurt, because nobody was going fast enough. When the winner arrived opposite 125th Street in New York, where Kate Smith would be standing on a barge singing "God Bless America", they would ask him about the race. Invariably it was the same answer "Oh nothing happened" - which meant that here was the first out of the 140 to 150 starters who had enjoyed a clear trip down the Hudson... Sprint races went on all over the country - from Maine all the way down to Florida. There were also closed circuit races, some of which were very exciting because we had such enormous entries. Most of us were interested in a race that we thought was going to be well organized, where there would be a lot of boats but especially where there was good water. I ran in Tulsa, Oklahoma, on the reservoir. At the start of each race, you had to go between the starting barge and a buoy on the other side to get to the first cornering buoy, possibly 100 yards down the course. This gave just enough room for 20 boats. But each start involved 60 boats. So we had our starting tricks. Everybody had a different system. I always found that mine worked extremely well. There would be a five-minute gun, a two-minute gun and a one-minute gun. At the two-minute gun, I would leave the pits, going out to warm up the engine so that at the one-minute gun, I would be oppo-

Fred Jacoby Jr. testing out one of the first boats built for him by his father "Pop" at their home in North Bergen, Jersey. Notice the forward fin ahead of the step to keep the boat on a straight course.

From his early teens, E.T. Bedford Davie helped Fred Jacoby in making outboard raceboats easier to control. Bud was one of the very first drivers to wear a crash helmet for racing.

By 1930, the 125-mile Albany-New York marathon along the Hudson River had become a very popular event, covered by several movie companies. Drivers tried to avoid a whole range of hazards such as fishermen's nets, mud flats, floating carcasses and every type of garbage.

site the starting barge, quite a way off course. Then I would go back for twenty seconds as fast as I could go, then turn round and come back so that I could hit the starting line with throttle wide open. The advantage was that I would start on the outside at an angle, come and by the time I got to the first buoy, I was halfway around it. I enjoyed racing so much. I would stick my hull on the top of an old Ford station wagon, and put the outboard engine on the back seat, then go down to a race meeting. Not that things weren't dangerous in those days and at those speeds. When you were going past a boat slower than you were, if he made a mistake, or turned right instead of left or hit a wave, or stalled, then you did not have much chance to get around him. Some people were hurt. Frank Vincent was thrown and then run over by his own boat. We did not have automatic shut-offs in those days. Lifejackets were compulsory. I didn't like this at all. During one race, the boat in front of me hit something and stopped dead. I could not go round him on either side because of the boat behind me. So I just plain turned over. I had been pretty far ahead at that time, so I just sat in the water, right on the first cornering buoy of the second lap and watched those boats whizz by. All they could see was my head, help up above the water by my lifejacket, which, in those days was certainly not a bright orange. Now I'd have given anything to have gotten out of that jacket and been able to swim underneath my boat if necessary. But I had to sit there for five laps, waving my hand in the air and hoping."

Whether it was a marathon or sprint race, there also grew up a breed of outboard engine tuners who often used some pretty unorthodox additives to get better performance from their waterbugs. These included TNT, alcohol, castor oil,

Mulford Scull built his own racing hulls named Shooting Star.

ether, peroxide, acetone, thinners and nitromethane. But they had to adjust their plugs, carb settings, venturi openings accordingly, or else. One such driver was a trained chemist, C. Mulford Scull of Ventnor, New Jersey, often seen coming down to his hull, *Shooting Star*, carrying a bottle and warning people to get "the hell out of his way." And set against those out to put the pep into their engine, there were others who wanted to take the pep out of their competitors. This ranged from filling oil cans with syrup, filling the petrol tanks with pyrene, inserting corks in the cylinders through spark plug holes, driving pins into coils and ignition wires, putting sugar in gas tanks and even loosening or nearly cutting through steering ropes.

By this time "Joe Public", whose interest was more often to go out with his family for a day's fishing, was becoming baffled - if not incredulous - at the rival claims made by each of the outboard companies that "they" had the most powerful outboard.

To sort out all the conflict and confusion surrounding racing outboards, their performance and legislation was overseen by the National Outboard Association

C. Mulford Scull from Ventnor, New Jersey, a chemist by training, was probably the first to use nitro-glycerine as a booster to outboard gas mixture.

(NOA), created by the manufacturers, with former Pulitzer Prize winning journalist, James W. Mulroy, as its very capable executive secretary. Among its aims : to promote outboard boating for pleasure, with such incentives as low-cost insurance. But also attempted "to adjudicate the sport and try to maintain relationships with the sales of stock outboards". By the end of 1928, NOA membership stood at a staggering 5,000.

And not all of them were men. Helen Hentschel, Marion Russell and little Mrs Red Atwood, to mention just three, crowded the boys at the buoys and neither asked nor gave quarter. In 1927, Helen Hentschel of Flushing, New York, had won the highest number of points of any outboard racing driver in the US. In 1928 she travelled to Europe with two boats and three motors to race on Lake Templiner, near Potsdam, Germany against experienced male drivers where she won against outboards of European manufacture and with larger displacement. But as British Outboard Racing Club Commodore Count Johnston-Noad stated : "Outboarding requires good nerves, good judgement and a light pair of hands. Given these, a girl of 14 could beat a strong man."

At the end of the 20s, the National Outboard Association organised the promotion of the sport in schools.

In 1927 Miss Hentschel won the highest number of points of any outboard racing driver in the US. In 1928 she travelled to Europe to race in Germany against experienced male drivers where she won against outboards of larger displacement.

Among those strong men was the famous French aeroplane pilot Michel Detroyat, works driver for Marcel Echard's *Lutetia I* and *II*, each powered by a 20 hp Lutetia "Sport" outboard, and unbeatable on such home waters as Monaco, Suresnes, Herblay and Maisons-Lafitte. In Germany, H.C. Krueger, already famous for his inboard-engined *Sigrid* hydroplanes as built by the Engelbrecht Yacht Works, introduced the outboard sport into his country with his Johnson-engined *Sigrid VII*.

Champion drivers were emerging in Italy, such as the Feltrinelli brothers - Egidio, Stefano and Dino. Then Count Carlo Casalini, sixteen years old, was beginning to notch up outboard race victories. During the next 45 years Casalini would take part in some 447 motorboat races, many of them outboard victories, many of them abroad.

After less than a decade of swift development, the "poor man's speedboat", using only 25 hp, was already climbing towards extraordinary speeds.

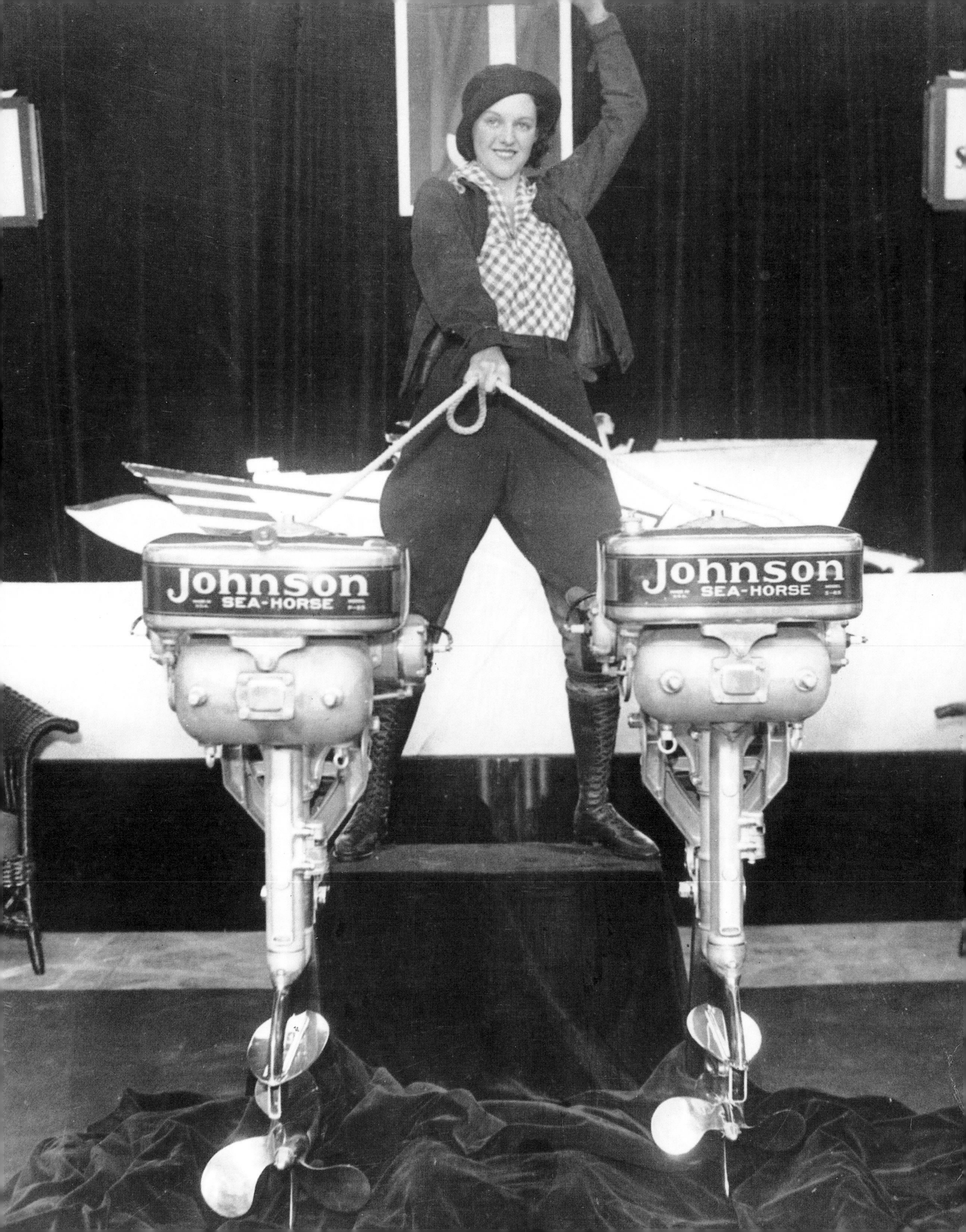
Johnson
SEA-HORSE
Johnson
SEA-HORSE

The Crash

In 1929, across America, a full-scale racing outboard engine war was taking place. Centre stage, Johnson Motors were determined to match and surpass Evinrude's Elto Quad horsepower by horsepower. Alongside the "Big Two", there was the promising Lockwood Motor Company of Jackson, Michigan. Benefitting from the talents of brilliant Purdue University engineering graduate, Finn T. Irgens, this company had brought out two successful units. In 1928, the 7 hp Lockwood "Ace", had competed in APBA Class A and reached a top speed of 27 mph and the 14 hp Lockwood "Chief had" competed in Class B with a top of 35.66 mph.

Finn T. Irgens.

Encouraged by success, Lockwood engineers launched a "Racing Chief" which would give 30 % more power. Test runs pushed boats to near the 40 mph mark. They were even planning to produce a Class D "Flying Four", a four-cycle, flat opposed 4-cylinder powerhead. Also-runs were the "Silver Arrow" recently produced by the Indian Motorcycle Co. of Springfield, Massachusetts, which in turn did battle with the Caille Motor Company of Detroit, Michigan. The 30 hp potential claimed for the Cross five cylinder radial type four cycle engine was also creating considerable excitement - even though the fewer moving parts of a two-stroke made it cheaper to run. With all this new equipment, races were springing up from coast to coast. Many were sanctioned by the APBA and the NOA. Specific motor size classifications were enforced to ensure fair competition.

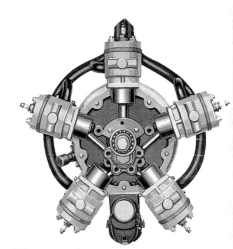

The innovative Cross 5-cylinder outboard engine in 1929.

To ascertain the exact horsepower that these engines were producing, Jim Mulroy at the NOA wisely arranged for a highly regarded laboratory in Pittsburgh, Pennsylvania to certify horsepower claims. Here accurate electric dynamometer readings were made of an engine and then its manufacturer agreed to abide by the NOA "Certified Brake Horsepower" figure measured, so guaranteeing accurate advertising and full protection to the buyer. No racing motors could be certified in so far as they were non stock. The tests were run in the

The new Sea Horse outboards were equipped with underwater exhaust, offset cylinders, a compression release-charger for easier starting and a twist-grip throttle. Such engines have since become collector's items, carefully restored by members of the Antique Outboard Club of America.

presence of engineers from competing engine manufacturers as well as representatives from NOA.

At first, Johnson engineer Kerizinsky and his team were unsuccessful in upsetting Elto. The Johnson opposed twin unit developing 25.75 hp, a 50 cu/in called the "Giant Twin" was beefier than previous Johnsons but not up to the latest Elto Quad, which with the "Speedster" had just been brought out in an "H" for its high-speed version. Elto engineers kept bumping up their Quad's displacement from 40 to 50 and finally to 60 cubic inches. This Class F Quad, dubbed "4-60" (4 cylinders, 60 cubic inches) gained an instant following and remains the granddady of all big outboard racing machines.

Then in 1929, Johnson produced the "Sea Horse 32" developing 32 hp at 5,200 rpm and the "Sea Horse 12". These units were equipped with underwater exhaust, offset cylinders, a compression release-charger for easier starting and a twist-grip throttle. The operator moved a horizontal lever to actuate the release-charger for starting. He twisted a sleeve, or grip, on the tiller arm to adjust the throttle. Most important of all was a rotary valve that boosted power by 50 per cent by permitting a larger charge of gas to be taken into the cylinders, partially contributed to a remarkable 50 percent increase in speed over the previous

Lou Johnson, the engineering member of the four Johnson brothers, contemplating his latest creation, the Sea Horse 24 in his office at Waukegan, Illinois.

The best of Italy's engineers participated in the outboard sport. On the shimmering waters of Lake Garda in 1931, Mario Speluzzi of the Milan Polytechnicum stands up in a Mariella-type hull with 4-cylinder Laros engine.

year's motors. Indeed 26 of the 39 world's records established by outboards during 1929 were set by Johnson Sea Horse units. Of the remaining 13 new records, 12 were established in classes in which Johnson didn't even compete. The top speed continued to rise. On March 23rd 1929, Harrison Fraser from Auburndale, Florida clocked up 43.76 mph. Two months later, on May 29th 1929, Julius Herbst from Wilmington used his Sea Horse 32 to set a new average of 44.54 mph, with one run at 44.83 mph. Herbst complained that the course was too smooth, claiming that he would have gone faster by two or three mph had there been a slight ripple. As 1929 continued, California's H. G. Ferguson (46.1 mph), Jacksonville's B. E. Lamb (47.33 mph) and Italian Antonio Passarin with an Italian Laros 600 on the stern of his " Mariella type IV" hull (48 mph), successively lifted the World outboard record. Across the pond, the pace was slightly less frenetic. In France, outboard races were now regularly held both in Monte Carlo Harbour and at Suresnes on the Seine where at one meeting 30 competitors took part. By now Marcel Echard's Lutetia fleet, was in healthy competition with the de Coninck boatyard, with Romano of Cannes, with Chauvière of Paris, with de Saever and last but not least with wealthy sports supplier André Tunmer, who raced several boats with his name reversed, such as *Remnut IV*.

Developing over 20 hp, the Class C Lutetia models enabled French enthusiasts to compete at over 30 mph in races organised in Monaco, Paris and Bordeaux.

André Tunmer, wealthy sporting goods distributor in France, played with his name to promote his business.

43

During an outboard regatta held on the River Garonne in Bordeaux in June 1929, Tunmer's Remnut IV *roars into the lead.*

Shingi Yano at the helm of Bullet II, *which he designed for the Watermota Company to further promote its engines. Tragically Yano lost his life with this boat when it capsized and he suffered a cramp when attempting to swim to the shore.*

One Frenchman campaigned *Elto II* - an imported American Boyd-Martin "Bullet" hull powered by the ubiquitous Elto Quad. In Scandinavia, Archimedes had developed a rotary throttle on the tiller of their 1928 outboard, following up with the robust 8/9 hp "B2" and 10/12 hp "B22" engines, fitted with reverse gear with slipping-disc clutch units. During the 1930s Archimedes would dominate all outboard racing events in Sweden and abroad with its largest B2 model. In Norway also, an annual outboard race was held as part of the Tvedestrand regatta.

In Great Britain, perhaps the most interesting hull designs at the 1929 motorboat regatta at Chiswick on the Thames were the Watermota-engined *British Maid II* with which Colin Fair won *The Star Trophy*, and her sister boat, *Bullet II*, kept in reserve. Both were the brainchild of Fair's innovative Japanese engineering friend, Shingi Yano. Only 8 ft long, each had a pointed, concave bow tapering flat aft which trapped air underneath that forward section and let it out halfway along. This was a primitive semi-tunnel hull. Each boat was constructed of cedar and spruce and allowances were made for the differing weights of Fair and Yano.

Not long after this meeting, Yano was testing *Bullet II* when the hydro overturned and threw him out. Minutes later, whilst apparently pushing the upturned boat to the bank, Yano suffered cramp and drowned.

Soon after, Fair vindicated his friend's design by once again winning *The Motor Boat Trophy*. Other British contests that year included a 40-mile marathon on the River Avon. The "Bann 100" was held for the second time in Northern Ireland, whilst in the 100-mile East Kent Outboard Marathon, two speedy Watermotas held their own among 20 competitive makes, being the only

Preparing for the start of the disastrous Dover-Calais cross-Channel race. That only two out of the thirty-six participants arrived at their destination proved that outboard skiffs were not equipped for offshore contests.

ones to finish the open sea course. But perhaps the most disastrous race of the year was when some 36 outboard-engined skimmers competed in a race from Dover to Calais and back. It began at four o'clock on a rainy afternoon when it soon became obvious to competitors that what had looked like a calm sea was, in reality, far too much for their little craft when driven at planing speed. Casualties soon occurred. Moreover, visibility worsened. Land was soon lost sight of, and navigation became a matter of guesswork, as many competitors who had taken the precaution of equipping their craft with compasses found that these were quite unreliable whilst running, on account of the motion of the craft.

When a long period passed without news of the arrival of any boats at Calais, the officials began to get anxious, and all possible means were taken to comb the waters of the Channel and rescue competitors who had spread out fan-wise and were now scattered in all directions. Jack Holroyd succeeded in reaching the French coast in *Sea Bee II*, powered by an Elto. Channel shipping was instructed to keep a careful look-out. Some of the competitors were out in their tiny craft all night, but eventually, and very luckily, all were rescued. That even longer-distance inshore races were within the scope of outboards was fully demonstrated in Italy, where on the 6th June 1929, a 257-mile grind took place from Pavia down to Venice.

By this time, the Italian Federation, with sponsorship from *La Gazzetta dello Sport*, had for three years been organizing the National Outboard Day with as many as 120 competitors taking part in some 20 championship elimination heats in Savona, Genoa, Viareggio, Stresa, Carate Lario and Pavia.

First in the outboard division was Ettore Negri of Pavia, and his Milan mechanic Calvi, who had been nursing an Elto bolted on the back of their Picchiotti hull. They completed the course in 11 hours, 26 minutes and 23 sec-

They did however get a medal for their courage.

Ettore Negri, winner of the first Pavia-Venezia marathon, motors across the Venice Lagoon in 1929.

Steven Briggs, president of the highly successful Briggs and Stratton industrial motors complex, bought up Ole Evinrude's firm. Briggs was to follow through by merging Evinrude with Lockwood and Elto. Whilst retaining their individual names, he formed the Outboard Motors Corporation (OMC) in March 1929.

Although OMC became the holding company, the strategy was for motors like this Evinrude Speedtwin and this Johnson Sea Horse to be designed and developed in competition.

onds at an average 22.15 mph. This was four full minutes faster than the winner of the inboard class in a Curtiss-engined Dodge runabout. Other outboard competitors included Dacco, Silvani, Speluzzi, Castoldi, Borromeo and Celli.

During the 1920s, the Evinrude Company's fortunes dwindled from bad to worse until Stephen F. Briggs, president of the highly successful Briggs and Stratton industrial motors firm, bought up the Milwaukee company in 1928. Briggs then followed through by merging Evinrude with Lockwood and also with Elto, and whilst retaining their individual brand names, formed the Outboard Motors Corporation (OMC) in March 1929. Whilst main offices were at the Evinrude factory, Ole Evinrude became president and Jake Stern, executive vice-president. Abruptly, Lockwood's Jackson, Michigan, factory was locked up, and its employees given the option of moving to Milwaukee.

On the hull side, a steady flow of "Flyaway" hydros was now leaving the Jacoby Boat Works at North Bergen. Fred Jacoby Jr. would always get the latest design to race, whenever he - or rather "Pop", brother Emil, or friend Bud Davie –came up with a better idea, and the old boat would be sold off to a hungry customer. By now their hydros had become shorter, wider and they were incorporating non-trip chines to help drivers get through the turns without flipping. The planing surface forward of the transverse step had been narrowed to reduce wetted area and most of the weight was carried on the aft planing surface. Longitudinal steps had appeared to further cut wetted surface, both fore and aft of the transverse step. They replaced the steering tiller with an auto-racing type

SEA BEE II 299

steering wheel which was slanted upwards, with a throttle control lever attached
to it. This enabled a more comfortable body position whilst racing. After this
innovation was revealed at the first official National Outboard Championships
at Peoria, Illinois, it was not long before others were looking for a way to copy
it. Alongside Jacoby, other boatbuilders in demand during this period included
Don Flowers, George Mishey of Cleveland and Phoenix, Worth Boggerman of
Texas, Humarock of Massachusetts and a few smaller builders. Also in 1929, an
outboard fleet took part in the Harmsworth Trophy regattas at Detroit, Michigan
where 16 trophies for runabouts, cruisers and outboards were up for grabs. The
race entry list totalled 351 powerboats, 100 of them outboards.

Whilst the best speed put up by an outboard on the choppy Detroit River was
35.14 mph, runabouts such as Dick Locke in *Hackercraft I* or Ed Gregory in
Chriscraft could only post winning speeds of 31 to 32 mph, albeit in a slightly
longer race.

A fortnight later, in England, Jack Holroyd took his *Sea Bee II* with a 655 cc
Johnson, out onto a six-mile course on Fareham Creek. With three passengers on
board, he kept lapping for 12 hours, covering a remarkable 363 miles and averaging 30 mph.

It seemed that from now on, the sport could only grow from strength to
strength. But then, on October 24th, 1929, "Black Thursday", the US stock mar-

ket went into a nosedive. Some 13 million shares were sold overnight and demands for repayment of loans started to be issued which bankrupted thousands of businesses. A global depression began whose repercussions would be felt for years. One of those ruined in the crash was Count Johnston-Noad. He was declared a bankrupt, his assets seized and his association with British outboard racing, to which he had contributed so much, brought to an abrupt end. With the order potential of 75 speed models being placed by the Watermota agent in Winnipeg, Canada, Colin Fair travelled out to secure the deal. On arriving, he was informed that the agent had also lost everything in the crash. Fair decided to pay a visit to OMC, Evinrude at Milwaukee and Johnson at Waukegan: "Ralph Evinrude was very hospitable. He showed me their very latest engines and took me into their experimental shop, where I was shocked to see one of our latest engines stripped down for analysis. With the knowledge that in 1929 Evinrude anticipated a sale of 35,000 motors and Johnson some 47,000, I decided to come home, where our humble outboard output was, maybe, 100 per year. For me, it seemed the writing was on the wall. It would be quite impossible to compete with the Americans and we had better concentrate on inboards. So I retired from racing at the peak of my career."

Small custom-built outboard engine manufacture at Watermota in Teddington, England was no match for the might of OMC in the US.

Super **Elto** Motors 1929

Beyond the Crash

The effects of the Depression on outboard speed took a little time to filter through. One of OMC's first innovations was the incorporation of experimental electric starting generators as developed by the Owen-Dyneto Corporation of Syracuse, New York, for Packard cars.

Some said also that the Lockwood company had been purchased by OMC, reportedly, to recruit Finn T. Irgens, their ingenious chief engineer. A wise investment because from "Irgy's" drawing OMC board now came the ingenious "Speedibee" racing unit. It put out 22.5 hp at over 6,600 rpm. Its dual, float-feed, side-draft Tillotson carburettors and associated air intake horns pointed defiantly towards the end of each cylinder. Steering bars were bolted to each end of the muffler assembly. Ball and roller bearings were used throughout this battery-ignited double gear-driven rotary-valve racing unit. Priced at a prohibitive $400 only thirty OMC Speedibees were meticulously hand-built and tested.

Legend has it an eager race driver fired up his Speedibee and easily accelerated to the front of the pack. In fact, he was so far ahead that even though the new engine broke down on a sharp turn, the driver was able to re-start it, handily win the race, and set a new speed record. Just before 1930, H. G. Ferguson had lifted the world outboard speed record to 49.48 mph at Balboa, California. Whilst his 11ft "Comet" hull had been built by the Crandall Boat of Newport Beach, California, his engine was a specially prepared Evinrude Speedibee. But industrially, things were not altogether rosy. The Lockwood brand was discontinued in 1930, whilst OMC tried to survive by selling left-over engines. This, however did not stop the race to be the fastest, with the speed target for outboards now closing in on the magic 50 mph. To achieve this goal, a great deal of innovation took place.

In July 1930, Ray Pregenzer with an Elto 4-60 on the back of his Century Hurricane had lifted the record to 49.72 mph on Fox Lake, Illinois. Although Brussels, Belgium's IMYU stated that Aldo Dacco became the first to break the "magic 50" when he was timed driving his 51 hp Laros-engined *Mariella IV*

Mr. E. Millot of Johnson's sporting goods store in Stockton, California, with his Hi-Speed Quad and trophies he won in 1929.

across Lake Garda at 50.77 mph, APBA reports suggest that Pregenzer had already lifted his speed to 50.93 mph some two months before Dacco's run. Could a British boat improve on this ?

The British Motor Boat Manufacturing Co. based in Ipswich had produced their 12 ft racing hydroplane called the "Rytecraft Demon", for outboards of up to 50 hp. Its chief and Elto concessionaire, Jack Shillan, had one of these specially prepared, called it *Non Sequitur III* and with a "4-60" on its stern, young Charles H. Harrison thought he had set a new average of 52.09 mph along the River Medina, Isle of Wight. But then his sponsor Shillan was informed that, due to a misunderstanding, as a silencer had not been fitted, the Marine Motoring Association could not submit the details for official recognition. Undeterred, Shillan and Harrison returned to the River Medina precisely five days before Christmas. Conditions were moderately good, but traffic on the river disturbed its calm, *Non Sequitur III* leaping out of the water and Harrison being forced to momentarily throttle down. The combined average of 53.28 mph and 50.67 mph worked out at 51.91 mph. This enabled Britain to boast five World Unlimited Speed Records: for inboard powerboats (98 mph), outboards (51 mph), aircraft (328 mph), cars (231 mph) and motorcycles (150 mph) - a formidable crown never since repeated. Hull designs improved. In New Jersey, Fred Jacoby Jr. and Bud Davie were among those who worked out that by kneeling down in the boat with the hand-throttle on the side, they would have even greater control of their beautifully-built hydroplanes. As the season progressed they fitted toe-holds to assist kneeling, then half-moon toe-holds for greater grip, then padded knee braces. And with factory-tuned Johnson "SR" and "PR" engines, Jacoby and Davie were almost unbeatable in B and C Class events. Alongside the Jacoby hulls, other yards were turning out equally effective raceboats. Gordon B. Hooton of Grand Rapids, Michigan, developed his tunnel hull and called it the "Wildcat" and sold quite a few to eager sportsmen. Thompson Brothers of New York offered their sleek "XQSME" racer. The Robertson brothers, an Elto 4-60 on the stern of their "Waterplane" built at their father's shipyard. Once underway, he used a foot pedal to cable-steer an underwater rudder.

Frank B. Bremerman of Indianapolis was granted a US patent for a more streamlined hull superstructure where the cowling was outwardly concave at the

bows and gradually changed to convex at or near the middle and rear end. There were some even who decided that outboards were a thing of the past. Malcolm and Dick Pope of Cypress Gardens, Florida, planned a rocket-propelled racer. A special hull was built by Mullins Manufacturing of Salem, Ohio, with a wooden bottom and a sheetmetal superstructure. *Pirate Kid* weighed 150 lbs and her thirty-two 10 lbs rockets weighed the same. They were activated in separate stages by switches mounted in the cockpit, connected to a storage battery. She had accelerated to 60 mph, when her rudder burned through and the boat went berserk, whirling round and round until all the rockets had been fired off. The second attempt, *Dixie Torpedo*, was of alloy construction and fitted with liquid-fuelled rockets. The boat might have gone fast if Malcolm Pope had not been nearly garrotted by a tow-rope from one of the escorting boats and the day's record setting came to an end.

*Rocketeer Malcolm Pope
grins nervously
in the Bossert-hulled*
Pirate Kid, *ready
for ignition of its 10 lbs
cordite rockets. They were
activated in separate stages
by switches mounted
in the cockpit, connected
to a storage battery.*

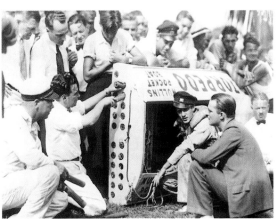

*Malcolm Pope,
in yachting cap,
waits while his brother
Dick fits liquid-fuelled
rockets to the aluminium-
hulled* Dixie Torpedo.

Malcolm Pope and Jack Kerr of Winter Haven, Florida went "outboard-barnstorming". Just one of their techniques was to go over an inclined ramp in two boats. They used hulls built by Penn Yann and Evinrude Speeditwin engines.

Over in England, experiments had also been taking place, not always successfully. See of Fareham built one prototype where a screwjack was used to slightly alter the shape of the keel, increasing its curve: "We never raced it. It wasn't all that good". They were also visited by an Italian propeller expert and experiments up and down the creek were tried with a whole range of screws. None proved at all effective. Stockbroker Harry Bomford, Sees' former customer, had a hydroplane built by Maynards which was almost a catamaran, where the driver and steering wheel were right up in the bows. But one test at Rickmansworth, however, was enough to show him that he had made the wrong investment.

Birmingham Aluminium Castings Ltd of Smethwick, built a 16 ft hydroplane and clamped a Johnson on the back of it. The hull was in one casting and the superstructure in another. They used a See hull as a mould. Neither were really watertight nor light enough. There were others who wished to push the sport in the opposite direction. The Marine Motoring Association of Great Britain decided to enforce a more restricted raceboat programme to make the sport safer. They had formed the National Utility Dinghy Class, with very specific rules. Only B and C Class engine were permitted. Boats had to be beachable, suitable for hanging in davits, and capable of being rowed with four people on board.

They must be no longer than 14 ft, no shorter than 11 ft, with a minimum beam of 4 ft 6 in, a bow of not less than 24 inches high, and 15 inches at the stern. Minimum hull weight, less equipment, must be 170 lbs. A round bilge rather than a hard chine was to be built; and the transom had to be not less than one inch thickness. Naturally, one of those yards which adapted its skill to fit with the MMA rules was See of Fareham. Percy See had now decided to hand over the challenge of designing such a dinghy to his 17-year-old son, Eric. Following trials with the first 12 ft of normal clinker construction, Eric observed how water was being trapped under the plank lands and not cleared from the bottom. He therefore reversed the clinker to take the place of the chine in throwing off water, reducing the wetted surface the planks acting as partial steps. Unknown to Eric See, over in the USA, both the Lyman Boat Co., of Sandusky, Ohio and the Pigeon Hollow Spar Co. used reverse clinker planking for their outboard race-boats.

The 14 ft See reverse-clinker MMA dinghy, powered by a 55 hp Laros, proved capable of 45 mph, whilst the 17 ft version with a 52 hp Elto 4-60 reached 42 mph in favourable conditions. Such performance at once prompted the Sees to patent their design.

The first major contest of the National Utility Dinghy Class was contested in May 1930 for the *Yachting World* Trophy. Jack Holyroyd entered his reverse-clinker *Sea Bee III*, and despite hitting driftwood at the start, pulled himself up

It required some bravery to enter long offshore marathons like Dick Cole and Gladys Clement did in 1930.

A typical Utility Dinghy race start. Safe but slow.

Out of gas or faster without the engine running ?

A rather efficient sun hat to resist the heat at Salton Sea in the California desert.

from 12th to 3rd and finally to 2nd in only 21 laps. The only man to beat him was Viscount Kingsborough at 22.7 mph. The following year, Italy's Count Salvi lifted the *Yachting World* winner's speed to 29 mph, but it certainly bore no comparison to outboard hydroplane speeds now being clocked abroad. Watermota was also in on the new class. Dick Cole, employed in the drawing office of Teddington, borrowed a 14 ft See "Utility Dinghy" and with a Watermota "Silent Speed Eleven" (11 hp at 3,750 rpm) on the back, crossed the Irish Sea with W. D. Elliott as crew. The following year, with Miss Gladys Clements as passenger, Cole made a 700-mile trip in a similar boat from Westminster Pier to Dover, Calais, Ostend, Bruges, Ghent, Antwerp and then back to Dover. By the end of 1931 the Depression in the US had virtually destroyed the sales potential of racing outboards such as the Evinrude "Big Four", the Elto "Big Quad" and the Johnson "XR" so that production of these units was discontinued. Higher speeds were now left in the hands of top tuners including Dean Draper, Marshall Eldredge, Walt Everett, Paul and Joe Wearly, Fred Nichols, Frank Vincent, Dick Neal, and several others. Bud Davie recalls: "The cylinders of our

Engineers at the NOA's Pittsburgh independent laboratory take electric dynamometer readings to give an "accurate"
Certified Brake Horsepower - in an effort to guarantee fair advertising and full protection to the buyer. Three different boats
were used to obtain a balanced average.

Once inside the van, not only the outboards, but an
Evinrude "Lawn Boy" motor mower were on show.

This is probably Thomas Alva Edison Lake waving from his unique pontoon hydroplane boat.

two-cycle outboards were often wearing out of round. We were always having to hone them and put in new pistons to keep the compression. Then a skilled engineer called Dean Draper, from Detroit, found out that by hard-chrome-plating the cylinders, they'd last a lot longer. Setting up shop to do just that Draper built up a big business".

In addition to which, if you could afford them, there were also experts on shafts and lower units, such as Randolph "Pep" Hubbell and Walker Baumann. Then there was the question of fuel. The Du Pont Company produced a combination of alcohol, benzol, castor oil and a couple of secret ingredients, and trade-named it "Dynax". This became the standard racing fuel. Whilst the PennYan Boat Co. of New York turned their "Ceestepper" into the largest-selling racing powerboat in the US, prototypes also proliferated. Thomas Alva Edison Lake of Milford, Connecticut, patented a three-point outboard hydroplane with hydraulically controlled outriggers as its two forward points and its rear point doubling as a rudder.

In "Hulls or Horsepower", an article published in *Popular Mechanix* magazine, LeRoy Malrose described the *No-Vac* outboard raceboat as built and tested in Chicago. The upper part of her hull, fabric-covered spruce frames, imitated an

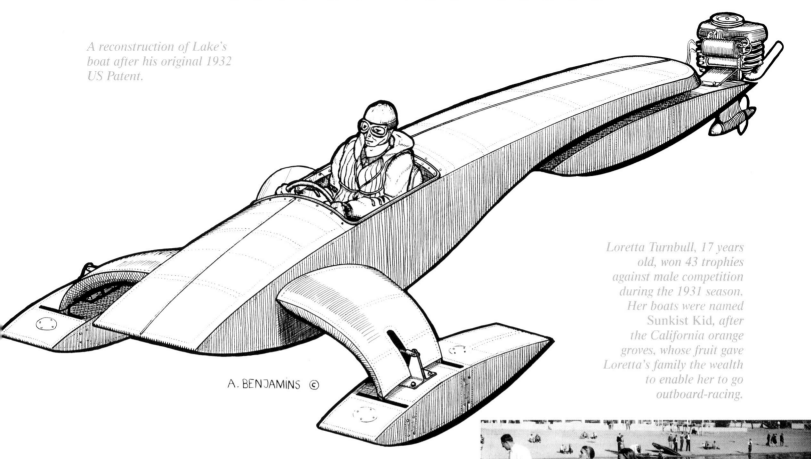

A reconstruction of Lake's boat after his original 1932 US Patent.

A. BENJAMINS ©

Loretta Turnbull, 17 years old, won 43 trophies against male competition during the 1931 season. Her boats were named Sunkist Kid, *after the California orange groves, whose fruit gave Loretta's family the wealth to enable her to go outboard-racing.*

aeroplane fuselage with even a streamlined windshield to encircle the pilot's body. The bottom planes were shaped like an arrowhead, one behind the other. Malrose claimed that with the same outboard engine, he had exceeded the speed of a standard racer by 7.5 mph.

This was quite an extraordinary claim considering that the unlimited outboard speed record was only just managing to increase. In 1931, the Pellegatti brothers, engineers behind the Laros, Italy's most successful outboard as manufactured by their Impresa Forniture Industriali of Milano, produced the F55, its prop turning at 5,500 rpm. That April, Aldo Dacco fitted a specially tuned F55 onto the stern of a futuristic-looking hull, designed by English naval architect Fred Cooper, and set up a new marginal increase of 52.64 mph across Lake Garda.

Where US vs Italy outboard competition was concerned, it was a teenage woman from Monravia,

Loretta Turnbull, obviously elated, after winning the 1933 edition of William Randolph Hearst trophy. Her father Judge Rupert looks proudly on.

California, by the name of Miss Loretta Turnbull who carried the Union flag. Loretta's father, Judge Rupert R. Turnbull, Commodore of the National Outboard Association, owned a very large ranch for growing citrus fruit and it was here that young Loretta decided, aged only 14, to race outboards, first with the boat name *Spirit of Bronchitis*, but soon after, with the appropriate name of the *Sunkist Kid* after the famous "Sunkist Oranges". By 1931, then 18 years old, Loretta had become woman American champion for Class C outboards and out of the 48 trophies she had captured, she won 43 of them in competition with men. Instead of sitting in her boat, which was only 10 ft 4 in. long, she would drive kneeling down, her right hand forward on the steering wheel and her left back at the engine controls so that she was riding almost sideways on a point of balance. Loretta was skilled in getting her boats quickly on to the plane, and the later models were fitted with a fin on their hull-bottom, which when lowered, enabled her to spin round the turns at high speed, but which could be raised for the straights. In 1931 Judge Turnbull, daughter Loretta and sons, Raymond and Rupert Jr. crossed the Atlantic with a Johnson-engined five-boat fleet. They only raced in Classes A, B and C. Loretta drove *Sunkist Kid II* against a small fleet of Italy and Spain's best male drivers to win the trophy. Raymond drove *Sunkist Kid IV* to 1st place in the Count Rossi Cup, whilst Rupert Jr. won 1st place on the River Po. The Turnbull family boats were not as high-powered as the European craft, but their American hulls were better designed. Returning in triumph, Loretta was racing near Syracuse, when *Sunkist Kid VI* flipped on a turn and clouted Loretta as it tossed her out. For some months it was feared she might never walk again - but when she did, Judge Turnbull tried to persuade his daughter to retire on her laurels. Without success. It was another four racing years later

The Turnbull raceboat fleet on tour during her Italian campaign.

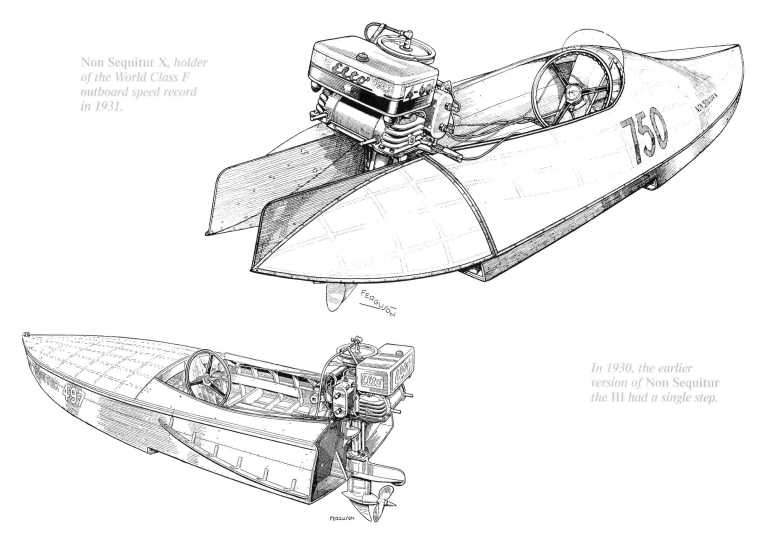

that this marine Amazon, failing to win the South California Championships in
Sunkist Kid XII, got married soon after and retired safely from the sport.

In the autumn of 1931 a new record was claimed as H. Ryan used a 973 cc
Elto to clock 55.28 mph. Although this was higher than Italian Dacco's mark,
because the runs were not made over a nautical mile, the speed could not be officially recognized by the IMYU. That October, American Tom Estlick used a
Johnson XR Special on the back.

After a suitable time of testing, *Non Sequitur X* was taken down to the river.
Medina and Charles Harrison had a long, arduous day in that boat, starting his
first runs whilst a light mist still hung about the river. Later, conditions
improved, although the air remained intensely cold; the sun came out and a light
southwesterly wind just ruffled the water. The roar of the big Elto, opened out,
was likened to "a continuous sounding of an ocean liner's siren - not unmusi-
cal". The combined average of 56.61 mph and 54.52 mph gave Great Britain
back the record with 55.56 mph.

Then, in 1932 outboard racing in the US continued to grow. In the month of
July alone, over eighty meets were held throughout the North American conti-
nent with hundreds of drivers taking part.

To further encourage the sport, APBA President George H. Townsend had
presented a medal for the American Outboard High Point Championship. Soon,
the Townsend Medal was to become the most coveted prize in the US outboard
racing fraternity. With a total of 11,738 points in 13 regattas, John B. Maypole
Jr. became its first recipient. 1933 saw some equally memorable highlights.

A bird's view over the pits in 1932 at Chicago's regatta. There are three men for a boat.

Many racing outboard motors had been seen in service on the sterns of collegiate racers' boats. Numerous schools sponsored teams where drivers usually purchased their own outfits. One such entrant was a 20-year-old student called Horace Tennes. On August 20th, against his doctor's orders and his mother's protest, Tennes, raced in front of 125,000 spectators gathered around the beautiful North Lagoon at Chicago World's Fair grounds to clinch the *William Randolph Hearst* Trophy for his second consecutive year. Three weeks previously he had suffered painful neck injuries after a dive from a springboard. Since several vertebrae had been knocked out of alignment, Tennes's neck had been rigidly strapped in a brace. Despite this, Tennes entered six races, won A and F Classes and took at 5th in the B Class for the winning total score of 1,056 points.

The greatest speed yet clocked by an outboard raceboat in competition was recorded in September at Lakeport, California. Joe Bansi, in a Class F hydroplane, zoomed around the 1 2/3 mile oval course at 52.879 mph.

Then, 22-year-old Lewis G. Carlisle of Long Island, who only two years before had placed last in his initial race, became the hottest outboard driver in the US, winning the Townsend Medal, his 18,807 points total better than some 430 drivers. But, as APBA President George Townsend reasoned, it was all very well for US pilots to race among themselves. How would they fare against a European contingent?

Pit scene from the races held as part of the Chicago World Fair.

Le Soriano

During the 1920s, both the importation of mass-produced US outboards and the smaller-scale manufacture of national outboards continued to promote the sport around the rest of the world. In 1922, the Austrian Motor Yacht Club in Vienna had made contact with the Brigittenau motorboat yard on the Danube Canal who had already been racing outboards and the sport began. As far away as Japan, alongside powerboat-building at the Sumida-Gawa shipyard, the Amagi hydroplane powered by a prototype Hinode outboard, built in Osaka, gave sportsmen the opportunity for competition.

On July 26th, 1931, forty-one drivers took part in Japan's first outboard circuit race on Sumida River in Tokyo. The following year the first 40 miles outboard marathon took place between Tokyo and the Arakawa Canal. Only four boats participated, the first one arriving in 2 hours and 11 minutes.

In Spain, Ricardo Soriano, Marquis of Ivanrey, a wealthy Spanish nobleman, decided to finance a motor which could take on the Americans. He approached Louis Coätelen of the Sunbeam Car Company, the brains behind the victorious Sunbeam-Talbot-Darracq racing car team. Working for Coätelen at the time was the bearded, diminutive French engineer Paul Bonnemaison, the brains behind the victorious *Ricochet* stepped-hydroplanes which Soriano had admired over twenty years before during the Monaco races. Bonnemaison developed a sophisticated 658 cc four-cylinder, four-stroke, unsupercharged unit named "le Soriano". Limited construction began in a cinema equipment factory in Barcelona by name of Maquinaria Cinematografica. It is reported that twelve units were completed. By May 1932, at St Cloud, near Paris, on the Seine, the Marquis of Ivanrey created the Paris Canot Club exclusively for Soriano engines owners and drivers. This was a houseboat with covered terrace, saloon bar, changing rooms, electric lighting, hot and cold running water, motor exhibition, research room and a library. The club committee could not have been more aristocratic. Count de Lapeyrouse-Vaucresson was president, with Soriano as vice-president. Jean Dupuy was Secretary, whilst on the Committee were

The Soriano on an aluminium hydroplane, being prepared by French genius, Paul Bonnemaison.

This is the Dupuy-Soriano, the most powerful and the most sought-after racing outboard of the 1930s. Less than half a dozen were built. Its streamlined underwater unit with its twin-rotating propellers was a work of art in itself.

*Sandro Salvi stands up
in his Passarin-designed
Mariella VI, after breaking
the 12 nautical mile Class C
Record at 47.41 mph.
His 500 cc Laros developed
33 hp at 5,200 rpm.
L.M.V. Head was
the powerboating
correspondant
for Yachting World.*

Viscount Sosthène de la Rochefoucauld, Prince Guy de Polignac, and Count Max Pourtalès.

On 14th July 1933, "Bastille Day", the French Motor Yacht Club organized an International race meeting for inboards and outboards. Drivers came from Belgium, Germany, Switzerland, Italy and Spain to compete with France's best in Classes A, B, C and X. Soriano arrived with his arsenal of engines and hulls. Watched by thousands of Parisians, a day's racing took place in the center of Paris. During the competition, the Soriano engine was tested in the unlimited class on the back of hulls built by de Coninck, de Saever and Chauvière (France); by Engelbrecht (Germany); by Feltrinelli and Passarin (Italy); and by Mendiguren and Soriano (Spain). The other outboards used - Lutetia, Laros, Sharland, Archimedes, Johnson and Elto - competed in Classes B up to F. On July 16th, the Marquis of Ivanrey attacked the world outboard speed record over the Measured Mile which he himself already held at a speed of 56.5 mph. With a Soriano engine on the back of his Italian Mariella-Passarin hull, he succeeded in breaking his own record obtaining a beautiful average of 59.40 mph.

Later that year, twelve of Europe's top outboard race drivers - including Bouchon and Dupuy of France, de Galdiz of Spain and Casalini of Italy - were invited down to Bayonne Canot Club near the Franco-Spanish border where the Marquis fitted each of them out with a Bonnemaison-Soriano rig and then raced against them during a five-day regatta.

Soon after, with growing political unrest in Spain, the Marquis of Ivanrey abandoned his outboard-building project. It was at this point that one of the Soriano pilots stepped in. Jean Dupuy, 34-year-old debonaire member of a rich family of press publishers, owning such major newspapers as the *Excelsior* and the *Petit Parisien*. Son of a famous sportsman, Dupuy began racing quite abruptly at age 12. The father came home one day and announced that he had entered the boy in a motorcycle race that afternoon. That began a racing career that included motorcycles, automobiles, International 6-metre sailing yachts, 1.5-litre hydroplanes and finally outboards that he named *Excelsior*. Anxious to make his mark on power boating, Dupuy acquired several engines, together with drawings, parts and patterns from the Marquis of Ivanrey. From now on Paul Bonnemaison, working in a highly sophisticated workshop in the Paris suburb of Courbevoie in the very centre of France's aero and motor industry, was able to bring his Soriano engines and hulls to perfection. Dupuy and Bonnemaison redesigned the Soriano, developing new cylinder heads for the opposed six-cylinders each with double overhead camshafts. With steel-lined aluminium cylinders and chrome-nickel-steel crankshaft, their engine became a potent 987 cc, which with a Roots-type blower developed a formidable 85 hp and more at over 5,000 rpm. They scrapped the original gearcase and replaced it with a gearbox location above the bottom of the boat. Most sophisticated of all, the 4 ft streamlined underwater unit comprised twin contra-rotating props spinning at surface level and fitted with cavitation plates up the leg to ensure that only half the prop was in the water. Very conscious of the power obtained, Bonnemaison produced a "roughwater" hull made of machined aluminium plating, slightly stronger, albeit heavier, than the standard timber and plywood currently employed.

From here Dupuy allowed one or two single cam engines to be sold, but at outrageous prices. Commodore Gar Wood, anxious that his 16-year-old son became as successful with outboards as his father was with his multiple aero-engined 120 mph *Miss America* hydroplanes, had one shipped across to Detroit.

Jean Dupuy, wealthy Parisian sportsman, having raced cars, motorcycles, 6-Metre sailing yachts and inboard hydroplanes, focussed his attention on the impossible: to beat the Americans at outboard racing. Dupuy's family owned major newspapers such as Excelsior *and the* Petit Parisien.

*The Soriano had
an opposed six-cylinder
configuration, each
steel-lined aluminium
cylinder fitted with double
overhead camshafts.
With a capacity of 987 cc,
a Roots-type blower gave
this pure thoroughbred
a formidable 110 hp
at 5,000 rpm.*

Count Carlo Casalini and Carlo Forni of Italy each acquired one. A hull and two engines were acquired by Arthur, Viscount Forbes, the 18-year-old son of the 8th Earl of Granard. For the past two years, young Lord Forbes had spent most of his holidays from Eton out on a lake at the family estate in Northern Ireland. Starting with a small Johnson engined sea sled, he progressed to a French hydroplane powered by a 500 cc Lutetia, gaining experience in races along the river Shannon. But when it came to graduating from B to C and even D Class engines, and racing outside Ireland he preferred to race abroad. Once he had tested the Dupuy-Soriano equipment, Viscount Forbes at once took them down through Europe on the top of his Mercedes SS sports car to compete on Lake Garda, Italy.

It was here that the young Viscount was introduced to APBA President George Townsend. Townsend was making a European tour encouraging entries for an international race meeting he was organizing for March 1934 in Florida. He believed that it was time that both the Gold Cup boats and the cream of the outboard hydros be given the best that Europe could offer.

Since European outboards were considered faster and more adaptable to rough water, the strict motor requirements enforced in American racing had been waived for those wanting to devise equipment that would match challengers. A new Class, " X", had been created for engines of unlimited horse-power. Several American drivers revamped their Class F motors, others built new motors to qualify for Class X designation, 61 cu/in or 1000 cc.

Twenty of these drivers turned up at New Smyrna, Florida, for timed trials to determine a four-man American team. Horace Tennes, Northwestern University engineering student; Phil Elsworth, Bucknell University student; Walter Everett, National Class F champion, and Art Sauerberg, earned their place.

The International races took place in Florida, at Smyrna and Palm Beach with some spectacular outboard races for the William Randolph Hearst Trophy.

Boats came from Sweden (Kurt Oldenberg), Hungary (Francis Luckavecz) and Spain (Manuel Giro). Sadly, Viscount Forbes was still at Cambridge, reading history and his family would not let him attend. For England, Edward

Bespectacled young English aristocrat, Viscount Forbes finds himself in Detroit, flanked by three great players in powerboat racing. Charles Chapman, editor of Motor Boating *magazine, George Townsend of the A.P.B.A. - and Horace Dodge, millionaire builder and driver of inboard powerboats.*

Viscount Forbes's Dupuy-Soriano on the top of his SS Mercedes. His mechanic was Jack Sopp better known for tuning racing cars at England's major autodrome.

*Horace Tennes
in* Hootnanny VI,
*a Century hull powered
by a factory 4-60 Evinrude.
To avoid fouling the plugs,
Tennes is idling here before
the start of one of the races
on Lake Worth in Florida.*

Treglown from Oulton Broad and C. J. Turner in *Non-Sequitur*, went in his place. But most formidable-looking of all was the Franco-Spanish armada immaculately equipped with shiny Soriano rigs: Jean Dupuy, Baron Alain de Rothschild, Soriano's son-in-law the Marquis Gonzalo de la Gandara, and Miguel Barella, an electrical engineer from Barcelona.

Star of the meeting was Horace Tennes, who had brought along *Hootnanny VI*, powered by an Class X Evinrude. Phil Ellsworth arrived from Bucknell University with *Blue Devil V*. The first of nine heats, held at New Smyrna, was watched by 12,000 spectators, who thrilled to Tennes' daring, reckless driving. Tennes' time for a 10-mile dog-leg course with sharp bends worked out at 52.63 mph. And he won heat two, with Jean Dupuy coming second after some desperate driving. Then Dupuy won heat three from Tennes. The contest now moved to Lake Worth, in choppy conditions and watched by 15,000. Driving the entire 10 miles on his knees despite *Hootnanny VI* frequently leaping out of the water, Tennes won heat four; half a mile astern was Walter Everett of Tulsa, Oklahoma, the National Champion. Whilst Dupuy (hull n° F53) won heat five, Tennes' victories in heats six and seven gave him the Trophy. So, despite all his investment, the Frenchman had been beaten by a mere student. Returning home he won a number of races against friendly rivals such as Prince Guy de Polignac.

Then on October 18th, Dupuy lifted the world outboard speed record to 65.21mph.

Riding on this wave of success, Jean Dupuy with his wife Dorothy, the millionairess daughter of Adolph B. Spreckels II, the "sugar king", decided to present a new international trophy for the sport that would carry with it a minimum endowment of 150,000 FF in cash. Any type of engine up to four-litre

Dupuy at speed on Lake Worth.

Boat n° 53 at Palm Beach. Jean Dupuy is flanked by reps from the Champion Spark Plug Company. At the bows, a crew member of Eileen of the Yacht Club de France.

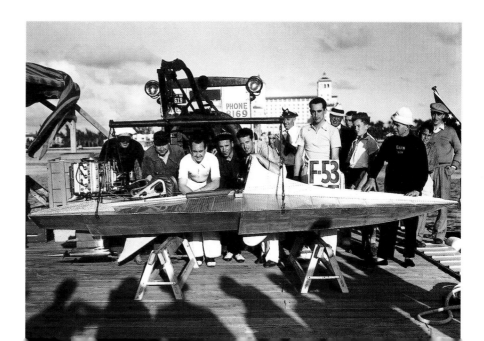

was permitted but the boat had to weigh under 710 lbs with empty gas and oil tanks. The contest was to be annual and to last two hours, with victory for the entrant who could cover the greatest distance. Publically announcing the Spreckels Trophy at the Waldorf Astoria Hotel in New York, Mrs. Dupuy announced that she would personally put up 50,000 FF before each contest to be distributed to the first three drivers.

Among those who took up the challenge were Viscount Forbes, whose new supercharger had been taken from a Delage racing car and fitted to his Dupuy-Soriano by Brooklands mechanic Jack Sopp. From America came Stanley Dollar in *Uncle Sam*, fitted with one of the latest four-cylinder "blown" Millers of 1,569 cc with transmission through a Riley outdrive. Dacco, Barberis and Carmagnani represented Italy. The French team comprised Jean Dupuy, together with champion racing car drivers Louis Chiron and Raymond Sommer. The race took place on Saturday July 6th,1935. Many thousands of spectators lined the course along the Seine, between the Louis-Philippe and the Carrousel bridges.

The three Frenchmen stayed in the lead, Sommer clocking lap record of 53 mph. When Sommer and Chiron retired, Dupuy's only serious contender was Stanley Dollar, for whilst the Soriano was good on the turns, *Uncle Sam* had the edge on the straights. But then the American split his fuel tank on the fourth lap and retired - as did Viscount Forbes on his eighteenth lap. Dupuy won averaging 44.08 mph.

Dupuy might have been unbeatable on home territory, but three months later, his world record was taken away from him.

This was achieved using a one-off Class X motor prepared to perfection by champion engineer-driver Walter Everett, who had taken the X version of the 4-60 which had four rotary valves instead of the standard two, then replaced its lower unit with a Walker Baumann tractor prop. That September the Everett "Special" was fitted on the back of the wooden-hulled *O-22* and entered into the

Jean Dupuy's armada was prepared in a fully equiped barge used as racing workshop on the River Seine.

One-Mile time trials that preceded the National Outboard Championships on Lake Spavinaw near Tulsa, Oklahoma. Following several hours of expert tuning, Everett handed the boat over to his sponsor, George Colman Jr. from Miami. Colman's first run timed at 68 mph, and his 2nd at 70.588 mph. This gave him an average 69.383 mph and the "bully barrier" of 70 mph had been broken.

Here is Everett getting near 70 mph full speed from his boat 0-22. But it was his sponsor, George Colman Jr. from Miami who had used it to lift the Class X record to 69.383 mph.

Perhaps an even more ingenious achievement than that was the one-mile straightaway record set by Herr Blankenfeldt of Germany. Using a König radial outboard engine of only 10.5 cubic inches, Blankenfeldt pushed his Pfennig hydro to 39.18 mph, and then completed a two hour extended run at 33.29 mph. These records for this size of outboard remained unbroken for 18 years.

It was not without reason that George Townsend, President of the APBA, pointed out that the Harmsworth Trophy appeared to be a dead duck, and that during last year's Gold Cup race the combined age of the three competing boats was 31 years, setting aside that two of them had broken down! Unless something

Walter Everett of Tulsa, Oklahoma, arguably the most successful Class F race-winner, record-breaker and engine tuner. He also dared to race in Texas where tough non-stock "anything goes" racing was held.

was done, outboards would become the faster class. As if to underline this, OMC– already comprising Evinrude and Elto–now purchased control of Johnson Motor Co. of Waukegan, Illinois. Johnson President Warren Ripple had been unable to sell his vast stock pile of engines and boats and between 1931 and 1935 Johnson Motors had gradually ground to an almost bankrupt halt.

So in November 1935, Steve Briggs, OMC Chairman and Ralph Evinrude OMC President, purchased two-thirds of Johnson outstanding shares. In 1936, Johnson Motors and OMC were reformed as the Outboard Marine & Manufacturing Corporation (OMMC). Despite top-level control, it was decided that Evinrude, Elto and Johnson outboards would remain arch rivals for sales at both dealer and consumer level.

As *Fortune* magazine pointed out then: "Chief Engineer Irgens of Evinrude and Chief Engineer J.G.Rayniak of Johnson get together for a shop talk once a week. If one of them has made some flabbergasting discovery he will tell the other, but mostly Irgens in trying to outsmart Rayniak, and vice versa..."

Not that the sport was particularly concerned with "big business", for as Bud Davie recalls: "Sprint races went on all over the country. There was closed circuit racing for collegiates, inter-collegiates, state, inter-state and national championships. Some of these were very exciting because we had such enormous entries. Not that things weren't dangerous. When you'd got a boat of 90 hp that weighed 200 lbs and you were going past a boat 40 mph slower, if he made a mistake or turned right instead of left, or hit a wave, or stalled, then you

Frank Harvey's beak-nosed racer was one of the more successful experimental-hulled rigs until...

didn't really have that much chance to get around him". But although Davie, as a Yale University student amateur would often beat the professionals, when he raced against the man whose father built his hulls, Fred Jacoby Jr., Davie was very seldom first over the finishing line.

Indeed if in 1934 Jacoby hulls had been placed in 300 different races, the 1935 season saw Fred become unquestionably the most outstanding outboard driver in the history of the sport. Driving A, B, and C hulls, he won 51 races as well as placings in 35 other races. It was a family team effort, with brother Emile as mechanic and sister Leonie helping with registration and scoring. During a weekend in Savannah, Georgia, he won 15 out of 16 races, on one day taking 7 first out of 8 races. In the Albany-New York marathon on a very choppy Hudson River, where out of 75 starters, 17 finished, Freddy crossed the finish line in a Class C outfit, some 20 minutes ahead of the 2nd. In the Shrine Regatta in Washington, he took 13 first places in one weekend.

Inside a fortnight, he lifted the Class B record for five miles five times in five consecutive heats, from 46.680 mph to 47.493 mph. Jacoby thus became the

A later Jacoby hull. Two handles on the nose and two on the rear enabled 3 men to lower it into the water. Steering was by steel wire cables and throttling was via a Bowden wire to the left of the steering wheel.

All out for New York.
89 boats, inboards and
outboards started
the 132-mile Albany-New
York Marathon of 1932.

first professional to win Townsend Medal with a 37,637 points total, nearly three times the total 11,836 points which had brought the trophy to Joel Thorne of Westchester in 1934. For this reason, Davie and Jacoby decided to team up to make an attack on Jean Dupuy and his Spreckels Trophy. Whilst Fred decided to use his victorious Albany-New York 12 ft hull, Bud Davie got a new Class X from "Pop" Jacoby of 110 lbs with the Jacoby hallmark, a deep-V with longitudinal steps and shallow cross step to reduce the wetted area and give improved roughwater handling.

For engines, Dean Draper of Detroit built three X special engines, with Elto 4-60 transom brackets and driveshaft housings, external Johnson "XR" rotary valves with Evinrude-adapted Vacturi carburettors and self-primers instead of choke. The gears were tractor units by Walker Baumann and the props came from Stannus. Such unit developed 90 to 100 hp but weighed only 150 lbs.

One week before Jacoby and Davie were to sail on the *SS Normandie*, Dean Draper delivered two engines to them by aeroplane. They got their hulls accelerating to 70 mph and over, up and down the local Hackensack River at Carlstadt, New Jersey. But there were problems with the Vacturi carburettor, still not solved when they took ship for France. Also determined to win the Spreckels Trophy was Viscount Forbes, who had now replaced his Dupuy with a new hull designed by Fred Cooper to incorporate alloy parts supplied by Birmal Boats of Southampton. Also that June, something happened which could easily have unnerved Dupuy. His brother-in-law, Adolph B. Spreckels, III, was also a keen speedboat pilot, who enjoyed racing under the burgee of the Seattle Outboard Association. On June 14th, 1936, Adolph was driving a Class F hydroplane in a race on Seattle's Green Lake. As he returned to the pit area after a heat, the throttle stuck open. Spreckels hit the beach at top speed. The boat flew over one woman's head, then struck several other spectators before coming to rest against the sound truck. Spreckels was thrown from the boat and landed on a telephone pole, a climbing spike impaling his upper left arm. He hung there until rescuers were able to lift him down. Spreckels was badly injured and needed several operations to restore his arm and face. More tragic, however, was the fate of spectator Ord Lockhard, who had been watching the race from his wheelchair. He was struck by Spreckels' boat and subsquently died. Concerned but not deterred, Jean Dupuy threw himself into putting the finishing touches to the

Fred Jacoby receives the Haynes-Griffith Trophy after winning the 1935 Albany-New York marathon.

Up and away! Fred Jacoby, with the champion of champion's boat number US-2.

Messrs. Davie, Jacoby
and Draper stand behind
the Class X-motor.
From left to right,
the finance, the hull,
the engineering -
and a team friendship.

*Messrs. Davie, Jacoby
and Draper stand behind
the Class X-motor.
From left to right,
the finance, the hull,
the engineering -
and a team friendship.*

*One of the rare examples
of Evinrude Class X
in original condition.*

*Close-up of one of
the special 4-cylinder
60 cu/in Class X motors
which Dean Draper
of Detroit built for Bedford
Davie and Fred Jacoby
to race in Paris.*

monster with which he would defend his Trophy. On the back of one of his 770 lbs alloy hull were twin Soriano engines, each tuned to develop 105 hp at 6,000 rpm, driving two contra-rotating props, one per engine. On trials this boat was reported to have reached 87 mph. To make up his team he chose Baron Alain de Rothschild and Louis Chiron. But Chiron withdrew at the last moment, to be replaced by Georges Monneret, French motorcycle champion, who had never before raced a boat. On July 4th, 1936, thousands once again leaned over Paris bridges or lined the banks of the Seine to watch the most powerful outboards in the world in combat around a 1.8 mile course. At the gun, Dupuy and Monneret were unable to start. They both got going some 13 minutes later, and with the power from his twin Sorianos, Dupuy roared into a lead which he lost on lap eight. His over-powered boat porpoised, slowing him down and exhausting him until he had to retire. Before an hour had elapsed, Fred Jacoby, Baron de Rothschild and Viscount Forbes had all slowed down with engine trouble but pressed on. On Jacoby's Draper Special the Vacturi carburettor was opened so much that Fred had to keep his finger on the jet during the last hour of the race. Davie, in the lead, cut off a sliver of wood and put it in the jet as he always carried a Scout knife when he raced in marathons. The initial results of this race stated that after 90 minutes, Monneret who had gained the lead, appeared the winner with 80 miles covered at 39 mph; that Jacoby came second at 34 mph, Viscount Forbes third at 31 mph, de Rothschild fifth and Davie sixth. But then things became a little less clear cut. Monneret was disqualified for taking a tow back to the pits. This should have made Jacoby first but then Fred was disqualified because the translated set of rules forgot to specify that the winner had to complete an exhibition lap unlike the French language version. So, as Viscount Forbes recalls: "I finished the race and my mechanic said I had won. We were packing up when an official said that I had been disqualified but I never did find out why."

And even though Bedford Davie firmly believed that he had won, the Spreckels Trophy was awarded to a Frenchman, Baron de Rothschild. After all, it had to be kept from America.

Back in January 1936, Dupuy had visited the New York Boat Show and ordered a custom wooden hydro from boatbuilder Don Flowers. Literally whilst Bud Davie was "en route" for the States, on July 12th, 1936, Dupuy accelerated his Soriano/Flowers rig up and down the Measured Mile opposite the Paris Canot Club and raised the world outboard speed record to 74.39 mph. News of Dupuy's record not only travelled to the United States–that August, some 900 km north of Paris, Norwegian motoring editor Odd Buhre, inspired by the Frechman's achievement, held a meeting of fourteen enthusiasts at his Oslo home. Their formation of a National Outboard Club soon led to Norway's first main outboard race, a successful coastal marathon around Oslo Fjord.

Meanwhile, soon after his return, Bud Davie ran his Paris boat and engine at Red Bank, New Jersey, and got the lap record at 68 mph. He was even thinking of running it in the Gold Cup because at that speed, he could have led some old inboards by a good 10 mph but may not have survived in the rough water they set up.

Dupuy in his twin Soriano-engined behemoth. On the back of his 770-lbs alloy hull, a potential 200 hp ready for transmission to two contra-rotating props.

*Viscount Forbes's Class C
hydroplane during
the Spreckels Trophy race
on the Seine.*

Instead, that October Davie took his Jacoby, complete with its Draper Special, to Green Pond, New Jersey, where he took the record back for the States with an impressive 77.75 mph.

Then, July 3rd, 1937, saw the third running of the Spreckels Trophy Dupuy won at 48.34 mph against competition from three American, three Italian and two other French Soriano drivers. This did not hold back Bud Davie. On October 17th, the irrepressible American lifted his world record one notch further with 78.12 mph. As Davie recalls: "I was working downtown in a bank and could only race on weekends. This record attempt was a weekend affair. If we had geared the engine slightly higher, fitted a smaller propeller and picked a lake to give the a longer run-up, Fred (Jacoby), Dean (Draper) and I felt we had a 90 mph boat."

Then there was Doug Fonda winning the Townsend Medal for that year with the inimitable Fred a close second. Reportedly Fonda got hooked on outboard racing when he fished Gar Wood Jr. out of the Hudson River after he flipped during an Albany-New York marathon which Fonda was watching. He was a wealthy industrial banker and spent money "to be the best". Fonda routinely towed five boats and seven motors for racing in Class A, B, C and F, complete with mechanics, to every race and drove with much ability too. In his drive to win the Townsend Medal, he allegedly flew his boats and motors from coast to coast on occasion in order to compete in more races on a given weekend and gather more points. For this reason, to enable Fred to regain his predominance, the Jacobys started to look around for ways to improve on straightaway speed and better cornering. Although they were not at first enthusiastic about the idea, one direction was to adapt their building methods to the three-pointer hydroplane for outboard power.

The first three-point hydroplane for inboard power had been built five years before. It arrived by accident. Since his 60 mph *Tech Jr* of 1912, Adolph Apel of the Ventnor Boat Works, Atlantic City, New Jersey, had maintained a reputation for producing successful raceboats. While testing his outboard hydroplanes, Apel noticed that as they rounded a buoy, their stern would slide but their bows dug into the water. To prevent this he fitted bustles or wingstubs. In 1932, the Ventnor yard built *Emanicipator Special* for Mortimer S. Auerbach, a wealthy local businessman. Although it had the Apel patent concave bottom and small non-trip chines, in cornering this inboard hydro behaved like the outboards.

Since the summertime work at Ventnor was to service raceboats, runabouts, aquaplanes and water-skis, Apel decided to turn a pair of water-skis into bustles. Fairing their front with the rising forward chine, they supported the 7/8-inch thick curved planks with brass tubing and braces. These additions gave the *Emancipator Special* just the stability it needed, and greater speed.

With subsequent inboard raceboats built at the Apels' yard, the Ventnor three-point system was refined to obtain optimum performance from two forward sponsons and the stern of the boat as the third point, so that drivers could use a cushion of air to race round the buoys. This configuration was so successful that in October 1937 Adolf E. Apel and his son Arno had filed a US patent which was granted some ten months later with n°2, 126, 304.

For twenty years, Detroit Yacht Club Commodore Gar Wood with his succession of ten multiple aero-engined *Miss America* single-step hydroplanes had remained the uncrowned Speed King of the world. Wood had encouraged his son Gar Jr. to become involved in outboard racing.

The controversial 1937 Spreckels Trophy race. America leads France, but not for long.

In the harsh shadow of a famous father, Gar Wood Jr. went outboard racing. As son of the unbeatable "speed king", with money no object, victory was the teanager's only option.

In 1938 Gar Wood Jr. and Texan boatbuilder Worth Boggerman collaborated to pioneer arguably the first three-point suspension outboard hydroplane. In September of that year, Gar Jr. ran the boat to a new competition record for class B at Chattanooga, Tennessee. Prior to this, other builders had stayed away from three-point designs, in part due to fear of the Apel patent for inboard hydros. Now the dam was broken and everyone got in on the act.

The adaptation of the Ventnor three-point system to smaller hulls was another five years away from perfection, but the Jacobys felt that they had better be the best, rather than anyone else. This would take time. Surprisingly, they were given permission by the Apels to use their patented design free-of-charge. Following his failure in the Spreckels Trophy race, Viscount Forbes pulled out of power-boat racing. He sold one of his Soriano 6 cylinders to a Milan car dealer and clever engineer called Guido Romani, whose garage was conveniently less than 1.5 mile from the Idroscalo lake. Since 1935, Romani's sons, Augusto and

Tight racing between two of Italy's great champions in 1937 on Milan's Idroscalo Lake.
Count Carlo Casilini in X 1-10 Mariella-Passarin hull against Augusto Romani in 16-X Rex,
both powered by 1,000 cc Laros F55 outboards.

Renzo, driving both Laros and Elto Quad-engined Century or Lotterio hulls had begun to tote up an impressive list of race victories. In 1938, using the Lotterio-Laros, 23-year-old Augusto Romani established World records for one hour and two hours, also clinching the Italian Championships. Soon acquiring a second Dupuy-Soriano from French pilot Eminente, Romani was to make such improvements on these two units - better water-cooling and driveshaft - as would enable his sons to become Italy's most successful outboard race drivers during the next two decades.

Somehow, the sport in Britain staggered on. A high point for many people had been the day the starting gun for the *Daily Mirror* Trophy on Oulton Broad had been fired by Commodore Gar Wood outside his boathouse in Detroit, some 4, 000 miles away, and its sound transmitted by a Tannoy loudhailer linked to transatlantic telephone to Everitt's Park, where it was heard by the 26 entrants and thousands of spectators. Following which, an exciting contest was won by

The annual outboard race across Milan gave spectators a bird's eye view at the Naviglio Canal. Here comes Augusto Romani in the Laros-engined 16-X Rex, named after the Atlantic record-breaking ocean liner.

A very rare "cigarette card" from a set called "Speed", produced by W.D. & H.O. Wills.

English concessionaire for Johnson engines, Harold C Notley drives the 22 hp Johnson-engined Chick III *at 36 mph.*

the local hero, George Treglown, whose *Black Magic*, powered by a Johnson "Racing A" enabled him to complete the 2.5-mile course at a sporting 31 mph.

In 1935, E. P. Barrus Ltd of London had gained the franchise to import the Johnson outboard into Britain. The sales director was a former Rolls-Royce car hire operator called Harold C. Notley. He determined that winning races and breaking records was the best form of marketing. In a series of reverse-clinker See dinghies called *Chick*, Notley did just that. 1939 came and promised to be a very healthy year for the sport. At Oulton Broad, the wealthy Edward Treglown, determined to reign supreme on outboard racing, had not only acquired Doug Fonda's Class X Jacoby hull, identical to the one with which Bud Davie had set his world record, he also acquired an identical Draper Special tractor drive.

Jean Dupuy had also seen the error of his ways. Although his champion teams had won the Spreckels Trophy three years' running, he would have to dispense with those beautifully-built, over-heavy, aluminium hulls if he was to beat the Americans.

For example, Marshall Eldredge, a meticulous machinist and great outboard engineer from Massachusetts put two Johnson PR-65s one above the other. Four individual PR cylinders were mounted on special crankcase with induction controlled by two PR rotary valves. Walker Baumann supplied the lower unit. Mounting this 90 hp Eldredge X motor on a Jacoby hull, on January 11th, 1939, Clinton Ferguson of Waban, Massachusetts, had lifted Davie's speed by 0.2 mph to 78.44 mph. Dupuy knew his engine had at least 10 hp power provided his boat was light enough. He therefore had it mounted on the 12 ft Jacoby hull specially built for him at North Bergen. On May 20th, 1939, the Frenchman created a new two-way average of 79.04 mph on the Seine. His best run was just over 84 mph. Dupuy claimed that he could push the world record over the 80 mph mark. World War II interrupted that claim and it was not until over a decade later that any higher speeds would be attained and then by Italians.

Last minute preparations for the starting gun at Middletown.

During World War II, single-step hydroplane racing,
although reduced to a small fraternity, remained fiercely competitive in the USA.

Post-War Revival

T he USA was fortunate that racing outboard motors were on hand when the Second World War began. The Evinrude 4-60 became the "Storm Boat" motor model 8008. It was modified from 60 to 55 hp and from 6,000 to 5,000 rpm and fitted with a bipod that allowed it to be placed in the middle of special Storm Boats that could carry eight soldiers at planing speeds. Thus a former racing engine, repainted in camouflage green, enabled some 300,000 Allied troops to cross the Rhine - over 125,000 men in a single day. Johnson also manufactured thousands of outboards for Army, Navy and Marine Corps use. A 22 hp twin-cylinder engine, modified to full-pivot reverse, was used on bridge pontoons. In one sector of the Rhine crossing, some 1,000 units were brought up by the Army to help facilitate the flow of supplies over the river. Pontoons in groups, tied together with cross members, were used to ferry trucks, tanks, and heavy equipment across rivers and other waterways.

Evinrude Storm Boat motor.

Johnson also turned out thousands of 5 and 10 hp outboards for use on rubber landing boats, and these saw action on both Pacific and European assault beaches. Evinrude's four-cylinder 9.7 hp "Lightfour" was used by the Navy in lifesaving boats which were dropped from bomber bays as survival equipment to rescue aviators forced to ditch at sea. According to US Navy records, this rugged engine was responsible for the "rescue of over 700 men from bombers or fighters forced down in the North Sea or Pacific Ocean as a result of enemy action." Johnson engineers modified the Evinrude 4-60 powerhead into a portable fire-fighting pump for the Navy. This adaptation, designated as "HP-500" pumped water out of the ocean at the rate of 500 gallons per minute at 100 psi, delivering a stream of water so powerful that it took three men to hold the hose. The Johnson factory had produced some 45,000 of these by the end of the war. In one case, three of these pumps were credited with saving a US destroyer when her regular pumps had been knocked out by enemy action. The three pumps worked steadily for 27 hours and kept the ship afloat until emergency repairs stopped the inflow of water. In Japan, 15 hp 4-cycle outboards manufac-

tured by the Shoda Aircraft Company were used by the Japanese Army to cross the Johore Buhru river before entering Singapore.

Although restrictions had been placed on the use of gasoline, outboard racing had not totally dried up. After three years of constant testing and re-designing, the Jacoby Boats Works had announced their Flyaway three-pointer. Alongside the North Bergen yard, Dick Neal, "Shorty" Fillinger of Texas and Don Flowers had also built their first three-pointers.

Most of these were built for the smaller classes A (15 cu/in) and B (20 cu/in). In 1941 Jacoby built a larger boat for class C (30 cu/in), intended for Fred's own use. It turned out to be a bit large for class C so Jimmy Mullen of Richmond, Virginia, class F record holder of that time, hung a 4-60 (60 cu/in) on it, winning in his class at that year's National Championships in Austin, Texas. After that, the Jacobys went on to build and sell smaller class three-pointers in 1941. Despite this activity, the conventional single-step hydros remained in the majority until the war stopped most race activity in 1942.

Following Pearl Harbor, the APBA closed its doors for the duration of the war, not to reopen until Japan threw in the towel. There was no racing on a national basis, most drivers went into the armed forces. There were exceptions. One was the annual Hearst Perpetual Gold Trophy for outboard racers that kept going in 1943, 1944 and 1945 at Long Beach, California. Another was in such highly-industrial midwest states as Ohio, Michigan and Indiana, etc., where many pre-war drivers owned or ran machine shops, foundries, pattern shops, making parts for the war effort. Such men were exempted from military service. Art Brown of Cleveland, Ohio, noted this and on July 4th, 1943, formed a new racing organization called the National Outboard Drivers Association to carry on racing in the above-mentioned states during the war years. NODA organized races in Detroit, Cleveland, Fremont (Ohio) and Columbus (Ohio). Gasoline being rationed, getting to the races was a feat in itself. Several drivers would pool their ration coupons, sometimes stretching the gasoline by adding more readily available solvents such as benzol. The NODA folded up when APBA re-opened its doors in 1946.

Powered by the Evinrude, such "Storm Boats" could carry eight soldiers at planing speeds. In this way, some 300,000 Allied troops crossed the Rhine.

Over in occupied France, outboard racing had continued, for a while. On June 17th, 1941, G. Caron used a Class X Dupuy on the stern of his Ralu-hulled Georgina to obtain a distance world record of 63.79 mph.

Fred Jacoby Jr. retired from active racing in 1942, with an impeccable record as American High Point Champion in '35, '36, '38, '40 and '41. In his brochure for that year, Fred claimed 4,000 first places in twelve years for both Jacoby single-steppers and three-pointers. Fred was to continue his job with Nolan Studios as scenic painter for top shows like "My Fair Lady", "Camelot" and "The Sound of Music". As for his friend Bud Davie, business involvements such as his hard chrome-plating factory in Detroit, decided him against returning to racing - for the time being, at any rate. Over in occupied France, outboard racing had continued some time. For example, on September 28th, 1941, there was a race on the River Seine, won by Bouchon. The same year, French pilot Caron used a Dupuy on the stern of his Ralu hull to obtain a world distance record of 63.79 mph. Jean Dupuy, turned American

Thanks for
your friendship
Pep Hubbell

*Randolph Hubbell
with one of his Johnson
PR replicas.
From his workshop
in El Monte, California,
he produced newly cast
parts designed to keep
the pre-war racers operable,
in kit form.*

citizen, was much criticized for his refusal to join the Free French. He might well have continued in the sport. But not long after the liberation, Dupuy and his wife were "en route" to a formal dinner. They were on a motorcycle because of the petrol shortage in France. Reportedly some part of their evening clothes got caught in the wheel, the bike flipped and Dupuy lost a leg in the ensuing accident. He was thus forced to sell all his race equipment

Following the return of peace, OMC continued their pre-war business strategy across the States of catering for the boom in fishing and family outboards but offered no new racing products. Whilst some 125,000 motors were sold in 1946 they were of little interest to racing enthusiasts. This vacuum pulled small firms into the picture. Names like Clyde Wiseman, Starnes, Fuller, Marshall Eldredge and Randolph Hubbell began producing newly cast parts designed to keep the pre-war racers operable. Both the Evinrude "Storm Boat" motor and the Johnson fire-pump based on the 4-60, now being sold off as war surplus, were quickly discovered by racing enthusiasts with a talent for pattern making and machining. Randolph "Pep" Hubbell of El Monte, California, began by supplying the fraternity with all necessary parts: copper heads, streamlined underwater units, 2:1 gears and much else besides, in kit form, to turn a Storm Boat

An early Mercury Rocket
"Racing" version
from 1947, nicely restored.

motor into a pukka racing unit. After that it rested on the ability of the machinist to build these diverse components into a racing unit. Later on Hubbell would supply an entire racing engine in the form of a "C-52" Class C unit. As they had done before the war, these rigs burned a fuel mixture of alcohol, methanol, and castor oil, and required some professional expertise forming what was nicknamed the "alky" drivers fraternity. But there was still a need for a "stock" motor a teenager could take out of a box, put on his homebrew hydro, gas up, and pull the cord to go fast. So it was that the outboard racing fans started talking about one solution: a brand new engine which had just appeared on the market, called after the Roman god of commerce, the winged messenger "Mercury". In 1939, Elmer Carl Kiekhaefer, an engineer in the field of magnetic separators, magnetic clutches and magnetic brakes, had purchased the assets of the Cedarburg Manufacturing Corp. in Wisconsin, including 300 "Thor" outboard motors that had been rejected by a major mail order firm because they would not perform satisfactorily. Sorely in need of capital, Kiekhaefer decided to rebuild and improve these engines to the satisfaction of the customer, who not only accepted them, but ordered more.

In March 1941, the US Government restricted the use of aluminium to military products - and by the end of the war, the Kiekhaefer Corporation was the largest chain-saw engine builder in the world and a recognized authority on radio-controlled target aircraft. Experience gained in manufacturing two-cycle engines for this purpose, saw, in 1946, the presentation of the 3.2 hp single cylinder Mercury "Comet" and the 6 hp alternate-firing twin "Rocket". Both motors incorporated anti-friction ball, roller and needle bearings in their connecting rods, crankshaft, driveshaft and prop-shaft. Both incorporated abrasion-resistant, rubber rotor water pumps and streamlined housings and cowlings.

Racing for Kiekhaefer Mercury began in 1947 when their latest model, the 10 hp Mercury "Lightning", was used in the first post-war Albany-New York marathon up the Hudson. One year later, the 1948 Albany-New York marathon was the largest so far in the history of the event. Out of 200 entrants, 141 completed the 134-mile river course–a feat considered impossible before the war. Mercury "Rocket" outboard drivers took the first five places in the 12.5 cubic inch Class I, beating those using Champion "Lite Twin", Martin "60" and Firestone engines. Class II had nearly fifty Mercury Lightnings and again the first five places in that class were won by the new comer at a speed of 27.9 mph. However, the majority of entrants in the higher-powered classes were still Evinrude and Johnson outboards as Mercury was not yet into the big leagues. Whilst such events now forced the APBA to officially acknowledge racing engines whose components were made by small manufacturers other than OMC, they also argued for the formation of a national organisation to handle marathon and sprint races for stock boats outside the existing structure of the APBA.

Racing for Kiekhaefer
Mercury began in 1947
when their latest model,
the 10 hp Mercury
"Lightning", was used
in the first post-war Albany-
New York marathon
up the Hudson River.

The Pro drivers in the 50s
raced mostly 3 point hulls.
Archive color photo.

A Fillinger hull powered by a Mercury Rocket at the beginning of the 50s. Archive color photo.

To give their motors a further edge on speed, Mercury also developed a more streamlined lower unit "Quick Silver". In fact, Martin Motors had produced a racing gearcase that outran the Mercurys until then lagging behind with their standard "fishing" type gearcase. In 1948, Kiekhaefer had instructed his chief engineer Reginald Rice, chief draughtsman Bill Spaeth and Dick Williams to produce a racing gearcase interchangeable with the fishing one so designed that the propeller shaft and gears would be inserted from the rear end of the propeller shaft housing, and the gearcase containing a water pump. Most racing units were pumpless, using speed to push water into the engine. In their attempt to accomodate this, the team arrived at a hydrodynamically inefficient shape. This Quicksilver lower unit was announced to the Mercury dealers on March 24th, 1950. Happily, its arrival on the racing scene coincided with another innovation. Among the vast armada of outboards, two alky-fuelled hydros raced by a Virginian called J. B. Broaddus would sometimes attract particular attention by throwing up a "roostertail" of spray in their wake. Technically Broaddus had "cupped" his prop so raising its pitch abruptly at the edge of the blades. This permitted the propeller to run on the surface, reducing drag and increasing speed. Stock drivers soon realized that using such wheels enabled them to raise the Mercury Quicksilver unit high enough out of the water to more than compensate for its hydrodynamic inefficiency when run deep in the water. During the next fourteen years, over 17,000 Quicksilver gearcases went into action. During that time, the lower fin or "skeg" was lengthened so that the unit could be lifted still higher our ot the water to take full advantage of propeller improvements while still maintaining steering capability.

At the same time and after exhaustive tests, the Michigan Wheel Co. had developed their two-bladed "AJ (for Aqua-Jet) super deluxe racing wheels, virtually custom-built to fit the specific individual motors on which they are to be used."

As the adage goes, nothing is new. In the 1920s, the propeller shaft of the inboard-engined Hickman "Sea Sled", an inverted V-bottomed craft, was brought out through the transom rather than through the bottom. With about half the propeller diameter above the bottom of the boat, Albert Hickman had created "surfacing" and the first boat to throw a roostertail.

I. E.White, vice-president of the Michigan Wheel Co., was well aware of the Sea Sled's half-submerged propellers, but stated that, at first, the props: "simply beat up a big foam and the boat didn't move fast enough to keep ahead of the following seas. Finally someone conceived of knocking over the tips of each blade. Strange things then happened. The boat actually ran along pretty well."

A Quicksilver propeller from Mercury.

Cupping had been born. And, the boat did run "pretty well". In 1921 an inboard Sea Sled set a class record of 58 mph, hot stuff in 1921! The cupping concept lay dormant for decades until White's company revived it so that the Quicksilver unit could be made to run in the surfacing mode. Almost simultaneously, Mercury also began making cupped stainless steel props under the name "Kaminc" which were fully competitive with the Michigan props. Kaminc stood for "Kiekhaefer Aeromarine Motors Inc."

Any driver whose Mercury Lightning was fitted with a Quick silver lower unit and AJ prop had a distinct edge on his competitors.

With the establishment of a new factory in a former dairy farm at Fond du Lac, Wisconsin, in 1949 the Kiekhaefer Corporation developed the Mercury "25 Thunderbolt". This was first four-cylinder-in-line, two-cycle, 25 hp Mercury outboard - with one-piece sand-cast aluminium block and integral single coil magneto system. Five years later sand-casting would be replaced by die-casting, beginning with the "Mark 55". Mercury's factory was on the banks of Lake Winnebago. This location presented the perfect opportunity to create a mid-western equivalent of the famed Albany to New York Marathon. Nominally it was a promotional event sponsored by *The Milwaukee Sentinel* newspaper, but it was really controlled and largely financed by Mercury. No wonder, therefore, that in the first running of the Winnebagoland Marathon in 1949, of the 300 entries, the majority of engines had been built locally. At the long-established Hudson marathon, to the amazement of race officials at Albany on the day before the race, drivers kept pouring in an almost never-ended stream until the total reached a record 315 entries. Many of these also used stock Mercury engines.

Mercury Motor Thunderbolt 25 hp 1949.

Also that year, when the Stock Outboard Racing Commission of the APBA organized the stock utility national championship on Lake Alfred, Florida, of the six events, Mercury scored a clean sweep in five of the six contests for which they were eligible. Indeed on many other circuits, Mercury Thunderbolt engines with Quicksilver lower units not only revived APBA Class D but won race after

A Scott Atwater engine with its "Streamline" lower unit.

Martin outboard engine equipped with an original Silver Streak racing lower unit.

race. In doing so, Kiekhaefer put the noses of at least two fledgling companies out of joint. Neither the 16 hp "High-Speed 60" and the 20 hp "Silver Streak 200" outboard with their "Torpedo" lower unit as developed by George W. Martin at his factory in Eau Claire, Wisconsin, nor the 16 hp outboard with its "Green Hornet" lower unit as developed by Scott-Atwater of Minneapolis, were a match for the Kiekhaefer kickers. Nevertheless, Scott-Atwater was not short of innovations developing the world's first separate fuel tank - freeing racing drivers from a dependance on the limited fuel tank of their engines, with less need for pit stops. It would also be Scars Elgin who developed the first lightweight fiberglass engine cowling.

None of this would have been possible if a reasonably-priced hull builder had not appeared on the Stock racing scene. That man was a former Eastern Airlines pilot turned rustic furniture maker, including clothespins, called Joe Swift, working in the citrus grove area of Mount Dora, Florida. Observing the great popularity of Stock outboard racing, Swift had come up with the idea of making low-cost hydroplanes to pair with Kiekhaefer's relatively low-cost Mercury engines. Until then, raceboats in the US were built with mahogany planks, fastened to spruce ribs and battens with brass screws. A typical Class A or B hydro of this construction sold for approximately $400 and was built to order with a delivery time of several weeks to several months. Swift upset the status-quo by developing a hydro which was similar in design to the existing three-point hulls but which was sheathed with marine plywood rather than with individual planks. Instead of brass screws laboriously turned into drilled holes he used a combination of glue and serrated nails hammered into place at great speed. The resulting boat could be sold for about $160. Boat n°1 was bought by Tommy Hagood of Orlando, Florida, who used it in regular Class A and B competitions with good results. Orders soon began to flood in.

Mass-produced in this way, most Swift three-pointers were sold through Mercury dealerships. Thus Swift made it possible for a would-be racer to walk into a Mercury dealership and buy a complete outfit, ready to race, right off the showroom floor. Swift added other models to the line and his business prospered. The 110-inch model "UH-092" was for Class A and B racing, whilst the 133-inch model "UHD" (known as Big Dee) was for Class C to D and F engines. Both had what the Swift sales leaflets called "negahedral afterplane and negahedral sponsons". Frames were of aircraft-grade Sitca spruce, planking of 7 mm Occume mahogany, finished with clear varnish. Decks were of 4 mm, three-ply mahogany, whilst the low turbulence cowling was oven-formed. During the next fifteen years, almost 9,000 Swift hulls were to leave the Mount Dora workshop; this does not include the sales of building plans. 1950 was the year in which the "Utilities" (soon to be termed "Stock outboards") felt mature enough to stage a full-scale National Championship Regatta - many of them sporting Mercury engines with Quicksilver lower units. It was also thanks to Kiekhaefer and Swift that, for example, at that year's Albany-New York marathon, officials were forced to artificially reduce the 600 entries down to the first 300 received. But starting 150 boats in each flight was still a formidable task.

Lest we forget the professional "alky" drivers, during this period Fred Jacoby's empty throne was taken by Doug Creech of Charlotte, North Carolina, who won the George H. Townsend High Points medal in 1948, 1949 and 1950. In his forties, ex-motorycle racer "Creech Screech" ran a Harley-Davidson dealership. He drove three-point hydroplanes built by Dick Neal of Kansas City, in Classes A, B, C, D and F from Florida to Washington D. C. to the Mississippi. In 1950 Creech's points score was 16,703.

Since the war, three-point development had been rapid, single step hydros soon becoming scarce. The early post-war leaders in hydro-building were Jacoby, Neal,

Doug Creech in contemplative mood. This Harley-Davidson motorcycle dealer from Charlotte, North Carolina, won the George H. Townsend Medal in 1948, 1949 and 1950.

*Just a fraction
of the jammed pits
at the 1953 Winnebagoland
Stock Outboard Marathon
- an ideal promotional tool
for Mercury. Between 200
and 300 boats would
compete annually.*

and Fillinger. The big problem was the tendency of the early designs to blow over backwards without much provocation. They were really hairy to drive !

In an attempt to counter this, the De Silva brothers from Venice, California, sold what they called " cab-over " hydros as early as 1950, moving the driver forward to hold the nose down.

At the beginning of the 1951 season, the Stock Utility Outboard Racing Commission of the APBA announced that from now on Mercury Quicksilver lower units and the Evinrude powerhead changes came under the rule stating that for any replacement parts to be accepted for Utility racing, the manufacturer must certify that such parts would be supplied as standard equipment on further models of the complete motor as sold by retail dealers. The APBA Commission also established Classes A, B and D for Stock hydros to go alongside " Stock Utility " runabouts, off the shelf racing gears, this alongside increasingly popular plans now available for home-built hulls. Stock hydro speeds were

respectable. Tommy Hagood of Orlando was showing a consistent 53 mph with a Mercury B/Swift three-point hydro using ordinary gas and closed exhaust system but with a Quicksilver unit and a careful prop. Elsewhere, Jack Maypole clocked 70 mph with a Mercury D Stock hydro. Most Utility drivers demanded that their motors be kept as "stock" as possible. They were against the "polishing", the tuning of a stock engine for racing. During the 1950 Albany-New York marathon, some "hop-up" modifications had been allowed on Evinrude engines. When the APBA banned "polishing" for the 1951 race, a breakaway "Stock Outboard Racing Association" was formed to organize a 1951 Albany-New York marathon where non-APBA members could race with non-stock modifications. The fleet would be limited to a staggering 360 boats, starting in three flights. By the end of 1951, APBA membership included 700 pro-outboard racing drivers as opposed to 1,300 Stock Outboard racing drivers. But early season predictions that pro-outboard racing classes would fold up under the onslaught

Bill Tenney illustrates the conflict which raged in the 1950s between the old-line alky drivers powered by Johnson, Evinrude or König and the upstart Stock drivers powered by Mercury.

the stock classes proved groundless. The 1951 season saw a total 79 sanctioned regattas in which stock outboard rigs could compete, and 95 for racing outboards. Despite the Korean War taking away a number of drivers to the armed forces, racing continued. The Townsend Medal for 1951 with the coveted race number "US-2" went to David Livingston of Arkansas, who toted up 38,245 points, more than twice that of Doug Creech. Aided by his family, Livingston competed in five hydro classes and two runabouts classes, making clean sweeps of many a regatta, as 2nd place went to Bud Wiget of Concord, California. Records in the stock division fell continuously. Florida's Tommy Hagood racked up record after record - almost two every weekend - in one class or another.

In the meantime, in Cedarburg, Carl Kiekhaefer had been approached by a brilliant young mechanical engineer named Charles D. Strang Jr., a research associate at the Massachusetts Institute of Technology. Strang proposed to assemble a tuned-up 75 hp Evinrude power head, a Johnson drive shaft, and one of Kiekhaefer's new Quicksilver racing lower units in an attempt to set a new hydroplane Class X record at over 85 mph. Kiekhaefer was not only intrigued by Strang's proposal, he offered Strang the job of head of a new research department at a salary he could not refuse. Although he never did build his record challenger, Charlie Strang's entry into the performance outboard field was to influence the sport for the next 40 years.

During the 1952 season in America, alky-fuelled pro-outboarders were becoming fewer and farther between in many parts of the US since the stock classes had jumped into prominence. All the same, drivers like Tenney, Wearly, Petermann, Wiget, Creech and other pro veterans held the fort.

Across America, the 25 hp Mercury Thunderbolt and 10 hp Super 10 Hurricane were regular winners in both Utility runabout and Stock hydro classes. Utility hulls frequently used were the Speedliners as manufactured by General Marine of St Joseph, Missouri, and a long, lean patented hull designed

Three point hydroplane P-100 at speed.

Here is a competitor in the stock runabout class anxious to appear conspicuous in the case of an accident. This was before the invention of fluorescent colouring.

by Frenchman Marcel Raveau of Lindenhurst, New York, and built over on Long Island, to mention just two. And, if you wanted maximum thrust from a Mercury engine, Carl Kiekhaefer had just introduced a four-cylinder, in-line, two-stroke 40 hp Mercury incorporating a one-piece, die-cast aluminium block and integral, single-coil magneto system. The 20th Albany-New York marathon, considered as a roughwater race for the pro/alky engines, now became a race for stock outboards - also because replacement parts for alky engines were no longer made by Johnson or Evinrude. In fact, the non-factory made parts were expensive for this killer of a race. Out of 254 entries, 246 started in six classes. First home was 22-year-old, Robert L. Switzer of McHenry, Illinois, in a Switzer hull designed by his brother David, powered by a Mercury Class DU (30-40 cu/in) in 33 hours 3 minutes, averaging 42.4 mph. The Switzer family had been building boats since 1945. Of the 88 finishers, 78 ran Mercury engines ranging from 10 to 40 cu/in The young Switzer not only won $500 for his first place in his class, but was treated to the special honor of having six beautiful girls bestow upon this day's hero some mighty luscious kisses which he took in stride.

In November 1952, 15-year-old Dean Chenoweth of Xenia, Ohio, became the first driver to win in three classes at a Stock Outboard National Championship : Class A stock runabout and Class A and B stock hydro. In 20 years of professional outboard racing, only two other drivers had been successful in notching up a three class victory, Clint Ferguson and Bud Wiget. Boatbuilders continued to tackle the instability problem with the three-pointer. As a former airline pilot, Joe Swift of Mount Dora had some understanding of aerodynamics, so it must have seemed reasonable to him that he could reduce the pitch instability so common in the three-pointers of that day by moving the centre of lift aft and closer to the center of gravity. So he built what he called "the lazy dog" because the forks resembled a dog sleeping with its legs stretched out in front. This configuration would later come to be known also as a "picklefork hull". In September 1952, Tommy Hagood, a top-notch driver, raced the "lazy dog" hydro, powered by a four-cylinder Mercury, at the Stock Outboard

Fifteen-year-old Dean Chenoweth of Xenia, Ohio, with his parents after winning a Class A stock National Championship. Dean went on to become a top driver in Unlimited hydros, eventually dying in the Miss Budweiser.

In January 1953, at Lakeland, Florida, Tenney, helped by his master mechanic Walt Blankenstein, drove his Hornet *boats to new competition marks in Class B hydro (53.6 mph), Class C hydro (60.7 mph) and Class C racing runabout (54.1 mph) .*

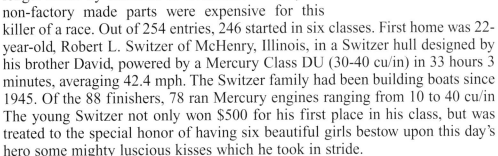

*Boatbuilder Joe Swift
with his star driver Tommy
Hagood of Orlando,
Florida, in his "Big-Dee"
hydro at the 1952 APBA
Stock Outboard National
Championships
at Oakland, California.*

National Championships at Oakland, California. Another driver was so intrigued by the boat that he bought it on the site and, powered by a Mercury KG-9, the lazy dog was seen again on the 1953 circuits. But Swift did not pursue the concept further, perhaps because he sacrificed some speed by reducing the total lift in the search for pitch stability. On the whole, most of the top alky-hydro builders were content to work with such variables as tunnel width, tunnel depth or sponson height, angle of attack of the tunnel floor, deck shape, etc., to stabilize their craft as best they could. They were conducting an evolution, not a revolution. But racing was not the only way in which Kiekhaefer was promoting his products. He succeeded in a much publicized "steeple-chase speedboat show" held on and around Lake Eloise, Florida. Six boats were specially designed and built with identical Mercurys. In a race where they not only had to ride across the water but fly over banks as well, Dick Pope Jr. from the Cypress Gardens water-ski show was the winner in *Lightning*. Among those who used Stock Mercury to take up the sport was William Errol "Bill" Seebold Jr., the eleven-year-old son of a Mercury dealer of St Louis, Missouri. Bill's father, himself an outboard racing-driver of twelve years standing, was soon teaching his son the tricks of the trade, whether with runabouts or hydros.

The rising supremacy of Stock classes over Pro continued. During the 1953 season, 286 sanctioned outboard regattas of all forms were held across the United States, although professional outboarders were faced with a real crisis, the destruction of Pro racing by Stock. Of the APBA expenditure on powerboat racing, 78 % would be on outboards and only 22 % on inboards. And, 70 % of the outboard budgets were spent on Stock against 30 % on Pro.

But the pros kept going strong. That year, of the 28 new speed records set in competition and one on the Mile straightaway, eight of the new records were set in 4 classes by one man, 38-year-old William Tenney of Dayton, Ohio. In January, at Lakeland, Florida, Tenney, helped by his master mechanic Walt Blankenstein, drove *Hornet* to new competition marks in Class B hydro at 53.6 mph, then in Class C hydro at 60.7 mph and in Class C racing runabout at 54.1 mph so breaking class records set in 1947, 1952 and 1951 respectively. Tenney was fast becoming world champion record-breaker of the post-war racing era. The 1953 season's largest race was the 5th annual "Milwaukee Sentinel" Winnebagoland Marathon where 272 boats in five classes competed. First five places in the Class DU were taken by Mercury-engined Switzer hulls, Bob Switzer himself completing the 92-mile course in a winning 1hour 47 minutes.

This young fellow is Billy Seebold, being weighed in after winning a National Championship. At the time he was driving for the Johnny Cash country music band in boats called Miss Folsom Prison, A Boat named Sue, *and other Cash hit records.*

Jack Maypole, famed PRO driver from Chicago in charge of his V-100, learning how the other half lives - or in other words up against a stock gladiator.

Throughout that year, to seduce Stock drivers to take part in the Racing Division, the APBA had made a desperate rule change. Any Stock engines had become acceptable for use in Racing Division of same class. Such engines no longer needed to be maintained in stock condition for racing events, open exhaust, alcohol fuel, etc., becoming acceptable as well as all the allowable modifications for racing engines. This intrusion bore fruit in 1954. Tacoma's Jack Leek ran his alcohol-burning ex-stock Class A rig on the Mile at Seattle and clocked 61.069 mph to raise that record over 7 mph. Leek's close friend, Burt Ross of Seattle ran his Class D hydro over the Mile at Devil's Lake and raised the Class F Record to 75.6 mph. The fraternity knew that even greater speeds would be reached if the trailing edge of the transom could be raised clear of the water, allowing the hydro to ride on its propeller. During the mid-1950s, in an effort to "trim under", champion driver Gerry Waldman of Milwaukee had mounted his four-cylinder alky Mercury engine low on the transom of his Swift, positioning its propshaft to point upwards towards the bow. Waldman managed to "pop the transom", as he put it, but could not achieve sustained flight. Nor could anyone else. It was also at this time that Hubert Entrop, a model builder for Boeing's wind tunnel in Seattle, began to race a novel outboard hull-shape designed by Ted Jones, the man behind *Slo-Mo-Shun IV*, the Allison aero-engined hydroplane which in June 1952 had lifted the World unlimited record to 178 mph. To take the weight off the transom of Entrop's boat, Jones designed a boat with the driver well forward, moving the centre of gravity forward and shaping the underside to move the aerodynamic centre of lift rearward. Ted, who was working for Kiekaefer, built the prototype and hung a Mercury 40 H Class F on the back. Try as they might, Entrop and Leek could not get it to prop-ride, although it showed promise. It was not, however long before they had solved the problem. As Joe Swift reported in an article in *Motorboating* magazine: "Entrop rides perched out on the bow handle while running downwind and then moves forward while running upwind! This latter trick enables him to take a casual glance now and then under the nose of the boat to see if his sponsons are getting too high. This at 80 mph. When this outfit gets up towards peak, the sponsons are flying about 5" off the water and the tail gets sufficiently airborne to transform the roostertail. An offset rudder is linked to the steering bar of his engine. When his rig hits a turn in the high 70 mph, it throws three columns of

For 1954, the APBA made stock engines acceptable to the Racing Division. Here is Tacoma's Jack Leek running his alcohol-burning ex-stock Class A rig on the mile at Seattle and clocking 61.069 mph to raise that record over 7 mph.

water: one from the lower unit and prop, one from the rudder and one from the fin carried on the left sponson. Entrop's Mercury is winding around 9,100 rpm and produces a tenor banshee wail..." In 1955 the spiral in numbers of drivers and regattas showed no sign of levelling out. Registered drivers in the stock division reached the 2,000 mark, while boat registrations reached a staggering 3,000. Stock drivers had the opportunity to compete in 280 regattas (an increase of 43 from the previous season), whilst the outboard pros had 114 chances (an increase of 12) to run their "alcohol burners". Craig DeWald, a Reading, Pennsylvania, 16-year-old, was outstanding on the marathon circuit. Limiting his activity to Class AU, he racked up 800 miles of racing during the season, equivalent to 160 heats of closed course racing. This mileage included three wins, three second places and two third places. Perhaps the peak was reached in 1956. At the 8th Winnebagoland Marathon, 223 boats started, but due to a west wind gusting from 20 to 40 mph, only 22 stock drivers finished in front of a large crowd awaiting the finish at Fond du Lac, Wisconsin. Among the champions, Bob Hering of Sheboygan, driving a Mercury Mark 20 H on a SidCraft, averaged 24.57 mph to win the Class BU. Doing so, Hering could never have dreamt that thirty-one years later he would drive an outboard boat to 169.531 mph. A staggering 530 outboarders competed in the 1956 Stock Outboard National Championship at Cambridge, Maryland. This was perhaps the largest regatta in stock racing and perhaps in the history of powerboat racing. And the end of such a season saw the retirement of Doug Creech of Charlotte, North Carolina, veteran of almost 2,000 boat races. At Long Beach, during the Outboard Nationals, Creech's Class A hydro caught fire and he had to jump ship to avoid being burned. He had won virtually every honor to be had in outboard racing, including over 1,000 victories, numerous National Championships, the John Ward Trophy, straightaway and competitive records as well as four Townsend Medals. From 1957 to 1960 there was a heavy drop in the number of APBA outboard racing members. Whilst stock outboards had dropped from 2,124 to 1,210 the drop in registered stock boats was from 3,155 to 2,446. This left a remaining core of enthusiasts with more than one boat. Over the same period, in the alky classes, 326 drivers and 1,122 boats had fallen to 272 drivers for 902 boats. This slower decline implied a core of multi-class enthusiasts helping to steady this group. But with lowered starting fields, sponsorship had become harder. A new approach would have to be developed

Ray Lenk, 29-year-old Detroit factory foreman, takes the winner's flag in the Mennen Outboard Marathon around Manhattan. Only 41 out of a field of 104 boats finished. 29 of them swamped by 6ft high waves!

The Class X elite in 1952 : n°1 Augusto Romani with his Romani-Riva, n°2 Renzo Romani with his Romani-Timossi and n°4 Massino Leto di Priolo with his Lesco-Swift.

Outside the USA

Elsewhere on planet Earth, outboarding had not been so frenetic. During the decade 1945-1955, at first there had been a rigid control on the importation of all new American models, including the Mercury range. Without such new marques, getting the most power from an outboard engine led to some extraordinary examples of ingenuity.

On May 26th, 1946, racing in Italy was resumed on Lake Como. Then on June 21st, 1947, one of the first international motorboat racing meetings after the War was run on the Seine in Paris with drivers from Belgium, Italy, Sweden and Switzerland competing with the French. In the European 1,000 cc Class X Championships, Paul Schiller of the Zurich Motor Club and the Italian Romani brothers, Renzo and Augusto, duelled fiercely due to the fact that they were among those who had acquired a number of potent pre-war Dupuy six-cylinder units. While the Swiss ran a double overhead camshaft version on the stern of his Portier hydro, the Italians ran singles, improved and tuned by their father Guido. Other Class X competitors included the three Leto di Priolo brothers and Dino Sestini.

Léon Rousset, France's most successful pre-war driver in Class C, relaunched the sport in his country with races in Lyon, Evian and Aix-les-Bains. Most hulls were Jacoby designs, built by Ralu and de Saever, whilst motors were not only recycled war-surplus Evinrudes and Johnsons, but also a converted 500 cc VAP motorcycle engine. In 1950, Rousset created the "Ile de France Motor Yacht Club" organizing two days of record-breaking per year on May 1st and the November 11th on the Measured Mile at Sartrouville.

Drivers included Delacour, de Candolle and Cheney. Set apart, Auguste Gerbaud, wealthy businessman in charge of an electric-starter manufacturing factory, had managed to obtain a pre-war Soriano. He had this fixed on the transom of a Ralu-Bréjat hull to compete in Class X racing around Europe.

For the 1950 Season, Guido Romani, the man who had sold Gerbaud his Soriano, now equipped his sons with three new "Romani" engines. Although based on the Soriano design, they were radically improved. Both head and shaft

Post-war races often saw the same hulls and engines competing as before the war.

were lighter. Better water-cooling. Improved oil circulation from a larger oil tank. Increased compression in modified combustion chambers, new roller-bearing based connecting rods, twin-carburettors and last but not least, a new supercharger custom-built by the Alfa-Romeo racing car department. Twin propellers were still used but gave greater thrust. Between 1950 and 1960, Guido Romani would increase the power output of his engines from the 90 hp at 5,900 rpm produced the Soriano to 130 hp at 7,600 rpm. In rivalry, Carlo Leto di Priolo also built three "Lesco" engines. Although they each developed 162 hp at 6,800 rpm, they were not as successful on the race circuits as the Romani units. Up until 1952, Team Romani used stepped hulls built by Riva of Sarnico, after which two hulls

by Timossi became their regular mounts. Scuderia Lesco used Swift three-pointers. By 1960, when the overexpensive and elitist supercharged Class X was finally abolished by the Union International of Motorboating (UIM), out of the 144 races in which they had participated, Augusto Romani had clocked 44 firsts and Renzo, his younger brother by three years, had totted up 60 firsts. They had usually come in 2nd and 3rd in the remaining 40 races. In sixteen years of racing activity, they won eleven Italian and six European Championships in Class X.

During this same period, across the Channel, English participation in the outboard sport gathered steam more gradually. Under the Presidency of Victor

A 6-cylinder Soriano engine modified by Leto di Priolo with a " homemade " blower made a fine racing unit before the development of the Lesco X4.

Lavender, British Outboard Racing Club members were using American motors modified with either Italian or home-produced parts.

S. J. Watson of Esher had acquired several experimental motorcycle racing engines, up to some 650 cc twins, developed by the late Eric Fernihough. Following experiments with one on the back of his hydro *Ninny*, Watson started commissioning Eric See of Fareham to build him a sequence of *Ninny* hulls to take those adapted engines. Others followed suit. As petrol was still rationed, they used methanol. Initially unable to buy US dollars to purchase Jacoby boats, the British had sized up the designs of successful boats in Europe, then chose the Italian Ralu hull. An example was imported, modified and adopted as a one-design class. A popular race site was an 87-acre gravel pit lake near London's Heathrow Airport. Before long, recycled war-surplus Evinrude and Johnson engines were soon joined by parts and whole engine replicas mail-ordered from the U.S. One of those who began to build up a business on this basis was Len Melly, whose Outboard & Hydroplane Services was soon supplying, servicing and repairing raceboats for the Lancashire Hydroplane Racing Club. To launch an all-British revival, Harry Guy Bartholemew, dynamic director of the popular British daily newspaper *The Daily Mirror,* commissioned C. B. Darby and Sons of the Commodore Boatyard at Oulton Broad to build six identical 8-foot 9-inch single-step hydroplanes. For horsepower, Charles Harrison, now chief of British Anzani Ltd of Hampton Hill had taken two standard-start, 4 hp rowboat motors and mounted them together at the top of a single-shaft drive and tuned them up to 20 hp for racing. Bartholemew then more or less gave these press-sponsored hydros to the Lowestoft and Oulton Broad Motor Boat Racing Club, who in turn hired them out for a year so that local young businessmen could be attracted into the sport. The idea worked, and the following year these sportsmen bought their own hulls, from either the Darbys of Oulton or from Russell Graves of Lowestoft. Perhaps less patriotically, Bartholemew went one stage further. From America he acquired a 1933, 350 cc Johnson replica engine, fully streamlined and "souped-up" by Hubbell and sent over to Britain. This was fitted on the

Idroscalo at Milan, 1949. Augusto Romani in the Soriano-Romani (n°76) closer round the buoy than his eternal rival Paul Schiller in the Soriano-Portier (n°89).

*9th May 1950:
Gino Alomati clocks a new
Class A outboard record
in Lina II, officially
homologated by the UIM
as Record # 220.*

back of a Darby-built hydroplane with bevelled chine on its rear plane, so that its freeboard came out of the water slightly higher and it could bank more easily round the corners. Called *Wicky 1*, after Bartholemew's helpful American friend, Wickman More, it enabled its driver, Alan Darby, to win the *Daily Mirror* trophy in 1948 for the second year running. In 1950, the 23-year-old *Motor Boat* trophy joined several old urns polished up to revive the sport in Britain. The British Outboard Racing Club had organized a Festival Regatta at Rochester, Kent, for Class A, B, C and X hydroplanes. With 52 entries from six clubs, some 42 boats competed together due to a clever delayed "cubic capacity start" handicapping sequence. Whilst first place was taken by E. H. Barnes in *Blackfriar*, a Johnson-Jacoby rig, the fastest boat was *Thunderbolt*, a one-design hull from

See of Fareham with an Evinrude Class X engine, handled by Len Melly of the Lancashire Club.

A similar revival had occured in Japan. Since 1949, in Tachikawa, the Far East Outboard Club, a group of U.S. Army and Occupation personnel, led by former Ohioan, Major Thomas T. Clarke of the U.S.A.F., had been working with the Japanese to revive the sport. Problems overcome included battling with a gambling syndicate seeking control of boat racing and six weeks of penicillin injections to clear up numerous and sundry infections accumulated by Major Clarke as a result of flipping an Class F hydro in the slightly contaminated waters of Tokyo Bay. A total of 40 outfits in classes BU, CU, A, B and C hydros took part in the initial regatta on Lake Sagami in the quaint tourist town of Yosi at the foot of Mount Fuji, north of Tokyo. Importation of racing equipment being prohibitively expensive, the Japanese had to resort to imported pre-war American engines or make their own. While H. Itoh was making copies of Johnson Class

A, B and C models, calling them "Kinutas", a Mr. Tamura made a Mercury look-alike. At first Japanese hulls were based on pre-war American Elsinore hydroplanes but then following Clarke's sketches, the Sumida-Gawa shipyard began to produce modern hydros and three-pointer copies. Soon after this revival, in 1951, thanks to the efforts of a certain Ryoichi Sasakawa, outboard racing in Japan was officially turned into a public sport followed the passing of a law. Like horse and bicycle racing, 3.3 % of revenues from the sale of both admission and betting tickets to stock outboard racing - annually amounting to many billions of yen - would be used in the reconstruction of post-war Japan, initially for its marine industry. In the decades that followed, under the aegis of a Prefectural Federation, over 170 municipal bodies have regularly organized outboard races at 24 races sites across Japan. This "Kyo-Tei" racing formula requires six 10 ft single-step hydros, each powered by a 32 hp-400 cc stock Japanese outboard, to round two turn buoys for three laps or a total of about one nautical mile. The race last 1 minute and 45 seconds so the gambling takes longer.

So far, England, however, had been deprived of Mercurys and three-pointers. In August of 1951, a race took place on the Thames at Chelsea that was worse than the cross-Channel fiasco of 1929. The National Hydroplane Championship was sponsored by *The Daily Mirror*. Ninety-four boats started. Thanks to river traffic, driftwood and rough water, precisely two finished. Even with outboards, the issue of whether the three-pointer was superior to the single-stepper was being contested and not only in America. This was evidenced at the contest organized in July 1952 by the British Outboard Racing Club at Ruislip Lido, Middlesex, for the *Motor Boat* trophy and televised for an unprecedented one and a half hour. Of the 13 entries in Class B, one was *Pet-Jet*, a three-pointer employing a semi-prop-riding Mercury outboard of only 350 cc. Although it would have been technically impossible for any Englishman to import such a rig, *Pet-Jet*'s driver, U.S.A.F. Sergeant Joe Estes, a ground crewman stationed at Lakenheath, Norfolk, and popular member of the Oulton Broad Club, had got his Mercury three-pointer over free on the system known as "PX", Post Exchange. Racing

November 1951: Swedish pilot Gunnar Faleij running a world record trial on Lake Siljan with Miss Sweden III.

against Estes was Englishman Alan Darby in the more conventional *Wicky 1*: "Oh, we had loads of lovely tussles together. On the straight, his was much faster than mine even though at that time I could do 50 mph, but I could corner better than him and would come out from the buoy in front, then he would reach me down at the bottom buoy and overtake me again."

Alongside this low-powered sport, there was one family in Italy who took up the pre-war World speed record and lifted it to a noticeable notch higher. The outboard and inboard racing career of the three brothers Dore, Carlo and Massimo Leto di Priolo started in 1946 with their using Laros F60 two-stroke outboard engines on Baglietto and Riva stepped hulls, typical of the late 1930s design, only to realize that it was an impossible task to beat the Dupuy-Soriano fleet. They therefore decided to import from the U.S., in 1948, two Eldredge two-stroke 60 cu.in., using two "P.R.50" 30 cu.in. racing Johnsons on a common crankshaft and crankcase with a tractor lower unit similar to the Draper design. Two years of development were necessary to get close to 80 hp, enabling the Leto di Priolo brothers set the Italian Class F record at 72.71 mph, using a "Big D" Swift three-pointer that they had to import from the Mount Dora factory in 1949. Since the Eldredge was not powerful enough to cope with the extra-large size of the Leto di Priolo brothers, they had to approach Manuel Giro, the owner of the "Maquinaria Cinematografica" in Barcelona, and buy two used single-cam Soriano engines from him. Brother Carlo then started to develop and change the supercharger

with a bigger one he personally designed and manufactured. For their hull, the di Priolo brothers went to the son of a furniture-maker called Angelo Molinari, who ran a little boatyard at the side of Lake Como. Molinari suggested that to take the 220 lbs engine, it would be best to scale up a Swift D hydro by 10 % to 12 ft. Although the engine was giving 95 hp at 5,800 rpm, Carlo arranged that via a 59-inch step-up lower unit, the speed of the small three-bladed prop reached 11,000 rpm. Thus on September 26th, 1953, Carlo's lighter brother Massimo climbed into the three-pointer named after him and, despite supercharger problems, went rooster-tailing up and down Milan's Idroscalo to a new average of 83.473 mph, an increase of five mph. Supercharging improved, soon after Massimo clocked an unofficial 88 mph.

By this time, Carlo had been invited to Fond du Lac by his engineering friend of four years standing, Charles Strang, who introduced him to Carl Kiekhaefer. "Lesco" machine tools supplied by Leto di Priolo's Milan factory were already being used to make Mercury engines. Following the world record, Carl was so impressed by Carlo's engineering prowess, that he invited him to join the company. As the Italian's primary income was building machine tools while keeping racing as a hobby, he declined. But he promised Kiekhaefer to operate the first Mercury dealership in Italy where, with his brothers, he formed "Marine Motors Italia" and began by importing a small batch of 32 engines, later to total 12,000 units. Where increasing his record was concerned, Carlo Leto di Priolo had realized that it was not possible to obtain a real "up-to-date" output by using a 1930 engine design like the Soriano. He therefore started to design a totally new four-stroke engine, with the invaluable cooperation of engineer Giovanni Savonuzzi, the father of the Cisitalia car. This was the true Lesco engine, and in 1954, the final prototype was eventually certified by Mario Speluzzi at the Milano Politecnicum at 162 hp at 6,800 rpm. One morning in December 1954, this engine again linked to the same long step-up lower unit and fitted onto a bigger three-point hydro called *Eduardo II* beat the 100 mph mark for the first time, averaging 100.382 mph on the Idroscalo, Milan's artificial lake. That afternoon Carlo Leto di Priolo telephoned Carl Kiekhaefer informing him of their success. When Carl told his Italian concessionaire: "Put the boat and engine on the next

20 December 1954: Massimo Leto di Priolo becomes the first outboard pilot to average 100 mph. His average of 100.376 mph is clocked along the Idroscalo of Milan.

*Balance reaches
a critical point.*

plane and send me everything", the Italian replied "No Carl, this is my toy." The first Lesco "X4" engine with a standard Soriano style unit was sold six months later to a Polish State sports organization and nobody knows what has become of it since. At the same time, Arturo Carniti, an Oggiono industrialist decided to manufacture and develop the small-powered outboard designed by Pietro Vassena of Lecco. In time, the Carniti would become known as the best Italy's racing outboards. The Swift three-point hull arrived in Britain. This was the achievement of the same man who had first introduced the Ventnor three-point inboards, the forward-looking Harold C. Notley. Now running a company called Outboards Ltd at Whitstable in Kent, Notley had also started to import the highly efficient little outboard designed and built by Dieter König of Berlin. Using his boats *Chick V* and *Silver Stream*, Notley went over to Europe with a team, including Dutch, German and British drivers. In 1953, they raced in Loosdrecht, Holland. In 1954, they raced in both East and West Berlin, Köln and Essen, Germany. The only man they always failed to beat was Dieter König himself, who in 1954 had acquired, secondhand, a Swift "Big D" three-pointer from someone who had imported it from America. Fitting one of his König engines on the back of it, Dieter immediately went out and won the European

*Eduardo II and its unique
powerplant are now looked
after by Gian Alberto
Zanoletti at the Museo
della Barca Lariana beside
Lake Como, Italy.*

Championships in the 500 cc Class on Lake Starnberg. König was to win the European title in that class an impressive eight times. In 1956 König made a new One-Mile record of 73.62 mph for Class C hydros ; he used a hull built from a stock plan by McCrea and owned by a U.S.A.F. airman, but of course fitted one of his own engines.

Mercurys had begun to make their mark in France. This was the initiative of Oreste Rocca, who with his brother Louis had several times won the French championship in Class C with Lutetia-engined raceboats built at the family boat-yard at Vitry-sur-Seine. On November 11th, soon after "le Mercury" presentation at the 1954 Paris Boat Show, Louis Devillié bolted a 640 cc model on the back of a Seyler-built American style hull and clocked a speed of 47 mph. Exactly two years late, Oreste Rocca won a class record on the Measured Kilometre at Saint Cloud, near Paris using a 500 cc Mercury to reach a speed of 50.21 mph, with a top speed of 50.96 mph. Soon after, outboard raceboatbuilder Pierre Matonnat of Arcachon in the Aquitaine region, dropped his Johnson agency to take on the Mercury agency for southwest of France. In the meantime,

Leto di Priolo's boat, a bigger three-point hydro called Eduardo II, *is powered by a pure Lesco engine, developing 162 hp at 6,800 rpm, again linked to the same long step-up lower unit.*

German 250 cc
König engine.

With fiberglass hulls built
by his brother Louis
at their factory in the Paris
suburb of Vitry-sur-Seine,
Oreste Rocca became
one of France's leading
outboard race drivers.

Charles Harrison, British
outboard record-breaker of
pre-war days, continued
to compete. As chief
of British Anzani Ltd, he is
explaining how
to adjust engine timing
to the glamorous "Yvonne
from Denver, Colorado".

English inventiveness continued. British Anzani brought out their 15 hp "Unitwin", a monobloc, two-cylinder, water-cooled unit, with a very streamlined underwater leg called the "Silver Streak". To promote this, Anzani Director Harrison bolted it behind the *Silver Arrow*, an eight-foot Canadian-designed three-pointer. With Alan Darby at the controls, this boat established a new mean speed in its class of 40 mph for four runs up and down Oulton Broad. At the Class B National Outboard Championships of 1954, held on the Welsh Harp Lake, first, second and third places were obtained with Anzani engines. Also that year, "Freddy" Buysse, President and Chairman of the UIM based in Brussels, stood up at one of their conferences and suggested the introduction of a type of raceboat other than the hydroplane, able to carry four people with luggage, with a maximum length of 13 feet nine inches, a minimum weight with engine of 286 lbs, but banning fiberglass and metal as being too expensive. Judging was to be in Paris in June 1956, where Jean Noel Bladinaire, President of the French Motor Yacht Club had already set up a gruelling six-hour outboard marathon on the Seine, with a typically low survival rate. The next move took place in January 1956 at the London Boat Show. Up to this time, runabout builders had tended to make exaggerated claims about the speeds of their boats. One man called their bluff. Naval architect Anthony Needell had just designed *Shark Tender*, a 30 hp Evinrude-engined runabout, cold-moulded in mahogany plywood by Souter of Cowes, for Newell Ltd. He now issued a challenge to other runabout builders to take part in an official speed trial. The first "Utility Speedboat Trials" took place in May 1957. It was organized by the London Motor Boat Racing Club on their gravel pit lake at Shepperton. With outboards up to 600 cc and inboards up to 1,500 cc, there were ten entries. Each had to complete three laps of a triangular course with the best lap time taken and set against the others. The fastest time, 32.55 mph, was set by Ceacraft Ltd's *Ceabird* fiberglass runabout, powered by a Mercury "55E" 40 hp. Second was Archie Peace in an Albatross aluminium inboard runabout and third Anthony Needell's Newell *Shark Tender* as driven by R. McDonald. Things might have ended there had not somebody asked: "But how do all these hulls perform in a bunch, riding in each other's wash?" The scratch race which followed was won by Alan Darby, champion hydroplane driver in the 35 hp Johnson-engined, light metal 13-footer *Pearly Miss*, built by Graham Bunn. Alan Darby recalls: "Archie Peace was driving an Albatross with a Ford 10 engine and while he was faster on the straight, our *Pearly Miss* banked well round those corners and we beat him to the finish." The importance of this stepless hull race on the future of the sport cannot be overemphasized. Compared to it, the "Grand Prix de Paris" organized the following month by UIM President Buysse for runabout builders was something of an anti-climax with Anthony Needell showing the only two French runabouts to turn up the heels of his *Shark Tender*.

"Les Six Heures de Paris" was created in 1955 by Jean-Noël Bladinaire to take place in front of and at the end of the Salon Nautique. His idea was to enable boatbuilders and engine manufacturers to put their latest product at work.

Rapport des Jaugeurs.　　　Measurers' Report.

Coque　　　Hull.

Nom du bateau:　　　Longueur:
Name of boat :　　　Length : 4 m. 25

Dessiné par :　　　Largeur:
Designed by:　　　Beam : 1 m 42

Constructeur:　　　Franc bord :
Builder　　;　　　Freeboard : 0 m. 47

Bois ou métal: *plastique*　　　Poids : 135 K°　　　Kgs ou
Wood or metal: *plastique*　　　Weight : 135 K°　　　lbs.

Autres détails selon la classe :
Other particulars according to class:

↓ Course Stroke

Date de la vérification : *9 Mai 1958*
Date of verification :

Signature des vérificateurs:
Measurers' signatures　　　:

Fabricating Plastics

Making an outboard raceboat of lighter material was another way to gain greater speed for the power bolted onto its stern. Immediately after World War II good marine grades of sheet plywood, developed for military use, had replaced carvel and clinker mahogany planking. Soon after, whilst runabout builders changed over to quantity-produced aluminium or molded plywood, the flat surfaces of the hydros limited them to sheet plywood. But then came fiberglass.

Glass fibre was invented in France at the end of the 19th century. It had remained a scientific curiosity until 1931 when the Owens Illinois Glass Co. had the idea of weaving this fibre to reinforce the new and different resins, generally heat-formed, which had begun to appear. These materials saw some industrial development during World War II, for example the radome of the Northrop P-61 "Black Widow" night-fighter, which carried out its first flight on May 21st,1942.

The very first glass-reinforced plastic dinghies were built in 1948 in the United States by Carl Beetle with General Electric, and by the US Navy Department with the Winner boatyard of New Jersey. While US boating magazines of 1954 made virtually no mention of glass boats, other than a small sailboat or two, the 1955 issues are full of photos and text about fiberglass outboard boats. In Great Britain, the first to present a glass reinforced plastic (g.r.p.) boat, was the Tod boatyard of Weymouth in 1950.

In France, the first boat in this material was a little dinghy produced in 1952 by the Swiss naval architect Pierre Staempfli. At the same time, Jacques Lestang, a chemical engineer at Arnaud Company, returned from the United States with the formula for gel-coat, a tougher resin destined to protect the hull exterior. Looking for French clients, Lestang presented himself at the Rocca boatyard at Vitry and met Louis Rocca: "Monsieur Lestang was supplying the builders of plastic caravans and he told me that one could also build boats". Both Louis's father and brother remained skeptical. For twenty-five years the Rocca family had been working with wood. So the risk for a well-known builder

The era of the white plastic raceboat has dawned. And here is the boat, powered by the latest imported Mercury outboard.
Here is a UIM Record certificate, dated 1958. One question in the questionnaire asks whether the hull is in wood or metal, the reply is neither, and the new word "plastique" is used.

to transfer to an unknown product was not to be underestimated. However, Louis succeeded in convincing his father, who in turn said to his other son Oreste: "Let your brother get on with it. In any case, it can only bring something valuable - if it does not work, well never mind we will have lost five or six months. That is not death in one man's life."

"My first boat in plastic", recalls Louis, "was a dinghy. I simply made a mould from a wooden boat. It was towards Christmas 1952. Very soon I noticed that the resins were not very efficient, so I had the products of Vibride Chemical brought over from the States. They were 30 to 40 % more expensive than what one could find in France, but I now had products which were very stable". This additional expense was made up for by one saving. The resin of the time required the addition of filler for thickness. These powders were expensive. Rocca discovered that plaster gave the same advantage of solidity for far less expense. Pioneer days where eventually such practices would change as soon as new resins appeared on the market. From 1953, Rocca began to market a small "grp" dinghy. Until 1980, they would be selling this little boat in its thousands. The Vitry boatyard thus gradually converted its entire range of boats to grp, including raceboats. Whether at Monaco, at the Paris 6 Hours, the Aix les Bains 24 Hours, or during competitions in Marseilles or in Italy, Oreste and his teammates Serge François and Robert Gérald were always among the first in the Class CU. In 1955, the first running of the Paris 6 Hours had been organized to take place at the end of the Paris Boat Show held on the banks of the River Seine. The idea was to demonstrate the motorboats on show at the exhibition. Although some twenty of the 55 competitors piloted Rocca hulls, ironically none of these won the race. This was left to Raymond Guyard in a 585 cc Johnson-powered Seyler. The second running of the Paris 6 Hours was also won

1957 - France versus Italy. The International Monaco Race Meeting saw some fiercely contested races, with France's Oreste Rocca coming through victorious in ever improved hulls built at the family boatyard.

This rare photo shows Carniti with Oreste Rocca (left) and Domenico Rocca (right).

using an Evinrude 585 cc on the back of a Ralu-Bréjat hull driven by H. Desfilles. Nevertheless the 3rd running of the Paris marathon in 1957 saw some 33 Roccas out of the eighty taking part. "Oreste was competing all the time" Louis Rocca recalls. "He had even raced in Morocco where he was lodged in one of the King's palaces." The same "plastic" initiative was taken over in England by Leslie John Derrington. Passionately fond of boats and the water, Derrington decided to see whether a little cockleshell made in fiberglass could really be seaworthy. Having built the first one in his potting shed at Shillingford, Oxfordshire, Derrington acquired an Anzani outboard from Charles Harrison

Rapport des COMMISSAIRES   OFFICIALS' Report:

Longueur de la base: 40 Km 9ᵏ.906   : Kilom – stat. mile – naut.mile .
Length of basis   Where :
           Lieu: Aix-les-Bains   Plan de la base/Map : à l'U.I.M.
Altitude:

N°	Durée Elapsed time	Vitesse Speed	N°	Durée Elapsed time	Vitesse Speed

6.10.57
Amon Ami Pietro BONNETTI
le "Fangio" du bateau. Amicalement

176

Photo
A. le Duc.

Calculs: 30 tours, soit 297ᵏ.180 en   5ʰ.5h' 53"

                                              9906
                                               3   5'7"= 307"
                                             29718

          reste à courir   5' 07" = 307"   11'37" = 697"
          temps du tour complémentaire   11' 37" = 697
          distance complémentaire   9906 × 5'07" = 4ᵏ.363
                                          11'37"

          En 6 heures: 297ᵏ180 + 4ᵏ363 = 301ᵏ543

                                                        301. 543 |6
50,   1 5   50257
    26   31. 069   34
            161   43   50.26
          3123   31.23 St.m. = 50ᵏ.26 ✓

Signatures des commissaires:
Officials' signatures:

                                              9906   6
                                               307
                                             69342   4
                                             29718
                                           2041142 |697
                                             2788   4363
                                             2531   3
                                             2091
                                             4400
                                             4182
                                             2180

Rapport des JAUGEURS

Nom du bateau   N° 46

Dessiné par : { ROCCA.

Constructeur :   Année

Long. 4 m.255 Larg. 1 m.420 Creux 0 m.400

Poids : 145 Kgs.

Moteur(s)

Marque MERCURY Type Mark 650 n°. 1378173

Puissance   Tours minute : 4 cylindres - 2 temps

Course 58,5 m/m. Alésage 72,8 m/m.

Cylindrée 973,5

Cyl.	1	2	3	4	5	6	7	8	9	10	11	12	13	14	15	16
Diam ←→																
Diam ↕																
Moyenne Mean																
Course Stroke																

Date de la vérification 12 Novembre 1962
Notes
Pesée au Laboratoire
de l'U.T.A.C. - A.C.F. à Cachan
sous le contrôle de M. Chapron

Signatures des jaugeurs :

Ajouter :
1° Liste dactylographiée des chronométreurs, des officiels, des jaugeurs et du DIRECTEUR de la tentative.

2° Photo du bateau avec indication des couleurs.

MEASURERS' Report :

Name of boat :   N°

Designer :

Builder :   Year :

Length .   Beam   Freeboard

Weight :

Motor(s)

Maker

H.P   Revs. per min.

Stroke   Bore

Cyl volume

Date of verification :
Notes :

Measurers' signatures :

Add :
1° Typewritten list of timers. officials. measurers and Supervisor of the trial.

2° Photograph of the boat with indication of colour scheme.

UNION INTERNATIONALE MOTONAUTIQUE.

AUTORITE NATIONALE	FÉDÉRATION FRANÇAISE MOTONAUTIQUE 8, Place de la Concorde PARIS 8e	NATIONAL AUTHORITY

DEMANDE D'HOMOLOGATION DE   APPLICATION FOR RECOGNITION OF
RECORD MONDIAL   WORLD RECORD.

VITESSE SPEED

| 1 | 2 | 3 | 4 | 6 | 9 | 12 | HEURES HOURS. |

FOND DISTANCE

| COMPETITION | 5 | 10 | 15 | MILES. |

CLASSE : F-U
CLASS

NOM DU BATEAU : N° 46
NAME OF BOAT

PROPRIETAIRE : ROCCA Oreste
OWNER

PILOTE : ROCCA Oreste   CLUB : Yacht Motor Club
DRIVER   de France

DATE : 11 Novembre 1962

Record précédent : Bateau :   Pilote :
Previous record : Boat :   driver :

Vitesse :   stat. m. =   Kilom.
Speed :

VIM :
1139
1140
1141

and attempted a Channel crossing: "The engine spluttered to a halt in mid-Channel and I was nearly run down by a French trawler from Boulogne. I paddled like mad, they spotted me just in time, veered past me and picked me up and took me to Boulogne." Derrington next decided to go into business as Fabricated Plastics Ltd and series produce a fiberglass-planing hull for racing. In October 1957, the Royal Motor Yacht Club teamed up with the London Motor Racing Club to hold the 100-mile Duchess of York's Trophy contest on their Shepperton Lake. Derrington and his son averaged a winning 22.51 mph, their boat, *Seamus John*, taking four hours 26 minutes cross the finishing line. 1958 was the year of the fiberglass round-bilged "Speed Derryboat". It began in May when 20 runabouts turned up at the London Club for the Boatbuilders' Utility Speedboat Trials. Whilst F. F. Dodson in 1.5 litre Healey Sportsboat led two inboards to the first three places in the scratch race, John Derrington with son Paul as crew, came in fourth with their *Paul Derry*, powered by a 327 cc Mercury. This boat also won them the 100-Mile Outboard Runabout Championship for the Duchess of York's Trophy at the British Outboard Racing Club's Bedfont Lake. Third place was taken by one of Fabricated Plastics Ltd's customers R. E. "Bob" May of Abingdon, with his son John as crew in their 35 hp Mercury-engined 11.5 ft *Grace Darling*.

By this time the UIM in Brussels had revised their rules for utility outboard runabouts, enabling Messrs Derrington and May to campaign abroad in the Class BU. At a 24-Hour International Prix d'Endurance at Aix-les-Bains, France, Derrington not only established a world six-hour Class BU record, but carried

John Derrington and his son Paul crewing the Fabricated Plastics flat-bottom hulled Paul Derry, *powered by a 327 cc Mercury to a new Four-Hour World record of 25.25 mph.*

March 1962 at the London
Motor Boat Racing Club's
meeting at Iver. Fabricated
Plastics Derry Cherry
hurtles round the course
like a molded bathtub
in a squall.

One of the many colours
available in the Mercury
Mark 55 range.

off the Redex Trophy for the fastest lap in their class. Recalling the experience of racing Derryboats, Bob May explained: "As they were flat-bottomed, we used to skid them around the corners, like dirt-track motorbikes. We used to broadside them. Although we tried to sit as still as we could on the straights, they'd still throw us about like a pea in a whistle! I'd be spending a lot of time putting my boat back beneath my passenger." In 1958, Derrington and May became the first Englishmen to race outboard runabouts in the Paris 6 Hours. "I did the whole run on my own, and although I'd put down carpets to lessen the hammering, I had to be lifted out of my boat. My backside was absolutely raw and there was blood everywhere. Although I wanted to retire on at least one occasion, in the end I won the Class BU, whilst John sank." If Derryboats or any other outboard runabouts were to go faster, they would need more powerful engines. Which is where the Kiekhaefer Corp. of Wisconsin now played an important part. Three years before, Carl Kiekhaefer had launched his four-cylinder "Mark 55 E MercElectric" on the market. Not only had this alternate-firing Thunderbolt unit developed 40 hp, but the customer also had the chance to select which two colours his particular engine was to be painted in. This two-tone "Merchromatic" range included marlin blue, gulf blue, sunset orange, tan, sarasota blue, sand, Mercury green and silver.

Two-tone cars had just become popular and Carl decided it would be nice to follow suit with the outboards. He loved to buy cars and everytime he bought a new one he insisted the factory duplicate the colours on the outboards. Before long there were engines of every colour combination which led to a difficult marketing problem. The engines were built and painted in large batches with the resut that Mercury never had the exact colour combination in stock that a customer wanted: "Marketing these colored beauties became a real mess" recalled Charlie Strang, "and our sales manager sadly told me that to sell an engine, we leave no stern untoned, a classic comment." With one of these engines, Jim

Wynne, former graduate of the Massachusetts Institute of Technology, now in Carl Kiekhaefer's employ, drove a slim 14 ft Raveau runabout to win its Class at the Orange Bowl Regatta. With two Mercury 55 E on the back, an identical Raveau was clocked at 60 mph. In 1957, whilst Carl Kiekhaefer was investing a great deal of time and money into national stock car racing, development work on outboards was supposed to be on the back burner. However, Charlie Strang had been conducting a secret development programme on an as yet unheard of 60 hp production model: "I nutted up a six cylinder outboard by taking some blueprints and cut three cylinders off one four-cylinder engine, and three off another and glued the blueprints together to make a drawing. Then we went out and got a couple of four-cylinder raw castings and sawed them off the same way the blueprints were cut. I got one of the race car guys who was a terrific welder, stole enough of his time to weld these things together to make a six cylinder block. Then we welded three two-cylinder crankshafts together and bootlegged them through the shop because Carl wasn't around. Edgar Rose made an ignition system for it out of autmobile parts and this, that and the other thing. We finally got it together and ran it. We finally put it on a boat and took Carl down to see it. It was pretty tall. He looked at it, and we pulled the cover off and he started to laugh. I asked him to try it out. He got in the boat and took one run up and down the river, he came back and said that it was speaking with authority, so let's build it. That was the decision process. Nine months later we delivered the first one". The Mercury "Mark 75", the world's first six-cylinder-in-line, one-litre production outboard, developing 60 hp at 5,800 rpm, was the most powerful production motor yet manufactured. It was offered in two versions - the Mark 75 Marathon, or as the Mark 75 H racing version, incorporating an electric single lever control which provided forward and reverse operation by using a two direction electric start to crank the engine in one direction or the other turning the crankshaft in one direction to go forward and in the other direction

The Mercury "Mark 55" had a superb bright finish.

Tommy Hagood of Orlando, Florida, clocks up a Six-Hour Class F runabout record using a Mercury-powered Raveau hull at the 1958 Orange Bowl regatta.

September 11ᵗʰ, 1957,
before sun-up. At the side
of Lake X, in readiness
for "Operation Atlas",
the 25,000 mile endurance
run to prove the staying
power of the Mercury Mark
75 outboard.
Carl Kiekhaefer is behind
the Mark75 on the left,
with Jim Wynne
to his right.

for reverse. The engine was stopped to provide "neutral" as Mercury engineers euphemistically called it. What had in the mid 1930s been only available to Jean Dupuy and his rich friends, could now be bought by many. To oppose the Mark 75 H, OMC-Evinrude presented 50 hp V-4 outboard called the "Four-Fifty" in plain trim, and "Starflite" in "Deluxe" form. It was soon nicknamed the "Fat-Fifty" because of its huge size. It guzzled fuel. At half to three-quarters throttle, a Starflite could quickly drink dry a 6-gallon gas tank. It was not until two years later that the "Fat-Fifty" would be upgraded to a 75 hp model, alongside Johnson's latest V4-75 hp Sea Horse, both two years behind Mercury. By this time, Kiekhaefer had become somewhat upset about OMC, whom he called "the enemy", accusing them of spying on everything he did. Indeed, industrial espionage between OMC and Mercury became fierce. Just round the corner from OMC's secret engineering labs at Sea Horse Drive, Waukegan, Illinois, was a restaurant called "Mathon's" - a favourite hang-out of OMC executives and engineers. Kiekhaefer would think nothing of sending spies down to Mathon's to sit at the bar and keep eyes and ears open for whatever info they could pick

up. In order to be able to test "in secret", away from "the enemy's" prying eyes, Kiekhaefer purchased Lake Conlin, near St Cloud, Florida, whose secluded waters he renamed "Lake X". To counter OMC's black-washing that Mercurys were "fast, but won't last", Tom King, Kiekhaefer's P. R. director, proposed a 25,000-mile endurance run on Lake X, using the Mark 75. "Operation Atlas" was planned and run by Charlie Strang and Jim Wynne. As the circumference of the earth at the Equator is 24,902 miles, this would require boats pushing for a 30 mph average, 34.6 days of non-stopping lapping the 5.5-mile circuit. In this way the Mark 75's could be throttled back from their top revs of 6,000 to 4,500 rpm. To monitor the event, officials of the United States Auto Club were hired for round-the-clock supervision. Four 15 ft Raveau family runabouts were selected, two as back-up hulls. They were equiped with windscreens and wipers, car headlamps and a 30-gallon tank to reduce frequency and danger of refueling operations. The buoys marked out the course were also fitted with lights. Two special refuelling and crew shuttle boats were built, with 50-gallon fuel drum elevated 5 ft above the deck on a cradle of angle iron. From September 11th, 1957 - 34 days, 11 hours, 47 min later - the lead boat crossed the finish line having completed 4,516 laps of the Lake X course and covered 25,003 miles. During this run, a certain number of "discreet" modifications were made at the halfway point, after the 25,000 miles were completed and before the second session was started. The engines were taken back to Oshkosh for "inspection" where the rod bearings were found to be rather well-worn. Following the inspection in the presence of the USAC official, the engines were re-assembled for the second 25,000 miles. In the process, a new crankshaft, rod and piston assembly was slipped into each engine. Carl was totally aware of what was underway while he was wining and dining the USAC man at nearby St. Cloud. Such information only came to

light many years later. Alongside endurance records, Carl Kiekhaefer was persuaded that Mercury should break the World unlimited outboard record. In January 1957, Charlie Strang had received a letter from Jack Leek, saying he and Hubert Entrop felt they could run at 100 mph and more if Mercury would help them with a model 75 H. After very little discussion, Strang readily agreed. Entrop would built a further improved version of the cabover hull design he had been developing over four years in conjunction with Ted Jones. Leek would serve as engine mechanic to specially prepare a standard Class F Mark 75 H, while Don Henrich, Mercury's resident prop wizard handled his speciality, all that in total secrecy. Kiekhaefer insisted that the attempts should be made on

The two Raveau boats maintained a steady 26 mph during 34 days of non-stop lapping the 5.5-mile Lake X circuit.

June 7th, 1958: Mercury have just gained the World Speed Record at 107.821 mph. From left to right: Jack Leek, Ted Jones, Charlie Strang, Carl Kiekhaefer and Hu Entrop - and a specially prepared Mercury Mark 75H developing 83 hp at 7,500 rpm.

Lake X to enable total security and publicity control. A stock engine was modified with special carbs designed by Charlie Strang to allow the engine to burn pure alcohol and a special racing lower unit was fitted with a very thin, high speed prop. With this arrangment the engine would develop 83 hp at 7,500 rpm. When Entrop's first trials on Lake X only reached 96.134 mph, Kiehaefer was severely critical. So much so that Entrop resigned, only agreeing to try again provided he could run on Lake Washington. Altogether some 68 frustrating runs were made up and down the lake's East Channel apparently in the 90 mph speeds. Then someone discovered that the pitot head speed indicator had been malfunctioning and that they had be reguarly topping the 100 mph. High speed photography of the boat's planing trim across the water enabled Ted Jones and his son Ron to modify the planing shoes and the prop geometry of the tiny 13.5 ft and 250 lbs hydro, called the *RX-3* to obtain improved performance. On the early morning of June 7th, 1958, Entrop literally flew the boat - sponsons tapping the calm water only occasionally through the APBA time traps at 109 mph then 106 mph, averaging 107.821 mph, increasing Italian di Priolo's record by 7 mph. Charlie Strang was a witness to the attempt: "For the first time, an outboard boat had lifted off the water and flown in sustained prop-riding attitude like a good inboard hydroplane. Indeed the *RX-3* exceeded 107 mph with only 82 or 83 hp because it was prop-riding, at time when nobody else was. Again this innovation soon spread like wildfire around the outboard armada. The Entrop "cabover" engine position and cupped prop soon saw an increasing number of prop-riding outboards. Nonetheless it was some time before anyone else reached the *RX-3* level of perfection". At first Kiekhaefer did not want the Mercury press releases to reveal the name of the driver. At the time, the space people were

sending rockets aloft with animals in the cockpit. Kiekhaefer gave in when Charlie Strang suggested to tell the press that a monkey drove the boat". That December, the APBA National Outboard Championships were held at Lakeland, Florida. The Class F race, a hot field composed of 4-60s, alcohol Class D engines and three of the new Mercury Mark 75 Hs. Immediate pre-race favorite, Hubert Entrop with *RX-3*, was hosed down in the pack, losing the services of one-cylinder in the process. He proceded to run the race on five cylinders, prop-riding all the way, finishing far in front of the pack with little or no fuss. In heat 2, although Entrop missed the start by one quarter of a lap, he caught up and forged into the lead. Never in outboard history had a field been annihilated so rapidly, but then Entrop threw a prop blade about one quarter of the way through the second lap. That heat and the National Championship was won by Joe Michelini, also with a 75 H. Entrop was to win the National Championship the following year with his world record-breaking rig. Just how far Mark 75 H power could reach would be demonstrated in 1959, when Dick Spelman, an air-conditioner technician from Miami, entered the Around Miami Beach Race, a rough run with half its 24 miles "offshore" on the open ocean and other half through Biscayne Bay. Spelman drove a 12 ft Holtcraft three-pointer powered by a Mercury Mark 75 H. Strong winds and white caps eliminated 29 of the 50 starters. This was the first time since the event's inception in 1949 that an outboard took top honours away from the inboard fleet.

It was also in the late 1950s that an improved cornering device, the sponson-mounted skid fin, made its debut on the outboard circuits. This was at the Pro National Championships at DePue, Illinois. Gerry Waldman had it on his SidCraft Class D hydro. Those watching never forgot the sight of the roostertail coming off that fin as Waldman went through the first turn on his way to the championship. It is not known whether Waldman originated the concept, but everyone soon followed suit, even the big Unlimited inboard hydroplanes. It was during this period that, over in Japan, several companies who had entered motor-cycle manufacture, also diversified into lower-powered outboards: Tohatsu, for

Entrop, shot from a low-flying plane during record trials. Note the propeller "chop marks" in the water and the pot-pot-pot marks left on the water as the sponsons tap the surface. RX-3 leaves clear water on both sides of the prop. This is true prop-riding.

The typical engine cover of the Mercury 75 H made its mark on outboard engine design.

Tokyo Hatsudoki, Tokyo engine factory; Suzuki, longtime textile loom manufacturer; Yamaha, longtime piano-manufacturer, and Yamato. From small beginnings, the Japanese four companies were thirty years away from competing against the "American three" on their own terms. Over in Europe, maximum-power outboard racing had so far been free from the revolutionary Mercury Mark 75 H and the 50 hp V4 OMC. But its arrival was inevitable. Arthur Bray of Poole in England, had gained the concession from Kiekhaefer to import Mercury outboards albeit at the initial rate of only two to twenty per year. When the 75 H engine appeared, A. Bray, looking for a network of regional agents, said that anyone mad enough to buy one could have an agency. Len Melly of the Lancashire Club acquired one to replace the tuned up Evinrude Storm motor on the back of his Swift Big D three-pointer, coincidentally called *Thunderbolt*. Although it did not give him that much more power, Melly did become the agent for the North of England. The Midlands agency was gained by John Merryfield, the bearded owner of a garage business in Ullenhall, near Henley-in-Arden. In 1957, taking a leaf out of John Derrington's book, Merryfield built an 11.5 ft fiberglass flat-bottomed runabout. At first, an 18 hp Johnson priced at £181 gave him 26 mph. Then he acquired a 20 hp Mercury Mark 25 with top end colored sand, bottom end tan, priced at £191, which pushed the speed up to 30 mph. Painting the sides and decks of his Meadcraft to match the engine, Merryfield, bearing his new Mercury agency in mind, called his runabout *Mr Kiekhaefer*. He became a member of the South Staffordshire Hydroplane and Speedboat Club and raced it first at Chasewater and then Shepperton. And he formed a new ambition: to beat the Derryboats. For 1959, Bob May heaved a 60 hp Mercury Mark 75 H onto the stern of the new 14 ft Derryboat he decided to call *Yellow Peril*. Such power ought to have put May in an unbeatable position. Indeed, at a 100-lap, 66-mile reliability trial on Oulton Broad, *Yellow Peril*, reaching top speeds of 45 mph, actually beat an over-confident fleet of inboard-engined Albatross runabouts, with the Mays using their characteristic Speedway-bike approach. *Yellow Peril* also scored a victory in the *Daily Mirror* trophy race on the London Motor Boat Racing Club's new circuit at Iver, Buckinghamshire. But May was not so successful at the Boatbuilders' Trials held that June on Chasewater Lake, near Brownhills, Staffordshire. Best speed taken for the three timed laps was 36.59 mph by John Merryfield in his less powerful Mr. *Kiekhaefer* - with *Yellow Peril* almost 5 mph slower. Then at the three-hour Grand Prix which followed, the first ever to have been held in Britain, Meadcraft again came first in Class B, whilst Fabricated Plastics' latest boat *Lilac Mist* and *Cutaway Derry* came second and third. In that contest *Yellow Peril* could only make the poor claim that it had won in Class E, over 700 cc. This, however, did not stop a journalist enthusing about her performance: "The crew of the *Yellow Peril* was one of the most energetic in the race. At every turn, his whole weight was thrown forward to keep the boat trimmed, and at the end of the three hours' constant, painful hammering, he was still using his weight, shifting about and generally straining every nerve to get the last ounce out of the boat." Three months later, at the 100-mile race for the Duchess of York's Trophy at Poole, although John Derrington and his business partner John Iddon led the sixteen-strong fleet for many laps, May proved the ultimate victor in *Yellow Peril* at an average 28 mph. Second, third and fifth places, however, were taken by

Meadcraft, one of them John Merryfield in *Mr Kiekhaefer*. Lest we forget, 1959 also commemorated the 30th anniversary of the last British-built Watermota racing outboard. It also marked the attempted birth of a new all-British outboard. Manufactured by B.R.D. Ltd of Aldridge, Staffordshire, the "Bermuda 2-40" had a healthy output of 40 to 45 hp. But like the Watermota, it was not long before the mass-produced US outboards forced the builders of the Bermuda to see reason. Year 1960 brought advertising and sponsorship to runabout racing in Britain. Thanks to the energetic efforts of John Derrington, the Regent Oil Company Ltd decided to sponsor the Boatbuilders' Trials at Chasewater. Not only did they provide free petrol and Havoline oil for the 48 competing craft, but set up the Regent Cup. The trials saw 14 inboards, four of them from the Claude Kirié boatyard at Les Sables d'Olonne, France. But the fastest boats in the trials were Fabricated Plastics Ltd's 39.47 mph *Orinjorra* with a simply enormous 1,247 cc Mercury and the 39.5 mph *Derry Cherie* with a simply enormous 1,479 cc Evinrude. Although his Meadcraft were absent, John Merryfield won the Regent Cup from both these boats in *Mr Kiekhaefer II*, powered by only a 179 cc Mercury. The World speed record remained a goal to beat. From Cologne, West Germany, came Rolf Friedrich Goetze, a businessman and former sports car world record holder. Persuaded by his Board of Directors to give up sports car racing, Goetze took up outboard racing. In June 1959, the German had arrived in Vienna, Austria, with boats and engines. Among the seven world distance records broken, Goetze himself annihilated the 12 mile records in Class D Stock hydro, Class F runabout and Class F hydro at 66 mph, 67 mph and 76 mph, set with Mercury/Swift-Molinari combinations. Most important in the fleet was Goetze's brand new "alky" Mercury 75 H Jones/Entrop Class F hydroplane. Although preliminary trials showed speeds in the 100 mph range, water conditions ruled out a serious attempt on Entrop's World record. Soon after Goetze won the Class X contest at Monaco with his alky 75 H on a new Molinari hull. He probably would have remained a challenger had he not been

...and meanwhile back in France and Italy. Utility runabouts continued to engage in combat.

May 5th, 1960:
The Ted Jones "cabover" RX17X during its 115.547 mph run up and down Lake Washington. Overcast weather and cold, with drizzling rain prevented the three-pointer from going faster still.

RX17X's driver was Burt Ross Jr., 32, a former star football player.

seriously injured in a race in Germany. But it was in the United States that the record fell. In 1959, C.W. "Doc" Jones, Evinrude distributor for the states west of the Rocky Mountains had approached OMC's Ralph Evinrude about getting an engine to reach over 100 mph. A Mercury dealer for nine years, in 1955 Jones switched to Evinrude which immediately made Kiekhaefer's old friend "Doc" Jones an "enemy". Jones also ran a special machine shop in Phoenix, Arizona, to build high performance racing engines. He was also a close friend with record-holder Hubert Entrop.

Jones suggested to Ralph Evinrude that with Entrop's help, the World record could swing back to OMC. So, Ralph Evinrude agreed to personally sponsor the challenge, although OMC directors wanted nothing to do with it at first. For the first time an engine larger than 60 cu/in would be used for a record attempt - namely the 89.6 cu/in-75 hp V4 Evinrude "Starflite II". Entrop built a 14-footer naming it *Starflite Too*. Jack Leek handled the engine, using a new gearcase designed for the purpose by Randolph "Pep" Hubbell, featuring a 1.5:1 step-up gear ratio and a propshaft which angled downward as it went aft in order to lift the rear end of the boat off the water at speed. This gave the Italian-made propeller some 7,400 rpm. On March 29th, 1960, Entrop dashed through the timing traps on Lake Havasu, on the Arizona-California border, at 114.65 mph, an increase of 7 mph with the engine burning ordinary fuel and revving at less than 4,900 rpm.

Kiekhaefer responded at Lake Washington two months later, on May 5th, 1960, with a new record of 115.547 mph. The 14 ft cabover *RX17X* was designed and built by Ted Jones. The pilot was Jack Leek's brother-in-law, Burt Ross Jr., 32, a Seattle outboard driver who had been a star football player. Overcast weather and cold, with drizzling rain prevented Ross from going faster still.

Kiekhaefer dispatched an entire team of private detectives to shadow OMC driver Entrop and "Doc" Jones's chief mechanic, Jack Leek. On September 16th, 1960, OMC responded with Entrop once again speeding down Lake Havasu in his home-built *Starflite III* lifting the average to 122.979 mph. Although tuned

exhaust pipes projected out from the Evinrude, stock spark plugs and a standard petroil mixture were used. Asked if the new mark was the best he could hope to get out of his rig, the bespectacled Entrop said: "Hell no! I might never know how fast, I can go with this combination. My speed isn't limited by the boat and motor but by my own intestinal fortitude in pushing it further."

Carlo Leto di Priolo of Milan, who eight years before had designed the Lesco-engined *Eduardo II* which had been the first to exceed the 100 mph average, now put together another challenger. This was an elongated cab-over three-pointer with a shorter version of the long step-up lower unit.

Unfortunately his record attempt made on January 1961 was unsuccessful, due to the excessive airborning of the hull and the impossibility of keeping it on a straight line. As Carlo recalls: "The speed was officially clocked by the Italian Federation at 115 mph even though I was driving at 130 mph. The same boat in a following version with a streamlined fully closed cockpit and trimable engine cover, was tested in the autumn of 1961, but I could not develop this beautiful outfit any further, on account of a family's request to stop any racing activity."

January 1961. Venue: Lake Iseo, Sarnico. Carlo Leto di Priolo helms the three-point Molinari with the last Lesco X4 engine. While the speedo was reading over 130 mph at one point, the official time was only 114.35 mph, just below the US record.

By the end of 1961, with radical streamlining, fully enclosed cockpit, trimmable engine cover, steering by handlebar, Carlo Leto di Priolo had hoped to improve Lesco X4's performance. But his family persuaded him to venture no longer into the dangerous unknown...

The Lesco X4 is now conserved at the Museo della Barca Lariana created by Gian Alberto Zanoletti. Since then, Italy has never regained the World outboard speed record.

133

Start of a new era of experiments in hull design.

Tunnel Vision

By the late 1950s, stock runabout racing had become a game for specialists. A hard core of experts had developed over the years and newcomers had little chance of success.

The mid-1950s were the also days when the racing outboard fraternity was sitting up and taking notice of the engineering supremacy of Dieter König's 350 cc and 500 cc racing engines, whether pushing hulls by Dieter Schulze, also of Berlin; or "Wetbacks" and "Jupiters" from the drawing board of Hal Kelly of Fort Pierce, Florida; or the ubiquitous "Atomic A", Big B and D from Joe Swift of nearby Mount Dora. Whilst the 26-year-old König had himself established a Class C record of 73.60 mph, over in England on Coniston Water, the 28-year-old Don Shead of the Midlands Hydroplane Racing Club had used a 350 cc König-Swift to break the national Class B record at 58 mph. But with increasingly greater horsepower now available, different configurations began to appear. Some ideas, such as the tunnel hull, were not new. Both the Hickman Sea-Sled, the Ventnor three-pointer and the Elsinore had been using the tunnel effect for over thirty years.

In late 1957, literally months after Hickman's death, Americans Dick Fisher and Bob Pierce, with advice from a naval architect called Ray Hunt, had built a 13 ft outboard-engined Sea-Sled to exploit their lightweight double skin foam construction. After a season's running with that hull they had still not overcome cavitation. As an experiment, they added a third hull in the middle to deflect away the air bubbles, so creating what they called their "Boston Whaler". By the late 1950s, Stock hydro and runabout racing had become a game for specialists. A hard core of experts had developed over the years and newcomers had little chance of success. This was reflected in the number of registered drivers which fell from 2,124 in 1957 to 1,210 in 1960, a 43 % decrease in only three years. Just as Stock racing was born in such marathons as the Albany-New York races of the late forties, so too was Outboard Pleasure Craft racing, or OPC. It offered people a chance to race their family pleasure boats, without the need for much expertise or the assistance of specialists. In the summer of 1955, Mercury's Charlie Strang and Jim Wynne co-drove a 14 ft fiberglass Crosby boat powered by a Mark 55 in an unorganized friendly race on Lake Winnebago. The

Roy Rogers, the "King of Cowboys" became a competitive pleasure boat race driver.

Ted Jones, of Seattle, Washington, better known for his designs for Unlimited inboards and outboard three-pointers, approached the challenge of a tunnel hull with characteristic ingenuity - as shown here.

following year, family racing took off in California, the prototype race staged from Los Angeles to Catalina Island, out in the Pacific. Roy Rogers, the "King of the Cowboys", a star of more than 90 feature-length Westerns, took part in many subsequent races and brought much publicity to the sport. Charlie Strang recalls: "Roy often upset the routine in my office in Oshkosh when he'd call after each race to ask me for more speed. The girls in the office would go nuts to speak with him, passing his call from one to the other before finally connecting him with me." In 1957, a real boost was given to sport when a 1,068 mile race from New Orleans to St. Louis was set up to commemorate the great paddlewheeler races of the 1800s on the Mississippi. These races were run with true pleasure boats, family boats with standard, gearshift type outboard motors available at any marine dealership. Glastron, Crosby, Yellowjacket (reputedly partially owned by Roy Rogers), Whirlwind and numerous other family boats of fiberglass or molded plywood were typical. Then in the late 1950s, Ray Leger, of Paramount, California, built a different sort of pleasure boat. This was the "PowerCat", a fiberglass catamaran with non-trip chines inside its tunnel, designed for use with two outboards, one on each sponson. The Mercury distributor for southern California told Charlie Strang about these boats: "We had one shipped to Oshkosh. I'll never forget that first exhilarating run on the river. It was a revelation. From then on we were cat enthusiasts. We put Ted Jones to trying to improve the breed and he came up with a nice 17-ft built of plywood. It did well but was no faster than the Leger boats. So, I used it as a family boat for a while." On August 30th, 1958, Mercury entered a team of these boats in the Mississippi Marathon, all powered by dual 70 hp Mercurys. Only 12 of the 28 starters reached St Louis and six of them were PowerCats. A Crosby runabout with similar engines driven by a couple of Mississippi River experts won the race, but the cats took second and third.

The following year, the first three places were taken by white Mercury-engined catamarans. Roy Fulton and Carlton Johnson drove a 16 ft "Magnolia" fiberglass cat powered by two 70 hp Mercurys from St Louis to New Orleans in 22 hours 37 min, second place taken by a "Jax Cat". Catamarans dominated the race. Fifteen entered and took eight of the first ten places, including the three first. In November 1959, a four hours pleasure type outboard race showed 68 starters quickly reduced to 35 due to hurricane winds stirring the waters of Florida's Lake Tohopekaliga into heavy swells. The winner was Chuck Mersereau of California, driving a PowerCat *Nice Kitty*, equipped with twin Mercury "700s". Eight of the first ten rigs in the unlimited class utilised twin-hull boats with 70 hp motors. In terms of "offshore" racing, that year's "Around Long Island Race" saw outboard catamarans take the first three places in a field of 42 starters and 19 finishers. Chuck Mersereau and Odell Lewis arrived a salty first in their PowerCat. Although by the end of 1960, there were at least 13 or 14 builders of cats for family boating, twin outboard catamarans never really caught on with the public at which they had been marketed. The need for twin engines was a cost hurdle and the tunnel down the center of the boat reduced the space available for seating. The limited planing surface on the sponsons made the boats rather sluggish at low planing speeds where the lift from the air in the tunnel was negligible. But they were great for hot-rodding and lake racing. Could single-engined cats achieve greater success? At Mercury, Jones and Leek got the 17 ft Jones cat to run fairly well with a single engine by putting a deflector in the middle of the tunnel just in front of the lower unit to direct the water to the prop. Ray Leger is reported to have run one of his small PowerCats with a single engine mounted behind the tunnel. And, in January 1961, Custom Craft advertised a 17 ft "Delta Ray" pleasure cat for single engine use, stating that they had achieved this with a "delta wedge" in the tunnel ahead of the engine.

Chuck Mersereau of Key West drives his catamaran 347 miles to victory in the Grand National 6-Hour Pleasure Craft Marathon at Lake X, near St Cloud, Florida, on December 30th, 1961.

Ted Jones in the cockpit, and behind him Ray Leger of the Power Cat Boat Company, two catamaran pioneers, discuss his battle-scarred race helmet with catamaran test-pilot Chuck Mersereau and Dave Craig, race chairman for the Miami Outboard Club.

Beside Lake Como, Italian boatbuilder Angelo Molinari, intrigued by articles published about these twin and triple-engined catamarans in the US, began experimenting with a single-engined timber-built hull which would run without a drag-creating wedge or planing surface ahead. APBA initially governed pleasure craft racing rather loosely, assigning it to the "Special Events Committee", a catch-all for every new areas of racing. They attempted a "suggested" set of rules but gave race organizers a "local option" to make up their own rules if they wished to do so. This proved unworkable, so in late 1960, Jim Jost, then Vice President for Stock racing and Charlie Strang devised the first set of rules to create a new division of APBA expressly for Outboard Pleasure Craft. The first major OPC race took place in January1961, on Lake Tohopekaliga, Florida. A total 63 boats, 14 of them catamarans, raced for six hours on the 4-mile course for a glittering $9,000 in merchandise prizes. Chuck Mersereau and Jon Culver averaged a winning 58 mph in a PowerCat, followed by Odell Lewis in a JaxCat and Johnny Bakos in another PowerCat, all with twin Mercury 800's of 80 hp. On the following day at Lake X, Jim Sewares of Miami set a kilometer record of 69.474 mph with a PowerCat and twin 800s. But then the Switzer Wing cataramaran turned up. It had been developed by the Switzer brothers, Dave as designer and Bob as driver, at their plywood boatbuilding company on Route 14, east of Crystal Lake, Illinois.

The start of an early (1961) Outboard Pleasure Craft race on Lake Winnebago, Wisconsin. U-11 is a Magnolia Cat, very similar to a PowerCat.

The original Switzer Wing. Bob Switzer (driver) in the port cockpit, Dave Switzer (designer) in the starboard seat.

Their father having been an early seaplane pioneer, the brothers were enthusiastic pilots of such light aircraft as the Piper Cub and the J3 and in Bob Switzer's own words : "We thought that if we could develop a boat with a Clark "Y" aerofoil section in between two fuselages, put the motors far apart and let the air work like a Ramwing principle, we'd have a pretty fast boat. The first prototype was conceived, designed and built in only eight days of June 1961 and fitted with a pair of 80 hp Mercurys. On our first go-around on the Fox River we kept leaping in and out of the water at 80 mph. There was nothing to keep the boat up because the 8-inch deep opening between the stern of the twin hulls was letting the air out. Then we fitted an elevator flap, and from that moment we were able to use ground effect, like a magic carpet. The same boat and the same engines gave us a speed of 120 mph. We could fly her up to three inches above the water".

In July 1961, at the 13th Winnebagoland OPC Marathon, Bob and Dave Switzer blew off the PowerCats with their astonishing Switzer Wing, powered by two Mercury 80 hp outboards with "Speedmaster" lower units, averaging a victorious 67.13 mph. The days of the PowerCats were numbered thereafter. During the 1960s, the Mercury-engined Switzer Wings became unbeatable in wide and open course marathons across the States. In the Miami Palm Beach contest along the inland coastal waterways, a Switzer Wing averaged 87.5 mph for 104 miles, a record still unbroken today. Altogether, some 67 twin-hulled racers left the Crystal Lake factory to be raced - or rather flown - by such champion pilots as Dave Craig and Gene Lanham of Miami, Bobby Massey of California and Kenny Kitson of St Louis. Small squadrons of them could also be seen on the Colorado, Potomac and Hudson Rivers. In 1963, Dave Craig's Switzer Wing, *Miss Skyway* pioneered enclosed cockpits. Although it was Dave and Bob Switzer's goal to produce a safe, fast powerboat capable of carrying a high fuel load, they did try to interest Carl Kiekhaefer in a boat to go for the straightway record, but without success. Among the up-and-coming fiberglass mass production boatbuilders was Bob Hammond of Standard Glass Products of Austin, Texas, with the Glastron range as designed by Mel Whitley. Unlike the Switzer

*In 1964, monohulls
of various design
were still engaged in fierce
competition.*

cats, Glastrons incorporated deep-V "aqua-lift" hulls. By 1965, Glastron had won more than 50 national race victories, including the 1962, 1963 and 1964 Long Island Marathon. It became clear that OPC was really established as a recognized form of racing when the 1962 Albany to New York Marathon eschewed the Stock classes and the race was run to the new APBA OPC rules. In the 1966 edition of the Albany-New York marathon, the first to reach New York from Albany was a Class "JJ" of unlimited engine displacement 17 ft Glastron powered by two black Mercury 100s, setting a record of 2 hours 2 min, averaging close to 64 mph. Third place was obtained by Robert Switzer in a Switzer Craft.

In the meantime, in Europe, the first English-designed outboard catamaran was strangely influenced neither by the Americans nor the Italians, but by sailing practice. Indeed, it had even originated in 1956. Roland and Francis Prout of G. Prout & Sons Ltd, Canvey Island, Essex, builders of sailing catamarans, decided that it might be an idea to build a motorized plywood catamaran to take with them to the Gulf of St Tropez on the French Riviera for waterskiing. Powered by twin 25 hp Gale outboards, their 14 ft prototype not only proved very seaworthy, but with a speed of 21 mph could even tow four waterskiers simultaneously. Two years later, they decided to put their little cat into production, marketing it as the "Panther 14". In October 1960, some 70 powerboats completed in the Paris 6 Hours. Retirements due to damaged hulls meant that only 38 finished the course. Two of these were British one being the Panther 14, as driven by Dimitrios, a French racing driver. Designers Roland and Francis Prout watched from the bank: "It was quite interesting the way he used to cut inside everybody at the buoys, gaining all the time. He ended up fourth overall". That the Prouts had set a trend soon became evident when Purbeck Marine of Swanage announced that their 16 ft "Cheetah" catamaran could achieve 38 mph

*A Prout catamaran
running down the Seine
at the Paris 6 Hours.*

from just three 35 hp outboards. The next indication of the coming of the cata-maran was at the Boatbuilders' Trials, held in June 1961 at Chasewater, which took three days, followed by weekend racing for the Regent Trophy and the Regent Cup. Among those 68 runabouts and speedboats taking part were five "Special Class" boats, or in another word, catamarans. Alongside the Prout Panther, there was Hemming and Morris's *Ellcat* with twin Mercurys; from Cheshire, Woodmet Ltd brought the US-imported "Mark 16" Catamarine and the "Mark 11" Baroda cat, each with two of the very latest 80 hp white-liveried Mercurys on the back. Then came John Merryfield's *Merrycat* built to US plans acquired from the Glenn L. Witt catalogue and powered by twin Mercury 45s, which were also used for steering. The fastest lap from all the trials' entrants was 39.387 mph by the Mark 11 Catamarine, capable of a top speed of 50 mph. *Merrycat* could only reach 36 mph whilst the more conventional *Mr Kiekhaefer IV* clocked 39.2 mph. The race was won by Denis Grogan in a flat-bottomed Blufin "12R". The Prout Panther 14's real vindication came when the following year's Boatbuilders' Trials saw 50 stock runabouts compete at Ruislip Lido, including Charlie Sheppard in his *Bristol Dart* and Norman Fletcher, former model-maker from West Bromwich, in *Flaming Arrow*. The highest lap speed ever attained was made by "The Tewkesbury Terror", Bill Shakespeare in his flat-bottomed *Shakespeare I*, whose 100 hp Mercury gave him 43.636 mph.

Paris 1961. Of the 80 entries, 43 starters featured in the Class XU - engines of between 1,000-1,500 cc. The first five places were taken by Mercury-engined French hulls, with Colombe and Fauré averaging 40.5 mph in their Simoneau-Chapron hull.

Racing the British way in March 1962, at the London Motor Boat Racing Club's Meeting at Iver. Jackie Wilson in his BluFin n°22, neck and neck with BITTA-L, both powered by Merc 800s.

Another Shakespeare boat made the second fastest lap at 41.499 mph. The Havoline trophy was won by the lower-powered 75 hp Johnson engined Panther 14, driven by Roland and Francis Prout, wearing newly acquired motorcycle helmets, neither having raced before. In the 1962 Cowes-Torquay offshore powerboat race, in a rough South Coast sea, where only 15 out of 42 starters finished, it says much that the winner of the outboard engine class was Doug Norvell, driving Dunning's Prout Panther 25 catamaran, *Thunderbird*, which indeed was the only outboard craft to complete the course. However, Prout catamarans didn't compete in the following years. Although they had built and sold as many as fifty Panther 14, Roland and Francis Prout abandoned further production in favour of their sailing cats such as the "Cougar". Had they not done so, British powerboat racing might have been a very different story. The successful rise to supremacy of the catamaran was to come from Angelo Molinari of Como, Italy. But the arrival of the second configuration that replaced flat-bottomed runabouts took place a little before. The deep-Vee hull as we know it today had its parallel but separate genesis in the Bahamas, then at Anzio, Italy, thanks to two designers - Ray Hunt and Renato Levi. Offshore racing was born in 1956 when Sam Griffith, a first-class aircraft pilot with a distinguished war record had teamed up with Captain Red Sherman Crise, to stage an offshore race from Miami to Nassau in the Bahamas. Whilst the race was won by Griffith and Dick Bertram in a 34 ft "sea skiff" powered by a pair of 200 hp Cadillac "Crusader" inboards, of the eleven starters, two were outboards. Woody Woodson, founder of Thunderbird Boats ran a 20 ft cathedral hull of his own manufacure powered by two 75 h. Mercurys. Danish boatbuilder Ole Botved ran one of his 18 ft "Coronet" hulls with two 35 hp Johnson outboards. That race was held on May 6th, 1956. A week later, May 13th, a 76 nautical miles ocean race was held around Bermuda island, limited to outboard boats. Ten started and three finished in 10 ft swells.The winner was Harry Cox in a 12 ft molded plywood boat driven by a

single 30 hp outboard. The premier ocean races of the late 1950s and early 1960s became the Miami-Nassau of 185 miles and the Around Long Island race of 280 miles. All had outboard entries. During that time, naval architect Ray Hunt, apart from helping Fisher and Pierce with their cathedral-hulled "Boston Whaler", had developed a 23 ft monohull whose deep-Vee section could cut through the water without pounding. The Essex Fiber Boat Co. produced four versions of this, one of which, a tender of the America's Cup 12-Metre yacht *Easterner*, was eventually acquired by crew member and Miami yacht broker, Dick Bertram. The first offshore race to be won overall by an outboard was the 1959 Around Long Island race. Jim Lacy won over a field of 29 inboards and outboards in a 17 ft Ray Hunt deep vee hull powered by a single Mercury 70 hp. Also during this time outboards went inboard - partially. Jim Wynne, Mercury test-driver, had tendered his resignation to Carl Kiekhaefer. For some time before his departure, Wynne and Charlie Strang had been secretly developing a project to locate a four-stroke inboard inside a boat's transom, whilst retaining the manoeuvrability advantages of the outboard in the leg and gear-housing - crucially linking the two by a universal joint. Wynne had first been told about this inboard/outboard by Mercury's Charlie Strang who had worked it out on the drawing board during his MIT graduate days, some ten years before. With Strang providing the sketches, specifying which off-the-shelf upper gearbox to use, supplying the lower unit and related components, then providing him with the money to finance the whole project, Wynne welded the prototype around an 80 hp Volvo Penta in his own garage. He installed it in a hull borrowed from Thunderbird Boats in Florida. Following the first successful trials in March 1958, Wynne managed to get complete financial backing from Volvo Penta at Gothenburg, Sweden. Following further improvements, secretly supervised by Strang, during the 1960 New York Boat Show, one hundred Volvo Penta "Aquamatic" units were sold. That same year, Dick Bertram of Miami asked Ray Hunt to design a

During the Havoline Trophy in 1962 the only catamaran (see on the left) competing makes his way up to victory.

Ray Hunt had specially marked hulls made to monitor the progress on his design.

The Volvo Penta Aquamatic is unveiled to the public.

31ft version of his deep-Vee hull for the Miami-Nassau offshore race. At the same time, Jim Wynne, with Volvo sponsorship, had the Palmer Scott yard in Massachusetts built him a Hunt deep-Vee, to be powered by two 80 hp Volvo Aquamatic stern-driven packages. Bertram and Griffith in *Moppie* and Wynne in *Wyn Mill* certainly proved the effectiveness of both hull form and engineering innovation by placing first and second in that Miami-Nassau contest. In 1962, having merged his corporation with the Brunswick Corp. of Chicago, Carl Kiekhaefer's assisted inboard/outboard inventor Charlie Strang to go round the Aquamatic patents of Wynne and produced the more expensive, 310 hp "Mercruiser" based on the "Big Block" Chevrolet truck engine. Among those grinding the props for this new unit was a new employee by name of Gary Garbrecht who will play an important part in a later part of this saga. By fitting two Mercruisers into Aokone, a 25 ft deep-Vee Bertram, Johnny Bakos was able to win the Miami-Nassau race of that year, covering the 184 miles in a new record time of three hours 42 minutes.

One other event in 1962 which helped to change the shape of the sport occurred when Clive Curtis, a marine retailer in Hammersmith, London, made a double crossing of the English Channel in *Baltic Spray*, a Healey "Corvette" runabout, powered by two 40 hp Gale outboards. Geoff Tobert, also known for making sea voyages to publicize his products and not to be outdone, challenged Curtis to race from London to Calais for a five-pound bet. Before long, other

Jim Wynne's patent for the inboard-outboard was filed in May 1960, but granted in April 1968. The thinking was Charlie Strang's.

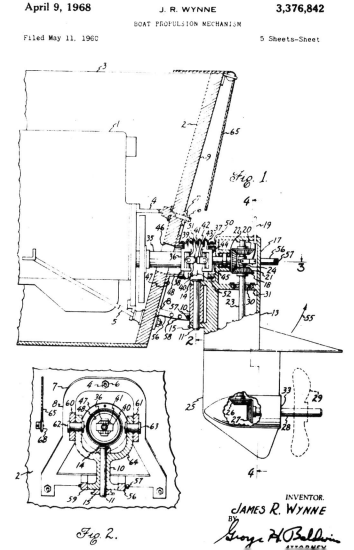

April 9, 1968　　　J. R. WYNNE　　　3,376,842

BOAT PROPULSION MECHANISM

Filed May 11, 1960　　　　　　5 Sheets-Sheet

Fig. 1.

Fig. 2.

INVENTOR.
JAMES R. WYNNE
BY
George H. Baldwin
ATTORNEY

A typical early offshore
outboard rig... in this case,
triple-engined!

marine dealers wanted to compete, each for a five-pound note. Thus took place the first Putney-Calais race, won by Curtis and initiating what became known as "Class III" in offshore racing. Also out of this contest was born the United Kingdom Outboard Boating Association founded in order to test outboards by racing them. Not that Mercury had the monopoly. Alongside Bundy and Gale, came Crescent from Sweden and Carniti of Italy making their presence felt. Carniti works drivers, Sergio Carniti and Angelo Vassena scored many circuit and marathon victories in 500 cc and 850 cc classes. Over in the United States, Carl Kiekhaefer had continued to increase the horsepower of his engines, the original 60 hp unit stepped up to 70 hp and then 80 hp, in chrome and white livery. So it was that John Merryfield and Len Melly teamed up with one particular ambition in mind: to become the first Englishmen to win the Paris 6 Hours marathon outright, using of course only the latest and most powerful Mercury for which they were both agents. Following the 1962 Paris race, where *Thunderbolt*, a Capri raceboat built by Toby Sutton of Oulton Broad, lasted just three laps before it fell to pieces, Merryfield and Melly approached Bill Shakespeare and asked him for a rear-trinimer with a ballast tank. Shakespeare refused them and instead offered to build one of his standard "strengthened rowing boats". *Thunderbolt VII* was only ready a fortnight before the race. On going to collect it, they were horrified to discover that their old rival had built two boats - one for himself and the other for Nigel Riley of *Watersport* magazine incorporating the very ideas he had refused to build for them. For the Paris race, therefore, not to be outdone by Shakespeare, Merryfield and Melly organized a refuelling system which was super-efficient for the standards of the time. Instead of clumsily manhandling four five-gallon petrol tanks they took over a 20-gallon Leyland lorry fuel tank, then had another one stuck up on legs in the pits with a 10 mm hosepipe attached. "Len's Loo", as they called it, thus enabled *Thunderbolt VII'*s team to reduce driver-swapping and refuelling down

Small inshore racing rigs
were able to run only
on smooth waters. Here
a Carniti 250 cc engined
Molinari hull.

WATER SPORT

NOVEMBER · 196

Vol. 1   No. I

MONTHLY

TWO SHILLINGS

Paris Salo

and

6 Hour Ra

At the Paris 6 Hours in 1964, Merryfield and Melly drove a Renato Levi designed V hull to victory.

to 20 seconds each time. "We had a good run with the Shakespeare and got about 48 mph on tap" Merryfield has recalled. "We just motored on through all the rough and didn't take too much notice. Len did the first hour-and-a-half, then I went in the middle and did the long stint, then Len did the last hour." A total 277 miles gave Britain its first victory on the Seine since W. W. II. Following a brief encounter with the naval architect Renato Levi in Paris, Merryfield and Melly met up with him again on the Regent stand of the *Daily Express* London Boat Show, where *Thunderbolt* was on show. The Paris winners told the Levi that they were anxious not to use Shakespeare again. Levi suggested they incorporate their transom design for mounting the outboard with his deep-Vee approach to make a faster and more stable circuit boat than had hitherto been produced. Levi said: "I'll design you a boat, then we'll come to an arrangement whereby you can build my outboard boats in Great Britain." Mr. Melly's tenth *Thunderbolt* was a 16 footer built by Watercraft Ltd of Shoreham and again the most powerful Brunswick Mercury was heaved onto its stern. This was the "Phantom" 6 cylinders 100 hp engine, which for reasons of its tallness had been styled in unobtrusive black, thanks to the advice of Charlie Strang's mother Anne who had made the remark: "Well, a large woman always prefers a black dress. Why don't you paint it black?". The Phantom soon came to be known as the "Merc. 1000". One of these units was on the back of Melly and Merryfield's new boat when it turned up for the 1964 Duchess of York's Trophy race at Chasewater. John Merryfield recalls: "You had never seen anything like it. There was a mass exodus from the pits to the car park to see our new creation. As Len was to drive at Carr Mill on Monday, I drove it. Where the other boats had about 40 mph, we had a good 60 mph. I won easily from Stan Pearce the favourite in a Shakespeare flat-bottom, indeed I ran rings around him". Perhaps fortunate for Shakespeare was *Thunderbolt X*'s absence from the 24 Hours marathon at Aix-les Bains, France. Despite the appearance of Tommy Sopwith and Jim Wynne in their two-litre Coventry Climax-engined *Thunderflash*, first and second places went to Bill Shakespeare and Jeremy James in their flat-bottomed Avons. Also at that meeting, however, was a catamaran built by Angelo Molinari of Como. As its drivers Carlo and Enrico Rasini brothers, from a Milan banking concern, showed during practise, the Molinari cat's vertical walls on each side of the tunnel gave it an incredible turning ability. Here was indeed a cat designed for racing rather than family boating. Almost immediately, as new Royal Yachting Association officials, Anthony Needell and Ralph Loosemore put in a protest that this hull simply did not comply with the rules. The Rasini brothers were therefore placed in a special "Experimental" class of their own though not allowed to claim a victory in the general classification if they were fortunate enough to get one. For 1964, France now offered two challenging races as the Rouen Yacht Club organized the first 24 Hours race on the Seine in the city's center, in emulation of the Le Mans sportscar race. Realizing the hazards from commercial river traffic during the Paris 6 Hours, it was decided to run the Rouen race on May 1st, a national holiday and hence far freer of such obstacles. Twenty boats, exclusively French and fitted with headlamps, lapped the 2.2 mile course. The race was won by Bouillant and Delestrez at an averaged 38 mph. The Paris 6 Hours contest was held five months later, in October. Determined to make a killing, Carl Kiekhaefer chartered a cargo barge and equipped it with the best servicing and pits equipment available since the days of Jean Dupuy. He also made sure that at least two Mercury-engined boats were racing in each class. Then he placed everything under wraps. Among his fleet was a "Torriggia" catamaran, beautifully built by Geremia Cetti of Como to be co-driven by Ancarini and Vecchi. Melly and Merryfield entered two Levi 16s, *Thunderbolt X* and another one to be driven by Jock Geddes and John Reed. Always curious, just before the race, Kiekhaefer entered the British pits and was about to take a photo of the revolutionary deep-Vee when Merryfield cornered him: "Look Carl, if you press that button, just once, you and the camera are going in the Seine ever so quick". The race began. Whilst a whole fleet of Kiekhaefer-sponsored hulls broke down or broke up, *Thunderbolt X* worked like a dream for John and Len except towards the end when it became a "pig" to control. But the British duo pressed on at reduced speed and won the race, computing 282 miles at an average 47.63 mph. When *Thunderbolt* was craned out of the water, they discovered that the thrust block on the engine had worked loose and virtually wrecked both the prop and underwater unit. To this day, both Melly and Merryfield still do not know how they managed to complete the race. Tragically, it was half a minute before the final gun that France lost one of her

These rare Molinari family photos show the secret weapon for the 1962 season - "il catamarano".

*Another victory
for a monohull
at the Rouen 24 Hours
marathon in 1969.*

most competitive pilots. Claude Kirié, aged 48 and designer of several competing craft, struck a bridge pier. His craft was submerged for six and a half minutes before rescuers could reach him. Kirié died in the hospital and the family
boatyard at Les Sables d'Olonne totally withdrew from raceboat building. As a
point of interest, the "Torriggia" cat came in fourth, averaging 45.13 mph. After
the race, Kiekhaefer tried his hardest to get Levi to design him a boat, only to be
told that Melly and Merryfield had got the exclusive rights on the outboard
deep-Vee design. It may well have been for this reason that he did a deal with
certain parties in Como, Italy, which in the course of time would make the deep-
Vees a thing of the past. The Italians, however, were not the only ones creating
the cat. Dieter Schulze, world champion in Class A, B, and C hydroplanes, built
his first tunnel-hull in 1964. "There is no way you can race against your customers. If you win, you are everything they can call you for. If you don't, then
what's wrong with you?". With such a philosophy, Len Melly and John
Merryfield hung up their own helmets and formed Double M Hulls Ltd. Plans
for both 16 ft and 14 ft production models were now put into operation by Chris
Tremlett at Topsham, Devon using his own special, hot-moulding process. Once
built, Double M hulls were normally fitted out for Merryfield's customers at
Studley, south of Birmingham, but if you were one of Len Melly's customers, it

would be fitted out at Ormskirk, Lancashire. Altogether some fifty Double M raceboats were to be built and raced during the next three years and they were almost unbeatable. Compared to the flat-bottomed Derryboats where the crew member helped to skid their flat bottom round the buoys, the Double M boats demanded a new type of driver. With the R.Y.A. Powerboat Committee wishing to come closer to international rules, the National Outboard Tourist Classes had been replaced by the UIM's Utility Racer Class, which called for only one competitor in the boat. One of those who went over to Double M hulls was Bob May and his son John, who recalls: "The Levis would suddenly dive off in the wrong direction. If you were cornering and laid them over and happened to get them with more water on one side than the other, never mind the steering wheel, they would simply dive off the other way. There was a certain technique in putting them round the buoy". Len Melly puts it another way: "It had a tendency to rock to and fro. It was a matter of holding the wheel in a manner to let the boat take its own course, but still control it. If you tried to correct it all the time, it ended up rocking from side to side. The trick was to slacken off once or twice because it tended to lay over on its chine. You could afford to let it do that three times, after which, look out!".

During 1965, Double M 16-footers swept the board with victories in the Regent Gold Cup, the *Daily Mirror* trophy, Duchess of York's Trophy, but only

Paris 1967 - One of the factors making the Paris 6 Hours dangerous was the presence of commercial traffic.

overall second in Paris, where Guyard and Monier won. Once again fourth place in the River Seine marathon was taken by a catamaran, a Mercury-engined Molinari, co-driven by Roda and Capalletti at an average 45.51mph. One journalist wrote: "The catamarans cornered extremely well. It was as if a guiding rail took them through the bends..." Indeed that same season, Angelo Molinari's inexperienced 18-year-old son, Renato, was clocked at a formidable 80 mph across Como Lake in one of his father's cats, some15 mph faster than the fastest deep-Vee. A Levi 17-footer as built by Double M Hulls also went campaigning offshore. Of interest for the future, *Mongaso*, which won three races in the Class III series, was crewed by Don Shead and his friends, James and Mike Beard.

Of course, the Double M deep-Vee had its imitators, not the least of whom was Bill Shakespeare with his latest Avon, slightly shallow in Vee and more bulbous for ease of cornering. And there was Charlie Sheppard with his Bristol hull,

Soggy Moggy, English slang for "wet cat", was built by Charlie Sheppard. Unlike those cats built so far, with rockers fore and aft to get the wind starting under the tunnel, Sheppard worked on the basis of a pair of waterskis, with no rockers but with an angle of attack on the top of the tunnel.

the most unforgettable of which, *Sheeza-B*, powered by a small 35 hp Mercury, enabled a 31-year-old called John Hill to win the National Championship Class CU at top speeds of 45 mph. None of these, however, quite came up to the professional supremacy achieved in 1966 by the Double M 16 and 17-footers; boats like *Uncle Den*, *Sch-Uno-Who*, *Miss Chief*, *Goldfinger*, and last but not least *MayVee*, which enabled John May to place second overall in the Berlin 6 Hours and first overall in the gruelling Chasewater 24 Hours marathon. Ironically, the one prize which eluded the Double Ms was the one which had launched them to success: the Paris 6 Hours.

For 1966, with the appearance of the most powerful outboard yet produced by Mercury, developing 110 hp and eclipsing even Evinrude's 100 hp Starflite,

Cantiere Molinari had decided to field no less than five catamarans, three of them powered by Kiekhaefer's latest "Black Widow". The other two were fitted with Rover "2S/150M" Marton marine gas-turbines coupled with Mercruiser stern-drives. Whilst these Mercruiser/turbocruiser boats achieved formidable speeds on the straight, they were unable to get swift enough deceleration for rounding the buoys. The Mercury-Molinari rigs, as driven by Roy Ridgell with Bill Sirois, Carlo with Enrico Rasini, and Renato Molinari with his older cousin Cesare Scotti, were an entirely different proposition. Molinari and Scotti came first overall at an average speed of 48.9 mph, with the Double M *Goldfinger* driven by Di Vito and Fusciard in second place. Even though his friend James Beard might have nose-dived the Shead-designed *Pussycat* in that choppy Seine marathon, Beard was far more successful with *Volare*, "a pure Levi", built by Double M Hulls. He won five Class III offshore races including first overall in

Scuderia Molinari, complete with "Black Widow" Mercurys, ready for the 1965 Season. With their appearance at Paris, they aroused considerable interest but proved rather disappointing in action.

the Putney-Calais. Not so successful was *Fatcat*, described as a Double M "Levi Ramwing 20 Catamaran" which was too sturdily built to give Lady Violet Aitken, Sir Max's wife, any winning speeds on the sea. A similar fate was suffered by Tommy Sopwith in *Flyover*, a sturdily-built cat from the drawing board of American Walt Walters. In fact, although virtually unbeatable, the Switzer Wing had one major weakness. They could not go round tight corners. In 1966, Dieter Schulze of Attnang, Austria, shipped one of his latest single-engined catamarans over to America in parts. He assembled it at SidCraft in New Jersey, bought an old estate car for $200, then towed the boat to Lake Havasu for the annual marathon. During the race, Schulze not only refuelled his own cat, launching it and recovering it without assistance, but whilst a Switzer Wing

1966 Paris 6 Hours - 86 teams took part. Molinari fielded five entries including one owned by the Kiekhaefer Corporation. Molinari and his cousin Cesare Scotti came first.

came first overall, Schulze came fourth and also won the single-engined class outright. His secret was tight cornering achieved by a full tunnel. Having sold his cat to an enthusiastic American for a good price, Schulze visited the Switzer Wing factory in Illinois where an agreement was formed for the Switzer brothers to build the Schulze cat under license and vice versa. Due to the problems of import duties, this never came to anything. Nothing, however, seemed to be able to keep back the introduction of the catamaran. At the end of 1966 Jackie Wilson from Sussex took the initiative of going out and buying a large cat, a small cat and a V-bottom from the "Torriggia" yard of Geremia Cetti at Lake Como, Italy. Taking them to the London Motor Boat Racing Club at Iver, legend has it that with only a 55 hp Carniti outboard, Wilson's small Torriggia was keeping pace with the 100 hp V-bottoms. Contrary to the evidence, many still put their faith in the Deep-Vee, particularly offshore. Although unsuccessful with his "Delta 28", Don Shead had now designed a 21ft fiberglass Vee hull powered by twin 110 hp Mercury outboards and called it *Avenger*. Driven by Pascoe Watson and Mike Beard, this Shead prototype finished fifth overall in the Cowes-Torquay contest and won the National Class III Championship with 20 victories. As for the Wynne-Walters variant, Don Aronow won the World Offshore Championship with two 28 ft deep-Vee "Magnums", costing $8,000 a piece. One of them was the first outboard-powered boat ever to win an international offshore race. The

unlimited outboard record continued to climb. Prompted by rumours of another Mercury record attempt, with sponsorship from "Doc" Jones of Phoenix, Hubert Entrop had developed a boat design around the low profile and low center of gravity of the 100-S Evinrude Starflite. The 17 ft hull was built by Wilbur MacDonald of Portland, Oregon. There was an enclosed cockpit and to gain a low profile and lessen wind resistance the pilot laid flat on his back in the boat, steering with a lever at each side of his boat. The pilot chosen was a 26-year-old undergraduate at the University of Washington by name of Gerry E. Walin, who had been racing outboards since he was thirteen and currently held the world speed record for Class A racing runabouts. On March 16th, 1966, Walin piloted *Starflite IV* to a new world's record of 130.929 mph on Lake Havasu on the Arizona-California border. As for circuit racing, the OMC had woken up after a sleep of several decades. The reason is that in 1966 Charlie Strang left Mercury for OMC, as director of Marine Engineering. The man who had helped escalate Mercury's horsepower supremacy now breathed R & D life into what his ex-boss Kiekhaefer still called "the enemy camp". The result was that for 1967, OMC announced their 115 hp racing unit: the Evinrude X-115 and the Johnson GT-115. This modified version of the 100 hp OMC had a new, slimmer lower unit. Perennial horsepower leader, Mercury only offered up to 110 hp in 1967, for the

An early Molinari catamaran taking part in the 1967 Paris 6 Hours, won by the brothers Rasini, Carlo and Enrico, again in a Mercury-Molinari cat.

first time in years, these flashy X-115 and GT-115 put OMC in the lead of the horsepower race. Indeed Strang had soon created a High-Performance Group in his department with the intention of getting back into factory-sponsored racing for the 1967 Season, ending at 25-year pit stop that began in 1942 with the onset of World War II. OMC factory racing was resumed in March 1967 when three boats were entered for the Parker Enduro at Parker, Arizona. Although none of its boats finished that race, by the end of the OPC (Outboard Performance Class) season, the OMC team had racked up 11 wins out of 16 starts. As for circuit racing in the UK, the deep-Vee was in contention. By altering the Vee and cutting the freeboard of a 16-footer, John Merryfield created *Thunderbolt XI*, a Levi design. With one of the new 110 hp Mercury "BP" units, Double M's unofficial works driver John May won the peak time TV World of Sport series and the Chasewater 24 Hours marathon. But then came the 1967 Paris 6 Hours.

Dieter Schulze, Austrian tunnel-hull pioneer sits in one of his revolutionary craft at Lake Havasu.

Bornhauser of Germany entered a Molinari cat powered by a rear-engined Porsche and was way ahead of the pack when his boat started to sink. Dieter Schulze raced his smooth-water Hydro-Cat, but also retired when he started to sink. Bill Sirois retired his Molinari when its Mercury blew up, and Keith Horseman, co-driving with John May, submarined *Thunderbolt XI*. The Seine marathon was won by Carlo and Enrico Rasini in their Mercury Molinari cat, although during the last stages, Rasini had to manipulate a snapped throttle. Following this contest, *Thunderbolt XI* was refloated, cleaned out, fitted with the latest 125 hp Mercury, and only 14 days after its Paris sinking, John May and Julian Bayley drove it to victory at the Berlin 6 Hours, averaging over 65 mph for 425 miles. John May recalls: "With the power we were getting, if you could keep the *XI* really tramping on and going, it was quite good. But if you were a bit unnerved and you let it wallow, then it became a petrifying thing and used to dart in every direction. It required a certain feel to drive it". May was not the only one concerned about the 125 hp BP Mercury brought out to rival to the Johnson GT 115. As John Merryfield puts it: "Apart from my own Mercury, Bill Shakespeare had one, two went to Germany and two to France, with an engineer to live with them. The instructions were that nobody save him touched them. As I said to Len Melly, that's the end of racing. Boats are expendable. Drivers are expendable. From now on it's merely an engine battle". There were others, however, who believed in the future, and started up a Junior Racing Class for 11 to 16-year-olds at the London Motor Boat Racing Club to get teenagers involved with learning to race powerboats. The first trainer monohulls, powered by tiny 10 hp engines, were designed by Anthony Needell and among those in the class of '67 was Jackie Wilson's 10-year-old son, Mark.

On March 16th, 1966, Starflite IV is shot here a few seconds before her record run

Gerry Walin takes Starflite IV down Lake Havasu at a scorching 130.929 mph

The competition between the two engines never ceased.

Elsewhere, with finance from Robert Glen of E. P. Barrus Ltd, Swordfish Marine of Twickenham, Middlesex, run by Clive Curtis and Chris Hodges, put together a modified deep-Vee Double M hull with no less than a 140 hp Johnson GT on the back. Called Hummingbird, she was to be driven by Curtis and his recent customer, James Beard. Among her features were air holes on the deck, leading to holes in the transom to improve airflow. But with all and sundry copying and modifying their original Double M design, Merryfield and Melly seriously considered building their own version of the circuit cat, but then decided they would be unable to beat Molinari or Schulze at their own game and called it a day. Double M Hulls Ltd reverted to John Merryfield Ltd and Outboard & Hydroplane Ltd. Their works driver, John May, also hung up his helmet: "A weird transition was taking place, with some very strange hull shapes about, driven by people who could not adapt their technique and were either flipping, barrel-rolling or submarining. Renato Molinari, whose cousin Cesare Scotti had recently gone over to the OMC camp and become his rival, actually asked me to co-drive with him in the marathon contests in Paris, Berlin, Rouen and Chasewater. But I realized that if a victory were scored, it would be by Molinari -with co-driver J. May- so I declined his offer". Although, in 1968, the Windermere Motor Boat Racing Club decided to allow outboard racing and

chose the V-hull built by Charlie Sheppard of Bristol Boats Ltd, by this time the bearded, bespectacled chief of that yard had decided to try his hand at a catamaran. Unlike those built so far, with rockers fore and aft to get the wind starting under the tunnel, Sheppard worked on the basis of a pair of waterskis, with no rockers but with an angle of attack on the top of the tunnel. Watching the performance of his plywood prototype, Sheppard's top drivers Carl Dawson and Brian Kendall agreed that it was really a "soggy moggy" or "wet cat". The name stuck. Before long, Sheppard had produced a fiberglass version of Airex-type sandwich foam construction ready for the 1968 Paris 6 Hours. Although he had initially fitted a pair of pendulum-operated, inset ailerons to avoid a flip, Sheppard decided not to risk disqualification from French officials and had them sealed up. He also filled the sponsons with buoyancy bags. Once again the Paris 6 Hours sorted out the men from the boys. Apart from Kendall and Dawson in *Soggy Moggy* and Curtis and Beard in *Hummingbird*, Jackie Wilson and colleague Don Ross had brought *Gawd-L-Pus*, a Saunders-built Rossinari cat, and Bill Shakespeare had arrived with three 19 ft forward-cockpit Avon cats. The French yards of Rocca and Cormorant had also entered cats. In addition, there were four, Johnson-engined Schulze cats, one driven by the American MacCune

From the pits, over 100 boats took part in the Paris marathon in 1967.

brothers, Hal and Tom. During the race, Carl Dawson stuffed *Soggy Moggy* coming down the straight, punching two holes in the deck, but thanks to the buoyancy bags managed to complete his two-hour stint. Back in the dock, with Bill Shakespeare, out of the race, bailing the water out of *Soggy Moggy*, Charlie Sheppard and team took some pieces off Don Ross's broken and retired cat to mend the deck. Following which Brian Kendall went out and won the 01 Class, placed eighth overall and beat a fleet of ON boats despite an attempted protest by the Johnson-powered Schulze cat team that *Soggy Moggy* had been powered by a 125 hp engine under a Merc 100 cowling, inaccurate as it turned out. The race was again won outright by Renato Molinari and Rosario Leonardi averaging 66 mph for 130 laps, but with one lap at 70 mph, although even with them it was rumoured that their Mercury was a 140 hp unit hiding behind a 115 hp cowling. Second and third places were taken by Schulze cats, whilst the first deep-Vee was *Hummingbird* driven to fifth place by Clive Curtis and James Beard. The same boat also went on to win the deep-Vee Class in Berlin. Indeed, the MacCune brothers were so impressed by Curtis and Beard's performance

Cesare Scotti, Renato Molinari's cousin, in one of his twin-engined tunnel hulls at Havasu Lake.

Monohulls are jumping high on the wakes of the River Seine.

that they invited them to race Schulze cats at the World Championship on Lake Havasu, Arizona. The Havasu race had first been staged in 1963 by Robert McCulloch Sr. of Los Angeles to promote his range of outboards through his special 3 cylinder 60 cu/in outboards winning the race. It would be accurate to say that outboard racing on Lake Havasu gave birth to the city. McCulloch had built the city on land, formerly called "Site Six" which he bought from the US government at the end of WW II for a few dollars per acre. His goal was to create another Palm Springs. He never quite reached that level but did build a very nice city from scratch and prospered therefrom. Curtis and Beard found themselves just one of 133 boats competing. Of this race, Curtis recalls : "I was leading the single-engined pack. We didn't know much about cats in those days. As

the fuel emptied from the back, the stern became lighter, whilst the front became heavy. This resulted in my going to the bottom of the Colorado River".

Competing alongside us were the Switzer Wings. I shall never forget one of them. It was called *Diabolo* and despite the wind and the waves, it ran 121 mph down the straight. But when it got to the corner it didn't turn, just carried straight on, careening sideways into the reeds. On our way home, James Beard told me that he wouldn't mind having a go at building an improved Switzer Wing that could corner. At the start of 1969, Jackie Wilson who had just acquired the König outboard agency, imported a green 17ft Schulze cat into Britain. Bob Spalding, a 28-year-old East Anglian driver, concerned that the big outboards were making the Vee-bottoms nose-dive, acquired this Schulze and finding it did not work very well with a König, replaced it with a 110 hp Mercury BP. Later that year, Jackie Wilson and Bob Spalding took their *Bobcat* down to Italy, to Molinari's Como yard. As Molinari thought they had no chance of matching his new 20 ft *Miss Titti*, named after his girlfriend, with its ultra secret "S-shaped" tunnel, he helped the two Englishmen with odd bits and pieces. *Bobcat* went out onto the Idroscalo Lake in Milan and started setting up speeds of 85 mph, 20 mph faster than the lolloping *Miss Titti* with her 125 hp engine. Because of poor assembly and not enough fuel, *Bobcat* failed to finish the race, but it had at least shown the Molinaris how incredibly fast a shorter cat could be. Bringing *Bobcat* back to England, Spalding then went out and nearly flew over Carr Mill Dam, Lancashire. The single-engined cat, it seemed, with the formidable horsepower available to it, was still in need of taming. This became evident when the London Motor Boat Racing Club organised a powerboat race on the River Thames. Despite barrages at each end of the course to prevent driftwood, most of the competing cats nose-dived into the chop. Brian Kendall flipped in his *Soggy Moggy* and was literally bowled across the surface, suffering "inside-out black eyes", albeit temporarily. The race was won by Don Ross in his latest

The British boat Gawd-L-Pus *shows how much competitors needed heaven's protection during the Paris 6-Hours.*

An early Schulze tunnel hull.

Angelo Vassena of Italy with engine problems with his 6-cylinder Carniti on the back of his cat built by Geremia Cetti.

Kenny Kitson in the Switzer Wing Diabolo at Havasu.

Gawd-L-Pus, a Wilson-imported Molinari, riding round at 45 mph to maintain an angle of 25 degrees and keep his cat's nose out of the water. Not long after this, Jeremy James was practising for the Liège 6 Hours marathon in a high-powered Shakespeare cat when he misread the course in the fog, drove over a weir at speed and was killed in a violent accident. Bill Shakespeare travelling behind in another cat, saw the accident, slowed down, went over, but escaped serious injury. Ironically, the race was won by a third Shakespeare cat, driven by Maxim Hilton and Wilf Gregory, the hull of which Gary Garbrecht took back with him to America. That Molinari remained the maestro was shown when, with Giovanni Pellolio, he averaged 67.62 mph to win the Paris 6 Hours, with the next three places taken by Como-built cats, whilst the MacCune brothers came fifth in the Johnson-engined Schulze. Back in Italy, Carlo Rasini became the first Italian to win the forty-year old Pavia-Venezia marathon, driving an outboard raceboat. His Mercury/Molinari clocked a new average of 86.9 mph. But even Angelo Molinari and Dieter Schulze realized that with outboard horse-power scheduled to go up even higher, unless there was some radical change in design, more than one death would occur on the European race circuits. Anyone looking at the twin-outboard-engined Switzer Wings would have at once real-

ized how the recessed centre section between the two fuselages avoided that backflip danger. Those few who were outboard racing in the early 1950s recalled Joe Swift's one-off three-pointer the "lazy dog" with its pioneer bow claws. Unlimited hydroplane designer, Ron Jones of Seattle had also been experimenting with bow claws in the outboard division: The name of the 20 ft tunnel hull was *Old Blue* and its pilot was Bill Seebold Jr. of St Louis, Missouri, fresh out of the alky hydro classes. Seebold had just come into contact with Gary Garbrecht, at that time working under Mercury's race manager Bill Steele. Garbrecht had set Seebold up with a couple of 125 hp "stackers" and it seemed appropriate to test them out on the latest Jones innovation. Jones, incidentally, had decided to call his bow claws by the more elegant name of "picklefork". This was not the only prototype that Jones built. In 1967 and 1968, a highly experimental "tandem wing" boat was built. It had a narrow central hull with a transverse wing at front and rear. Sponsons with planing surfaces were at each wingtip. This was, in other words, a four-pointer. The project was sponsored by Mercury at Ron's request but not very generously, with the result that the boat was rather roughly constructed. During the initial tests, water streaming off the sponsons drowned out the engine before the boat even went on plane. Mercury

proposed to send an engineer to modify the engine cowling to correct the situation, but he never appeared and the project died on the vine. Mercury picked up the boat and took it back to Wisconsin. Ron never saw it again. Later on Phil Rolla and Angelo Molinari would ship the Jones four-pointer across to the Italian lakes for a planned project to lift the World speed record, a project which never materialised. Whilst four-pointers have never been introduced into outboard racing, there are now several four-pointer unlimited hydroplanes on the American race circuits.

Ted May, from California, gets a little high above the River Seine... But he finished the race.

Renato Molinari drives his tunnel-hulled Miss Titti during the 1969 Paris 6 Hours which he won, with Giovanni Pellolio.

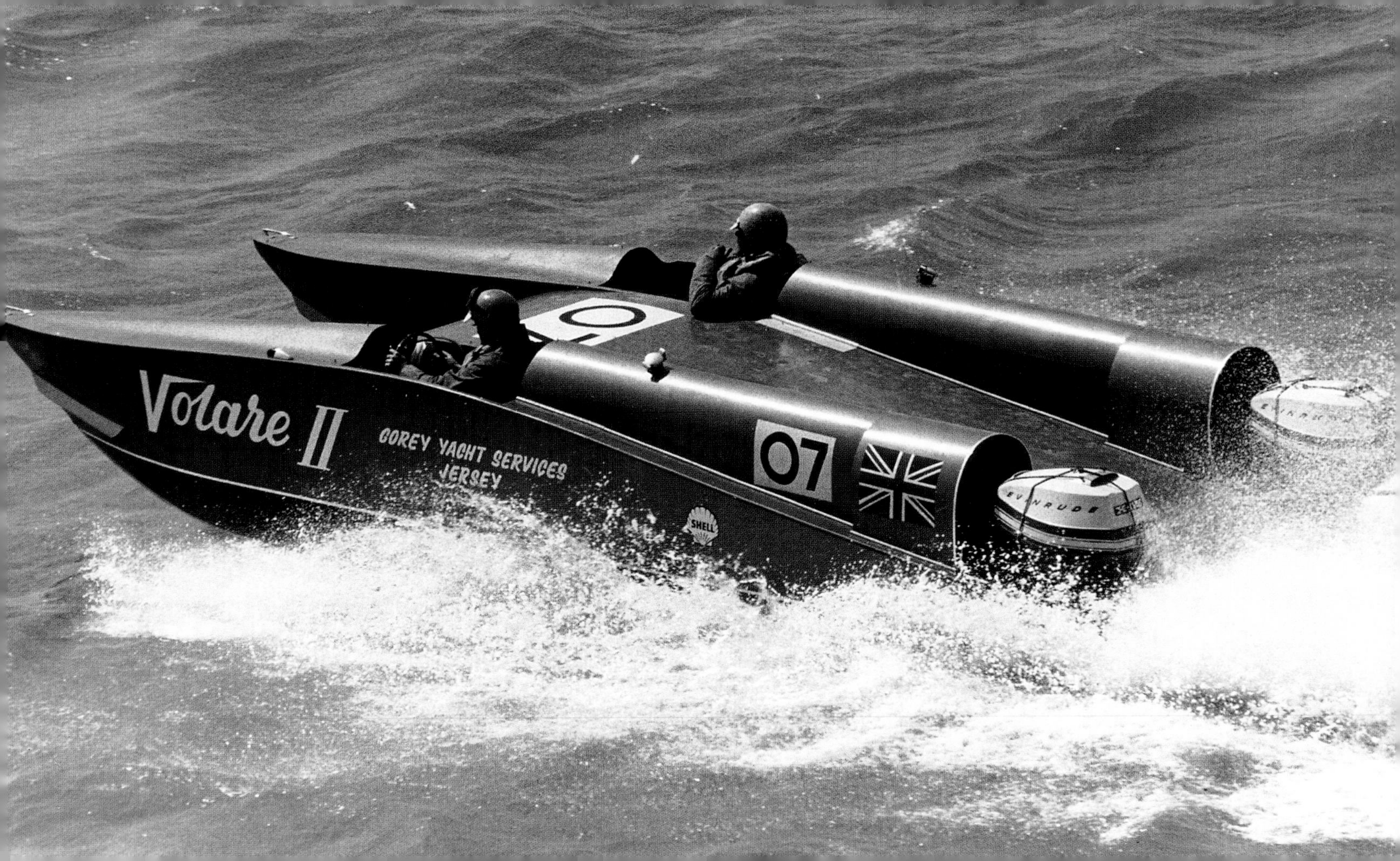
Volare II
GOREY YACHT SERVICES
JERSEY
07
SHELL
EVINRUDE

Pickleforks

Following a disastrous outboard-engined fiasco on the River Thames in 1969, Charlie Sheppard of Bristol Boats worked on a way to make his *Soggy Moggy* cats safer: "I knew I had got to do two things. The lift had got to be started further back and I had got to take the leading edge of the tunnel further away from the surface of the water. I achieved this by cutting the foredeck out and raising the leading edge of the tunnel by about four inches."

At the Rouen 24 Hours race of April 1970, Sheppard and Mercury's racing manager, Bill Steele, were watching the rainsoaked marathon from the comfort of a hotel bedroom when Sheppard described his new cat configuration. Steele at once remarked that Ron Jones of Seattle had also been working along exactly the same lines with his latest aero-engined unlimited hydros, and then added that Ron has given them the name "picklefork". Sheppard and Jones were not the only ones working on such concept. Following his return from the 1968 Havasu race, James Beard persisted in his ambition to build a Switzer Wing type cat that could go round buoys and Chris Hodges was consulted as to the best way to make it strong enough not to break up at sea. Hodges' considerable skills as a carpenter enabled him to give good advice. Almost 22 ft long, the prototype was built in England by Osborne and was finished off and rigged with the latest twin Evinrude X115 outboards totalling 300 hp, at Swordfish Marine in Twickenham. Painted dark metallic blue, it was called *Volare II* with racing number "07". At first, the offshore fraternity laughed when they saw Beard's experiment. But on 18 May 1969, *Volare II* silenced at least some criticism by beating the higher-powered favourite, Martin Jensen's *Scavenger* by a mile and averaging 50 mph. On being taken out of the water, one of *Volare II*'s props was missing, and both of her large steps, positioned amidships on each hull bottom, had split due to the lack of waterflow continuity in the bottom planking and the tie between aft and forward plane. This was rectified by fitting stainless steel turbulence deflectors under each step. After that, *Volare* enjoyed a very successful season and won

One of the first, if not the first, of the Ron Jones picklefork tunnel hulls powered by twin Mercs, at Long Beach, California.

nearly all the Class III races she entered, at speeds in excess of 56 mph. The critics persisted. Maybe the catamaran might work in Class III, but where the faster classes were concerned, the deep-Vee was surely unbeatable. Italy's Balestieri, for instance, had bought Don Aronow's *Maltese Magnum*, renamed it *Tornado* and become the first non-American to win the World championship. As for Aronow himself, during 1969 he campaigned a new 32 ft fiberglass deep-Vee, powered by twin 475 hp Mercruiser 482s and called *The Cigarette* after a famous Brooklyn express cruiser of the 1920s. He set an all-time single season record of eight wins, including the Bahamas 500, Miami-Nassau, Cowes-Torquay-Cowes and Viareggio. In the meantime, the only other British-built hulls which could offer anything like competition came from the drawing board of Don Shead. One of these, for example, was the 28 ft *Avenger Too*, cold-moulded by Souter of Cowes, powered by three Mercury outboards totalling 375 hp and driven to victory in the 1969 Round Britain marathon. Watson took 39 hours to complete the ten-stage 1,403 mile circuit, where only 24 out of the 42 starters finished. Meanwhile James and Mike Beard and their associates, Clive Curtis and Chris Hodges, with requests for them to build *Volare II* -type catamarans, decided to form a new company named Cougar.

Indeed, during the 1970 offshore season, the Class III "Cougar" cats, the Earl of Normanton's *Black Panther*, the Countess of Arran's *Badger V* and Liverpool cotton broker Ken Cassir's *Hy-Mac 580*, all powered by twin Mercury outboards, and the single-engined *Catapult*, were among the twin-hulled raceboats seen on the sea. James Beard remained determined that a British-built cat could win Paris. To this end, he designed *Miss Cougar*. Like Charlie Sheppard's new *Soggy Moggy*, *Miss Cougar* also had picklefork sponsons, but far more pronounced ones. She also had stern flaps, and an anti-trip chine panel which prevented the deck from dipping underwater during a corner, normally the cause of barrel-rolling. She also had an hydraulic lever made up from car parts and bits of tube, to enable her driver to use power trim, to "kick" a boat out of the turns. Built at Cougar Marine, Hounslow, this revolutionary, green prototype was four years ahead of her time, but her center of lift provided too far forward for the horsepower on her stern and *Miss Cougar* rolled over at speed in the 1970 Paris marathon. Her driver, the Earl of Normanton was badly injured and never raced circuit again. During the same contest, Brian Kendall and Simon Fleming driving Charlie Sheppard's slightly less radical picklefork, *Soggy Moggy*, won the 01 Class in Paris and came fifth overall. Since the late 1920s, outboard racing categories had gone by letter up to "X". In the 1960s the UIM added the letter "O" (for outboard) to these classes. It was now decided to split the "OX" into two classes: "ON" (2000 cc) and "OZ" (unlimited). Paradoxically, in the USA, the pro-drivers decided to drop the letter designations and move to metric units of displacement as 250 cc, 350 cc, etc. This was largely prompted by APBA pro division President Harry Bartholomew, a Californian driver who enjoyed racing in Italy and picked up an urge to follow European car and motorcycle practices. If the 1970s decade was marked by a battle in the most powerful ON and OZ Classes, it was between two race managers - OMC's Leek versus Mercury's Garbrecht. With cross-flow Evinrudes and Johnsons matched against Mercury loop-charged efficiency, works drivers became courageous pawns in a fiercely fought war. Whilst Entrop's friend Jack

Sean, the Earl of Normanton, at the wheel of Miss Cougar, *her revolutionary sponsons some four years ahead of their time.*

Leek of Tacoma was a seasoned veteran since the 1950s, Gary Garbrecht had arrived on the scene slightly later. In 1968, whilst already manager of Mercury Marine's racing department, Gary Garbrecht had also established a private company of his own as a tax shelter through which he and his son and his son's friends raced go-karts, motorcycles and even boats. He called his team by words used by Wisconsin football coach, Vince Lombardi - who often demanded a "second effort" to his players.

No choice of phrase could have been more apt, particularly following Garbrecht's appointment in 1971 as Mercury race director responsible for world-wide activities. The 12-boat team he formed was soon dubbed "The Black Angels", among the finest kicker jockeys in the history of the sport. They included Bob Hering, Mike Downard and Tom Stickle from Mercury's home town of Oshkosh; Bill Sirois from Fort Lauderdale; Bill Seebold Jr. from Fenton, Missouri; the Dutch national champion, Cees van der Velden; and last

*To make Gary Garbrecht's
"Black Angel" team really
dynamic, the pit support
had to be as effective
as the pilot dedication.
Here is just one of the fleet.*

Bill Shakespeare racing across Lake Windermere, England, only seconds before the accident that cost this experienced builder-driver his life.

but certainly not least, Renato Molinari, whose father supplied their hulls behind each of which was fitted the latest Mercury, the formidable 140 hp "Twister 6C" specially prepared at the factory.

At the 1971 Paris 6 Hours, the winning "Angel" averaged 77 mph. With twin Mercurys, Bill Sirois won the Lake Havasu marathon at an average 79.25 mph.

The force of the "Black Angels" was first felt in England when the 1971 race for the Duke of York's Trophy contest was held on Lake Windermere. Its "Deed of Gift" had now been altered, with permission from the Queen Mother, to specify outboards instead of inboards and to allow for an American engine on a British, Italian or Austrian hull. The three-hour race was won by Renato Molinari.

Tragically, a fatal accident occurred during pre-race practice, which once again underlined the lethal dangers of racing a cat with too much lift in it. Bill Shakespeare, whose experience in racing went back to when the largest outboard available, was testing his forward-cockpit *Shakespeare Special* with its 150 hp Johnson "Stinger" engine, when the red cat started a backward flip, shot upwards, then slid back down and sank like a stone. Neither boat nor pilot was found by the divers. Like all deaths in powerboat racing, Shakespeare's caused some to pull out, and made others more determined in their resolve to make a more stable powerboat.

OMC driver Brian Kendall, who had nose-dived his Sheppard-designed picklefork, *Soggy Moggy*, in Paris, decided to hang up his helmet, whilst Charlie Sheppard himself stopped building cats and within a year had organized a new race at his local Bristol docks, which was to become a crowd-pulling classic known as the Embassy Grand Prix. Up to the end of 1971, Garbrecht's "Black Angels" had been racing full tunnel cats. Fully aware of the backward flip problem, some of them, particularly Renato Molinari, had incorporated a six-gallon ballast tank in the bows of their powerboat. Racing into the wind, the driver would pull a lugger allowing water to fill the tank via a scoop on the back of the boat and then when he turned and headed downwind the water would be jettisoned. But it was not always possible to use this makeshift device in the short time available.

No wonder, therefore, that for the 1972 season both Molinari and Hering of Oshkosh, raced what they described as a new Italian made secret weapon, a cross between an tunnel and a pickle-nose hydro or in other words, a "picklefork" cat. The changeover to the Sheppard/Beard configuration at once paid off. At Dayton, Ohio, Hering averaged 82.873 mph for five miles and then went on to score overall wins at the Milan 3 Hours, Miami 225, Wisconsin 2 Hours, Amsterdam 3 Hours and Paris 6 Hours. At Paris, co-driving with Renato, Hering set a 93.6 mph lap record and averaged 87.15 mph for the 523 miles they covered.

The Paris 6-Hours marathon remained a harsh testing ground for different design approaches to racing catamarans.

Neck and neck! OMC's newly developed V6 engines arrived "fresh" at the 1974 marathon held in France's capital city: they not only gave as good as they got – they went better by winning the first four places.

For James Beard and Cougar Marine, based in Hampshire, England, such a vindication of their design ideas spurred them on further. They made a second and more successful attempt at a Class II catamaran. Some four years before American Doug Silvera had won the Bahamas 500 offshore race in a 31ft Bertram powered by no less than four 140 hp Mercury outboards. The 33 ft four-seater catamaran which Cougar now built, called after its paper-making sponsor *Wiggins Teape* was also powered by four Mercs. Driven by Keith Dallas, she was reasonably successful in 1974, coming second in the Cowes-Torquay-Cowes race. But then the following year, Dallas had it re-sponsored as *Penthouse Inverhouse*: "We changed it from a four-seater to a two-seater, which reduced the front end weight of the boat; we took the wing extension off the back and we fitted four new Mercury outboards, each tweeked to 230 hp. In that guise, she became an extremely successful boat - even coming third overall in the Miami-Nassau race". With such power under its black cowling, this latest Mercury also enjoyed a formidable supremacy in 1973 around the race circuits of Europe and America. Garbrecht's had now developed two separate forces: Team Mercury Europa at Molinari's yard at Como and Mercury Marine at Oshkosh.

Not that Charlie Strang and OMC could not hit back. He had been trying to convince his management and particularly the marketing people that they should have a V-6 to sell: "At that time I was not yet CEO and had to be persuasive rather than demanding. After hearing dozens of reasons why such a large engine was not saleable and meeting much resistance to putting a V-6 in the production plan, I said to Leek to build a few V-6s on the racing budget instead of the production budget and run them at Paris. As I built the first 6 cylinder engine at Mercury, we surreptitiously built those V-6s in the racing shop, welding up crankshafts out of bits and pieces, as well as everything else. They were finished just before leaving for Paris and were virtually untried". The gamble paid off. At the 6 Hours, the first four places were taken by Scotti catamarans powered by those OMC V-6 250 hp Evinrude and Johnson prototypes. Those initial V-6s built in the racing shop were built at 2-litre solely to mislead Mercury into think-

ing that the production engine would be 2-litre and hence about 200 hp when, in reality they were designing a larger engine of 235 hp for public sale. In Paris, Strang went so far as to toss a scored piston to a Mercury engineer who had been assigned to keep an eye on OMC's pits, asking him: "What do you suppose caused that?". He ran off happily, clutching what he supposed would be the piston size for the soon-to-be announced production V-6. They were totally stunned at the horsepower certification tests a month or two later when the OMC V-6 pulled an easy 235 hp versus the Merc's 200. Going home with a victory in my pocket, I was able to convince my boss to let us design and build a production version with the marketing people protesting that they would never sell more than 1,600 units a year. We sold 26,000 the first year, limited only by production capacity, and onward and upward in succeeding years."

A Mercury Twister II propels James Merten to a new World Outboard Speed Record along the Fox River. The date is August 8th, 1973.

As if to get the edge on their old rivals, on August 8th, 1973, Mercury's American race manager, James Merten, came out after two years' retirement from a very successful 20-year racing career and lifted the world unlimited outboard record to 136.381 mph, clocking a maximum of 138 mph down the Fox River. The 17 ft three-point cabover hydroplane, as designed by Merten, was powered by a Mercury "Twister II", very similar to those sold to independent OPC drivers competing in the APBA unlimited class, known as the "King Kong" brigade.

This record was backed up at the annual national five-mile closed course championships on Lake Eufaula, Alabama. Out of a total entry of 216 drivers, 12 class champions emerged and Billy Seebold Jr. of St Louis, Missouri, upped the unlimited record to 85.592 mph, beating the existing mark of

On board the record boat with shirt-sleeved Mr. Merten at over 137 mph!

*Behind the pits
at the Bristol Grand Prix:
"probably the most
competive drivers
in the sport" become pals
over a tin of lager.
Left to right:
Bob Spalding, Cees van der
Velden, Bill Seebold Jr,
and Renato Molinari.*

83.026 mph set by Reggie Fountain Jr. of North Carolina, only one week before.

Seebold, who like his father before him had just arranged for his own 13-year-old stepson, Mike, to go racing, also visited Europe for the first of many times. Teaming up with 1972 ON Class World champion Cees van der Velden, they won the Amsterdam 3 Hours in a Molinari picklefork. Molinari himself won the 1973 World ON Class championships at Koblenz, Germany, whilst nearest rival Bob Hering miraculously survived a spectacular high altitude flip in an identical hull. While Seebold headed east, Bob Spalding of Ipswich, England, headed West and became the first British driver to work at Mercury's Lake X as chief test-driver for one year. This involved endless testing of the fuel-injected V-6 engine on the back of a Molinari hull. Another Englishman fortunate enough to benefit from the Twister II was Spalding's colleague, 30-year-old Tom Percival. A third Englishman was Freddy Miles of Birmingham, whose Mercury-engined Milesmaster cats were being built by the late Bill Shakespeare's apprentice Dave Burgess, also carrying on a tradition of racing success.

To answer all this Twister power, OMC bravely decided to replace their Stinger and Strangler models with a form of alternative engineering with a phenomenal power potential. In 1971 OMC engineers had built the first US-made triangular rotary combustion engine based on the design of Doctor Felix Wankel. In February 1973 their racing team introduced the world's first rotary-powered outboards at a press presentation in the Miami Marine Stadium. They were, they claimed, equivalent to a 12-cylinder piston engine and capable of a potential 300 hp. The best that could be said for them was that though they failed to finish, the two rotary-outboard boats were spectacular in holding down first and second place during the first lap of the Parker, Arizona 9 Hours race, not against the outboard competition but against 7-litre, three-point, inboard racing

The sheer walls
of the Bristol Docks were
unforgiving. They forced
drivers to use all their nerve
and experience around
the tight corners.

hydoplanes which had a long tradition of leading that race while they lasted. Campaigned by drivers like Mike Downard and Tom Posey, the OMC rotary had its victories, such as the contest for the Duke of York's Trophy on Lake Windermere, in England. The team acquired two more rotary-powered craft and went on to take first, second, and third place in its third competition that year. On May 6th, driver Jimbo McConnell set a record of 112.7 mph in the quarter-

Straw-hatted Joe Swift takes a quiet look at Johnson's latest weapon: their rotary outboard.

Cover off showing
the innovative inners
of the world's first
triangular rotary
combustion engined
outboard.

Dr. Felix Wankel

mile speed trials at Marcy, New York, using a four-cylinder rotary motor. During the Paris 6 Hours, the rotary-engined Evinrude of McConnell/Woods led the race for five and a half hours.

The OMC Wankels ran in more US races than European because of a highly technical disagreement with the UIM as to how the displacement should be measured. In the US, the displacement was computed at 2-litre while the UIM's technical expert declared it to be 4-litre. This esoteric argument led OMC to use the engines primarily in the big US enduros where they could put a lot of running time on the engines and where their goal was to beat the inboards, since no outboards could provide enough competition for the Wankels.

OMC stopped racing these engines when it became clear that manufacturing cost considerations would prohibit mass production of such outboards for sale to the public.

In 1972, Commander Peter du Cane of Vosper-Thornycroft shipyard had attempted an alternative in the shape of a three-point "ramwing" boat, a reverse three-pointer called *Advance*. Following model tests done by the newly-established Cougar Marine, du Cane's friend Fiona, Countess of Arran, managed to accelerate *Advance* up to speeds of 80 mph but found it impossible to take it tightly around the buoys. Four years later, James Beard again tried a reverse-three-pointer circuit powerboat, only to nose-dive it during the Amsterdam race. But then Cougar Marine also experimented with three circuit boats whose right and left picklefork sponsons were of a slightly different width and length to enable them to go more tightly around the buoys - only to discover that due to outboard engine torque, these experimental hulls tended to tilt a few degrees when running. In Italy, Molinari certainly did not have any design patent on their own configuration. Cesare Scotti had certainly shown this with the cats he built for the OMC factory team, until he was killed in the 1974 Paris 6 Hours marathon when his boat veered off course, slidded along the concrete embankment and smashed into a bridge buttress. At 90 mph Scotti had little chance of survival. Indeed the following year, Mercury were to pull out of the Paris race on the eve of the event because they considered the course too dangerous. Experiments aside, J. Beard and Cougar Marine certainly came up with some winners. The 15 ft *Wood Mariner* had not only enabled him to win the first staging of the Embassy Grand Prix at Bristol, but to average 78.30 mph during a 400-mile marathon at Chasewater. There followed the "Circuit Two-Pointer Model E" of which the Netley Yard might have built some 10 hulls had not the 1973 fuel crisis nearly threatened to wreck their business. Following "Models F" and "G", came "C2H", three of which were built and raced successfully by the Embassy racing team Peter Thorneywork, Roger Jenkins and Beard himself. OMC felt they had to improve on Mercury's 136 mph World speed record. On September 12th, 1974, Gerry Walin was back at Havasu. His team had told him he must not exceed 135 mph in the *Starflite IV*, the critical speed for a lethal blow-over. Although the first run was timed at 135 mph, on the return run the boat had accelerated to 147 mph when her nose lifted, she rocketed, flinging Walin across the

Starflite IV at 147 mph, beyond the point of no return, seconds before her blowover.

hard water. His back was broken, paralysing him from the waist down. He was over a month in intensive care in critical condition from sinal, thorasic and leg injuries. When his wife left him for another man, Walin killed himself.

For the 1975 Embassy Grand Prix, of the 18 "Formula One" hulls, nine were Cougars powered by Evinrude or Johnson V4s and V-6s developing 200 hp at 5,750 rpm; whilst there were only five Molinaris powered by the V-6 loop-charged Mercury "Black Max", developing 175 hp at 5,500 rpm and for racing renamed the "T3" or "1750 XS".

Cougar was not the only yard offering an alternative. Disenchanted that he was getting slightly inferior boats to those driven by Renato Molinari, Bill Seebold Jr. of St. Louis, Missouri, had persuaded friend and hydroplane-builder Andie Lawrey to help him build his own full tunnel hull for the ON Class, to be powered by a Mercury Twister II. Six were sold before they even built the first one. Then in 1975, they evolved a system for building tunnel hulls with pickle-fork sponsons. With this hull, Seebold beat Renato Molinari in all three heats of the St. Louis Grand Prix. The third driver to decide that Molinari cats were not the only way to go was Cees van der Velden. In March 1971, Molinari and Bob Hering had used a V-6 Mercury T3 to win the Parker 7 Hours marathon at an average 100.285mph. Van der Velden was not allowed a T3 for Parker and then was told that when the second T3 arrived in Europe it would also go to Molinari and that he would be left with a lower-powered "Twister II X". The Dutchman, therefore, decided to go over to OMC. Requiring a hull, he got a local boat-builder to make him a copy of a Molinari, but with less lift in it. The builder

Great Britain's Tom Percival upheld a family powerboat racing tradition which went back to his grandfather before World War I.

Italy's winningest family:
Angelo Molinari,
and his son Renato (above)
in these rare out-of-cockpit
photos.

made a complete mistake and gave it more lift. Nevertheless, with sponsorship from Marlboro, and the latest Johnson V-6 with its experimental middle unit on the back, Cees campaigned his "Veldenari" in what was left of the season.

At the World ON Class championships held at Cardiff, Velden's boat was perfectly suited to the rough waters and won the first heat, albeit that the inside rear of his left sponson blew out. After agreement with the organisers, the 'Ceesinari' was taken to Cougar Marine at Netley Abbey where Chris Hodges worked all night to repair it. Absent from heat two, Velden now had to win heats three and four to clinch it. This he achieved, so taking the title for the second year running, but this time for OMC.

At this time Hodges had design ideas in conflict with those of partner James Beard. At the Windermere Grand Prix, Velden, now determined that he should replace the late Scotti as OMC's European boatbuilder, asked Chris Hodges if he

would like to build boats for him. At first, Hodges did not wish to leave England
for Holland, but after added financial inducement, he went over to Boxtel for
several months to show Velden's apprentices, Peter and John, how to build
Molinari-type cats. By the beginning of 1976 the Dutchman had 18 raceboats on
the water, some of which, disintegrating at speed, soon taught the team the way
to improve.

Very quickly, some extraordinary changes had taken place elsewhere. It had
begun when Seebold told Garbrecht of Mercury that he would like to run his own
designed and built boat in the big 142 cu/in class. Frustrated with Molinari,
Garbrecht agreed. Having only completed the boat one week before, Seebold and
Velden (back in the Mercury fold) maintained formidable speeds of 120 mph to
win the Parker Enduro. Immediately afterwards, Garbrecht offered Seebold a
$150,000 one-year contract to build boats for Team Mercury in America. This
was followed in quick succession by a better two-year contract, an even better
three-year contract, then an excellent contract for life.

Realising that Velden could also build good circuit boats for Team Mercury
Europe, Garbrecht decided that he need no longer pay Molinari such a large sum
for building factory's entries. When he offered Molinari one third of the pay, the
Italian resigned and took his very considerable skills to OMC who were only too
pleased to accept him.

From now on, Garbrecht at Oshkosh, with his brilliant Irish-born chief engineer William Les Cahoon, worked closely with Seebold and Crum at St Louis,
exchanging requirements, changing, for example, from a left-hand to a right-
hand gearcase for the T3; moving a step here or altering the angle of attack of
the wing there. And perhaps most advantageous of all, Garbrecht had also
recruited a 24-year-old ace driver Earl Bentz from Nashville, Tennessee, who
could pace and often beat Seebold at his own game. Indeed, Bentz lifted the 5
mile outboard raceboat record to 96 mph, 4 mph faster than Seebold's fastest.

Not that the British had been ousted from the 100 mph outboard race scene. Tom Percival and Bob Spalding, unbeatable national champions, became the first English duo since Melly and Merryfield to win the Paris 6 Hours marathon doing so for two years' running in 1976 and 1977.

During the 1970s there seemed to be absolutely no limit to the cu/in and horsepower that could be packed under the cowling of an unlimited outboard engine. As each factory leap-frogged the other in additional pots, it became difficult to know who had the greater challenge; the boatbuilders or the few works-drivers trying to adapt their test-pilot skills for ever higher speeds with ever greater chances of accidents.

By the mid 1970s the Mercury-versus-OMC capacity battle presented an almost insurmountable problem to designers and builders. Every raceboat has a critical speed, and a limit to the amount of air that can be scooped up and compressed along the tunnel-hulled bottom. What is ideal is to match the critical speed with the maximum engine-power obtainable so as to achieve optimum acceleration.

But whenever a more powerful engine appeared, once mounted on the back of a boat, performance became unstable. By the end of the season the balance would have once again been sorted out with new boats being built for those engines. But then come a new racing season, a more powerful engine still would arrive and the whole procedure would begin again. Such quantum leaps in horse-power became quite hairy, except perhaps for Renato Molinari and Bill Seebold, who always got their factory's latest powerhead in advance. It was not long after OMC's 3.3-litre 235 hp V-6 Evinrude and their 240 hp Johnson first went roaring up and down Lake Como in early 1978 that Mercury replied by sending their 3.5-litre, 200 hp V-6 Black Max Mercury up and down both Lake Havasu City and Lake X, so that Seebold could develop the best hull for it. The main prob-

Earl Bentz, Mercury race driver, was known as the "Tennessee Tiger".

Time for explanations: Mercury engineer Les Cahoon explains the finer engineering points to the no-nonsense Gary Garbrecht, whilst drivers Seebold (in cap) and Jenkins listen intently.

lem suffered before the 1978 season in both camps was that their cats would not "sit down on the corners". So Seebold and Les Cahoon, Mercury's maestro-engineer, came up with air-brakes. These were air-cylinders that rammed a little wedge down in the water at the back of the sponson. After 45 days of continuous testing of these brakes, four of Garbrecht's latest team - Seebold, Bentz, Sutter and Fountain - introduced their secret weapon at the St. Louis race. Seebold's winning average of 115 mph certainly proved the air-brakes' effectiveness. By mid-season, Renato Molinari was also testing out air-brakes. In July, the World OZ Class championships were held for the first time in Britain, at Chasewater. Watched by thousands of spectators, including Princess Margaret, Renato applied the brakes on his cat and disintegrated at 100 mph, mercifully with no injury to himself. The contest was won by Seebold. Chasewater was the first of the six-race, Formula One series, sponsored by Canon, and won on a points basis by England's Tom Percival, Seebold's team-

It was never easy to refuel a floating racing boat during the Lake Havasu marathon.

mate in a sponsorship deal by Long John whisky. The supremacy of the V-6 Mercury was further hammered at the Paris 6 Hours marathon where Percival's rival Bob Spalding, co-driving a V-6 Mercury-powered Velden rig with Bill Seebold's 19-year-old son Mike, maintained a winning average of 91mph, a record-unbroken to this day. Faced with this new threat and with what OMC might have brewed up for the 1979 season, Les Cahoon now progressed to the most monstrous Twister, the T4, a tuned exhaust V-6 with longer stroke Mercury never admitting to the phenomenal 370 hp packed underneath its black cowling. But although the T4 offered phenomenal

potential it was not always reliable; its big heavy pistons tending to blow up at the wrong moment. There were, however, two races in which it stayed together.

The Embassy Grand Prix that June was watched by an estimated 258,000 spectators crammed around the confined area of the Bristol docks. During the qualifying heats, Earl Bentz, "The Tennessee Tiger", who had never raced at Bristol before, went out in a boat which had not been fully tested and, with only a T3, posted a lap at 98.24 mph; the race was won however, by his boatbuilder Seebold, using a T4 in a slightly older,

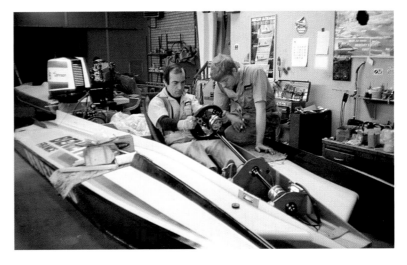

damaged boat who clocked up a best heat average of 88.39 mph. Throughout the contest Molinari's Saffa cat, powered by Evinrude, had been plagued by mechanical problems. Three months later, the Italian determined that no T4s would beat him at the OZ Class World championship contest, especially as this was to be held near Milan in front of hundreds of thousands of Italian supporters. Although back in 1974, Mercury and OMC had made a gentleman's agreement that no more twin-engined rigs would be run, Molinari showed up with a 20 ft cat powered by a pair of Evinrude V-6s, totalling six-litre. Garbrecht was furious. He telephoned Charlie Strang of OMC and delivered a strong protest. Although Mercury had already broken the agreement by showing up at Havasu with two twin-engined rigs which ran away from its rival singles, Strang sportingly called Molinari, who remained determined to run his twin engined boat. The contest began. In heat one, Bentz was disqualified for jumping the gun, but his colleague, Seebold, managed to beat Molinari, the latter hitting the pits and buoy. At first the Italian officials turned a blind eye to this but changed their minds when the Mercury team were able to prove Molinari's error by using a

Cees van der Velden at his Boxtel boatyard in the Netherlands, fine tunes the driver's control position.

Renato Molinari (left) and Cees van der Velden (above) in Paris, 1977.

Breaking "the gentleman's agreement". Twin Evinrude V-6s totalling six litres on the back of Molinari's 20-footer

A chevalier of speed afloat, ready for the race…

video of the race. Sunday saw the three remaining heats. Molinari won heat two, with Seebold second. Molinari won heat three, with Seebold second. Thus the Italian had two firsts, whilst the American had a first and two seconds. To win the world championship on points, Seebold not only had to win heat four but also post a faster heat time. Garbrecht now took all the single-engined drivers aside and worked out a plan of campaign on a bench as to how they were going to "wet out" Molinari from winning. If they could get the Italian to start from the back by going off in line abreast, each one could then take him out as far as possible. Mercury mechanics now raised the single T4, leaned it down and changed the prop for a ten-lap showdown, and Seebold recalls: "That was the best start I made during the whole weekend. We caught him napping". During the first two laps both van der Velden and Jenkins managed to hold off the Italian; the Dutchman actually taking him off for a tour round the pits. This allowed Seebold to gain a valuable 9 second lead. But then, with its formidable acceleration, the *Saffa* boat started to reduce the lead. On the 7th lap, Bentz who normally would never let anyone lap him, actually slowed down to let Seebold past and then proceeded to block Molinari, though not for long, but for long enough to let his fellow American complete the heat in first place and with the fast time which he needed.

OMC's shrewd and seasoned race manager, Jack Leek once said "The public were familiar with the old reputation that Mercury knew how to build race engines. Well, we knew how to build a race engine, too so we ran their arse off whenever we could!"

A Lethal Business

By 1980, the seven-race series for the "Canon Formula One" trophy had become a circus of survival for some 12 veteran works drivers. Unless they had the latest and lethal "King Kong" engine from Evinrude/Johnson or Mercury/Mariner, there was virtually no chance of taking top honours. This lack of a sizeable fleet to take the starter's flag was beginning to alienate both sponsors and race organizers. During the Parker Enduro race, British officials approached both OMC's Jack Leek and Mercury's Gary Garbrecht and asked them to propose a limitation on outboard engine capacity. Although both race managers had agreed on a 2.5-litre limit, by the time they had arrived back in England, the capacity was further lowered to 2-litre as for the ON Class. So, it was announced that the 1981 Bristol Grand Prix and the Duke of York's Trophy would only be open to the ON Class, which was renamed "Formula One". At about the time of this decision taken by Charlie Sheppard, Mercury not only decided to suspend any further investment in developing big racing engines, but withdrew their powerful T4, then developing over 400 hp, from the circuits. They announced they would support a 2-litre limit. Some cynics said they had done this because they realized that whilst their T4 was not coming up to full expectations, they had also discovered that, in truth, OMC did not have a 2-litre engine. After 18 months of service, Gary Garbrecht resigned from Mercury: "I was totally disenchanted by the politics between the department which I was running and the non-racing attitude of the company's executive staff under its new president Richard Jordon. We were disbanding a very successful factory racing team and replacing it with a far less efficient customer race program. Anyway I needed a rest." True to form, Garbrecht did not leave his loyal drivers totally unprovided for. Each one of them was sent a crate of racing equipment (two blocs, two pistons, gearcases etc.) should they wish to continue racing.

The last race in the Canon Trophy series was the Paris 6 Hours marathon. Just before this race, OMC, who had also been expected to fall in with the two-litre

Collision racing at Chasewater, England. The third cat's backwards flip slices the stern off the second cat.

Renato Molinari was forever shadowed by Giorgio, his helpful brother and sometime co-pilot.

limit, held a controversial press conference to announce their intention of producing a new OZ Class engine for the 1981 season, an enormous 3.5-litre V-8, burning 94 octane gas and developing 400 hp at 10,000 rpm. Up to that time Canon Business Machines had shown a keenness to support the new limit. But they now decided to pull out "until powerboating puts its house in order." By this time, veteran driver Jackie Wilson decided to hang up his helmet but was keen that his son Mark be given a chance. Wilson and a host of other drivers formed the Formula ON Drivers' Association (FONDA) with a £2 membership fee and Wilson as chairman. By this time, Mercury's London publicist David Parkinson and Bristol's Charlie Sheppard planned to add a second race to the FONDA series. A meeting was arranged with the Paris 6 Hours' founder, Jean Noel Bladinaire. Sheppard wagered Bladinaire a bottle of champagne per boat that the following October he would have 30 ON Class cats take the starter's flag. Following this meeting, a FONDA point-scoring series now grew to include Brussels, Bristol, Linz, Milan, Paris and an American race at St. Louis, Missouri. Meanwhile, the John Player cigarette concern had signed a three-year contract to sponsor an OZ Class series around the new OMC 3.5-litre V-8, with a formidable amount of prize money. Although they had initially expressed an interest in a capacity limitation, veterans such as Molinari, Velden, Colombo, Jenkins, Percival and Spalding were lured away to that class. OMC's racing team entered six new V-8 outboards in a race held at Brodenbach, Germany. These strong powerplants easily captured first and third places in their

Britain's Bob Spalding in perfect control of his Velden-hull powered by a Mercury V-6 during the 1978 Season.

initial outing. A 3.5-litre Evinrude V-8 pulled down the top spot, while second was captured by a Johnson V-6 and a third by a Johnson V-8. Some may have wondered where was the real competition and which series could now claim the prestigious title "Formula One".

In the spring of 1981, at a controversial meeting of the UIM, a vote was taken to decide this very issue. Although 17 of the 27 countries represented, voted that ON Class should be the Formula One, General Secretary José Mawet reminded delegates that the opinion of the sport section pointed towards OZ Class as the preferable candidate. There was a revote, and OZ Class became Formula One as FONDA was pensioned off to the alternative title of "Formula Grand Prix". Significantly, when OMC formed a committee to prescribe the rules for their Formula One series, José Mawet was made Chairman. Whilst some have suggested that the UIM had been bought off by OMC, others have hinted that the FONDA lobby was in the pocket of Mercury. There is no proof for either allegation. But one thing is certain that both series saw some fine racing. By the end of 1981 some ten OZ Class rigs had seen combat, and OMC were announcing that they would have at least fourteen V-8s on the circuit for 1982, available to approved buyers at $14,500. Altogether some 24 drivers took part in the FONDA series, eight of them British, seven American, two Italian, and not to forget the German Michael Werner. Because only 22 drivers turned up at the Paris 6 Hours, eight short of the figure wagered by Bladinaire, Charlie Sheppard had to buy two crates of champagne. But Peter Inward and Nick Cripps's victorious 86.8 mph average in a Mariner-powered Hodges cat, round a very rough River Seine, certainly made it all worthwhile. For Chris Hodges, this was certainly a vindication of his continued abilities as a designer-builder,

The Formula One fleet, formerly OZ, during the 1981 season. The "King Kong" powerplant is the 3.5-litre OMC V-8 unit.

particularly in competition with hulls built by Molinari, Velden, Seebold and Dave Burgess. In winning with a total score of 31 points, Tony Williams was presented with the FONDA trophy. Then as if to further hammer home his supremacy, Williams took his boat up to Lake Windermere and lifted the world unlimited outboard record to 137.96 mph.

By 1982, the John Player World Championship had been extended to nine crowd-pulling events at Leon, Como, Bristol, Vichy, Dramman, Pittsburgh, Liège, Holme Pierrepont and Milan. Despite their experience and the lure of big prize money, the OZ Class drivers certainly had their work cut out as they took their lightweight 17 ft cats, almost dwarfed by their 3.5-litre V-8 outboards, around these courses at speeds of up to 130 mph, with split-second deceleration down to 100 mph at each and every buoy turn. Whilst building hulls for five other Formula One drivers, Cees van der Velden had no time to do his own testing and experimentation. At the Liège Grand Prix, on lap 18, the Flying Dutchman's own boat nose dived at nearly 120 mph and exploded into fragments. Following his release from an intensive care unit, internal injuries did not stop Velden from returning to his workshop just six weeks after his accident and planning for the 1983 season. Ironically, the championship was won by Roger Jenkins with an Evinrude on the back of his Burgess hull; second was Molinari in his Martini-sponsored aluminium and carbon fibre cat; and third was Tom Percival whose hull had been built by Chris Hodges. Coincidentally, the only contest of the FONDA seven-race series to take place at the same venue and on the same weekend as the John Player series was at Bristol. And it was

The "OMC circus" at the start of the Pittsburgh Grand Prix.

here that, once again, "the man from Missouri", aged 41, achieved a feat such as legends are made of. Seebold and his expert mechanic Leo Molindyke arrived in the pits with one blue, white and red-striped Tissot catamaran and two Mercury engines, one conforming with the two-litre FONDA limit and the other bored out to 2.4-litre to enable him to take on the Formula One 3.5-litre OMC fleet. As heats for the two optional series had been alternated, with Molindyke achieving speed records for engine-swapping in the pits, Seebold raced a gruelling total 130 high speed laps to win round three of the Formula One series and the Duke of York's Trophy for an unprecedented fourth time. That weekend, hundreds of thousands of British spectators went wild in their support for an American because as an underdog, he had triumphed. It was around this time that Bob Spalding noticed that he and his fellow drivers were reaching higher speeds in competition on the race course than the existing straightaway speed record attempts. In October 1982, he took his V-8 Johnson-engined *John Player Special* up to the Lake Windermere and cranked it up to a new outboard record

Roger Jenkins takes off during the 1982 Champion Spark Plug Grand Prix on the Mississippi River in Minneapolis. Miraculously he suffered only bruised legs.

Start of the more popular 1982 FONDA 2-litre race series at Casale Monferrato, Italy.

of 139.66 mph. In 1983, 19 drivers from six countries competed for star prize money through some nine extremely well-attended Formula One races, while 26 drivers from nine countries went point-scoring for the seven-race FONDA series. Both series had begun to introduce a new generation of drivers prepared to take their 3.5-litre and 2-litre cats up to top speeds of 130 mph around demanding sprint-style courses. Once again, Molinari proved himself the Formula One maestro with a winning 66 points to Cees van der Velden's 48 points. Both veterans had come up with cockpit-to-engine cowling shapes differing in their streamlining. Molinari's had evolved at Fiat-Lancia's wind-tunnel thanks to his Martini sponsors. The FONDA series, made up of 15 minutes heats, was equally spectacular, with Germany's Michael Werner scoring maximum points in his Seebold-hulled *Liqui-Moly*. In a season which saw the deaths of Peter Inward (GB) and Ken Stevenson (US) and the reluctant retirement of Miss Fiona Brothers following a near fatal and crippling accident, perhaps the most interesting innovation of all was a composite cat built for FONDA competitor Steve Kerton. Built at Barracuda boats, this hull used carbon fibre, Kevlar and fiberglass. Although Kerton's composite lacked the same feel that a plywood hull can give, the following year at the Bristol Grand Prix, where Billy Seebold won his sixth Duke of York's Trophy, Kerton barrel-rolled his cat at over 100 mph and survived, though badly shaken and bruised, to find his cat still all in one piece. Once again, at the end of the season, as if to emphasize the superior edge of the high capacity cats, Rick Frost accelerated his Johnson-powered Burgess *Trimite Paints* down Lake Windermere to a new world outboard record of 144.16 mph. Again Mercury rose to the challenge and George Andrews Jr., using a 200 hp Mercury V-6 on a special Karelsen 3-pointer, reached a startling 157.424 mph at Moor Haven, Florida. The extreme danger involved in flying these boats at these speeds became clear when Andrews was killed during an attempt to raise his own record. Following this tragedy, both factories seemed to lose interest in pursuing the record. In 1984, the FONDA series acquired one further feather for its cap with the 81-year-old Harmsworth Trophy. Four years before, the rules of the legendary bronze plaque had been altered to a four-heat offshore series Great Britain versus America. This became an expensive procedure given that contenders had to start in at least one of the heats on the other side of the Atlantic. Indeed, the 1983 winner was the only competitor from America to enter the British heats and merely had to finish to qualify. This was no good, so in 1984 the Harmsworth Trustees and FONDA organizers again re-wrote the rules for a two-heat contest. The first heat at Bristol during the same weekend as the Duke of York's Trophy contest, and the second in Nassau, Bahamas. Whilst some regretted that a trophy once contested by unlimited powerboats had not gone to the Formula One contingent, it was certainly well earned by the British team of Jon Jones, Tony Williams and John Hill. At a seasoned 49 years old, John Hill, the master from Cheltenham, also used his Burgess hull to win the FONDA trophy for that year. To understand what happened with the Formula One championship in 1984, and since, one must once again return to the Unlimited hydroplanes, to the water speed record, and to Gary Garbrecht. With characteristic ambition, Garbrecht had always felt that an outboard tunnel hull could beat the Unlimited aero-engined hydros "at their game". At the 1983 Miami Boat Show, this ex-Mercury race manager met up with his old enemy Charlie Strang of OMC. Strang inquired whether Garbrecht would like to set up an OMC hi-performance center like the one he had run at Mercury. A five-year contract was signed whereby Garbrecht would put four of the Johnson 425 hp V-8 outboard engines onto the back of 30-foot tunnel Unlimiteds renamed *USA Racing Team (U-19)*. The first boat was ready for the last race of the season, at Houston, Texas. With two of its motors turning clockwise and the other two anti-clockwise, *USA Racing Team*, driven by Jimbo McConnell, finished a stunning second overall, clocking speeds in excess of 150 mph. This boat, or a development of it, might well have been a winner in the 1984 season, but Garbrecht wisely decided to postpone his attack on the U-hydros. Investigating carefully, he had learned that there would be three new

USA Racing Team (U-19) with four Johson 425 hp V-8 outboards on its stern, giving it speeds of over 150 mph.

hydroplanes powered by Lycoming gas-turbine engines for the following season. Garbrecht's had also a new contract to build all the 3.5-litre V-8 motors for the 1984 season, a particular challenge in as much as Mercury had just decided to bring back a select number of their T4 outboards to try and undermine the OMC monopoly. With such forces back at work, combat could only develop in a lethal way. Nobody will ever deny that the 1984 Formula One season was both a futile and a tragic one. The futility related to the American Formula One scene and to whether Mercury would be allowed to use their updated 3.9-litre T4 engines against the OMC. Formula One circuit regulations specified that at least 50 engines of a given model must be manufactured and offered for sale in order to prevent special prototypes being supplied to a select few drivers. On June 7th, Mercury threatened legal action against OMC, the APBA and the Formula One Association, if the rules were not changed to allow their Mercury T4 engines to be raced, among others, by maestro Billy Seebold and his son Mike. On June 13, OMC went to the US Federal Court in Chicago and asked that the Court prohibit Mercury from inducing Mercury owners to boycott the Chattanooga race. One day later Mercury filed a legal suit in the Tennessee Court at Chattanooga against the APBA, Formula One and OMC to force admission of the T4 engines. Although the Court ruled that the race be run under special event rules, those at Mercury, in Chicago, and such APBA members as agreed with them, voted to run the race under UIM OZ Class rules, creating a breech of contract between the APBA and the US Formula One Association. But the Tennessee Court was very unhappy about this and issued orders that Messrs. Jordan, Hauenstein and Miller be arrested and put in jail for contempt of Court. Hauenstein and Miller were " put inside " for one day, before bail was paid and they regained their freedom. The Chattanooga race was held as a special event and Mercury T4 engines were excluded. Prior to the Sacramento race in early July there was more Court action, more lawsuits, more money out of the APBA pocket. Finally, after a settlement, the T4s were allowed to race at Cincinnati but were totally ineffective against the OMC V-8s. Ironically, the only time that the T4 was seen on the World Championship circuits was at the British Grand Prix in London, throttled by Billy Seebold, and even then, it was

Renato Molinari, Formula One maestro on yet another victory podium.

only able to gain him one heat. But by the time of this race, a tragic sequence of fatalities had taken place. There were four deaths in four months: Luigi Valdano, Gérard Barthelemy, Saverio Roberto, and in August, during the first heat of the Belgium Grand Prix, Tom Percival, the 41-year-old, English champion. Within days of Percival's death, Roger Jenkins announced his retirement from the sport, whilst 41-year-old Bob Spalding announced his decision to retire at the end of the season. Before August was over, Cees van der Velden, with team-mates, Arthur Mostert and Francois Salabert, announced the withdrawal of their team from the London Grand Prix. "All drivers accept an element of risk in the sport" Velden commented, "but the equipment we presently use gives us no margin for error, and it has resulted in four deaths in four months. It is more important to correct the safety problems than to continue to race". The only veteran who did not pull out immediately was Molinari, determined to place in both London and Milan and so log yet another, if hollow,

In over twenty years, Molinari had endlessly refined the design of the circuit cat to the point where, with this Martini-sponsored aluminium and carbon fibre cat, he was able to post regular speeds of 140 mph with such "king-size" engines.

In a backward-flipping accident the pilot became very vulnerable.

championship. The season over, the 39-year-old Italian, with 16 World and European titles scored over 19 years, finally hung up his helmet.

One of those particularly upset by Percival's death was his boatbuilder, Chris Hodges. During the winter of 1984/85, Hodges carefully studied many photographs of accidents where people had been maimed or killed. In many cases, the flimsy fibreglass seats were still in place when the wreckage was brought back in. From this Hodges deduced that it was easier to control the possibility of injuries inside a cell than try to cope with the limitless number of possibilities when drivers are thrown out. The next stage was to research the best materials to build such a safety cell and in this Hodges was assisted by the composites industry, the Motor Industry Research Association, the helicopter industry and the helmet manufacturers. With the further involvement of Cyanamid Fothergill, suppliers of composite materials to Ferrari and Lotus car racing teams, a prototype safety cell was constructed of carbon-fibre, Kevlar and Nomex honeycomb. In January 1985, a helicopter dropped a scientific dummy equipped with numerous accelerometers strapped aboard the prototype Hodges cell, at 115 mph from a low altitude to simulate a power boat crash. The injuries sustained by the dummy not only encouraged Hodges, but also Cees van der Velden, an eyewitness to the test. Indeed, the Dutch champion publicly announced that all his future crafts would be equipped with a safety cell. Two months later, to make the final test of his safety cell, Hodges had himself strapped into one which was fitted into a circuit powerboat donated for the purpose by Bedford Davie of Arizona. This was then lifted up by a crane and then dropped upside down into the water. The craft surfaced in 2.8 seconds adopting the attitude of a fishing float with Hedges some 2 ft clear of the surface. Hodges now waited to see how his safety cell would stand up to the rigours of Formula One racing. Pro-F1, a new sports agency, announced that they would be promoting a thirteen-race "Champion Spark Plugs World Championship", with Garry Garbrecht's providing the fuel-injected 3.5-litre V-8 OMC engines and engineering back-up throughout. Instead of three short heats, each race was to comprise a 30 to 50 laps around courses of approximately one mile in length. Despite his retirement, Hodges was persuaded by Pro-F1 to revive his team with Bob Spalding and Sweden's Bertil Wik as drivers. Whilst both drivers' boats had safety cells, so also did the Velden rigs of six other drivers, including Velden himself, Ben Robertson and Gene Thibodaux from the US. Indeed, with removable steering wheels and five-point safety harnesses, perhaps the most noticeable feature of the 19 catamarans was the way

For a long time, both wheel and dashboard of a Formula cat had remained very basic.

March 11th, 1985 – Chris Hodges played "guinea pig" by being strapped into his safety cockpit and dropped into the North Sea at Shotley, in order to test the flotation. Hodges came above water level in 2.8 seconds.

in which all that was now visible of the driver was his helmeted head ready to recoil like a tortoise in case of accident. And accidents there were, but they were no longer fatal. Had he not had a safety cell, Bertil Wik would have lost both his legs when his engine came away and his cat sliced open an aluminium rescue boat. Arthur Mostert would no longer be alive as his safety cell saved him during a double barrel-roll. Jimbo McConnell nose-dived in an old Molinari cat, without a safety cell, and was seriously injured. The only shadow cast on the potential of the safety cell concerned the 1985 Formula One champion, Bob Spalding. At Seville, Spain, with his Championship secured, his cat did a singularly undramatic barrel-roll and landed upside down. Because too much buoyancy from the fuel tank prevented the boat from righting itself, Spalding remained underwater for up to three minutes before a rescue team pulled him out unconscious. Unhurt, he decided never to race again. As for the 1985 FONDA series, with its less powerful 2-litre Mercury engines, 26 drivers from seven countries took part in races at Nassau and Miami, in South Africa, then at Hanover, Bristol, Lignano, Milan, London, Copenhagen and Paris. A 50-year-old John Hill showed the value of experience by skilfully handling his Burgess *Beefeater Gin*, with its streamlined Mercury cowling, to score a total 58 points and received the trophy for the second year running. At this stage, FONDA did not seem interested in the advantages of the safety cell. But, to understand what happened in 1986, it is necessary to look at the World unlimited outboard record and to one of the sport's longterm enthusiasts. In 1984, Bedford Davie, having been in and out of the sport for over half a century, decided that he would finance the development of a turbocharged outboard engine. A 2.4-litre Mercury was taken and twin-turbocharged to raise its horsepower from 430 up to 520 hp at 9,500 rpm. This was then clamped on the transom of a 19.5 ft three-point hydroplane built by Ed Karelsen, Seattle, to be test-driven by seasoned 49-year-old campaigner, Bob Hering. Following the 1984 season, Mercury chief engineer Jim Hauenstein had resigned, leaving a great deal of confusion between his department and the main engineering center. Unable to get any co-operation regarding assistance with the fuel flow adjustments on his " special ", the 72-year-old gentleman from Arizona almost called the whole project off when his hydro hit a turtle during a trial and virtually disintegrated, with no

The record-breaking team:
Les Cahoon,
Bob and Carla Hering,
Gary Garbrecht
and the inimitable
Bedford Davie.

injury to Hering. With the hydroplane rebuilt, Davie now took it down to Garbrecht's Second Effort team, where a fuel-injected 3.5-litre V-8 Evinrude, with custom-built gears, was fitted. The average to beat was still 157.424 mph. The vulnerable aluminium skeg on the V-8 gearcase was replaced with a stainless steel rudder, whilst the whole motor was fixed in a straight-ahead position. Propellers were machined out of a solid billet of steel by Boeing in Seattle and designed to spin at 8,800 rpm. "We spent about 60 hours of testing on Lake Hamilton before we were ready for the record attempt", Garbrecht recalls. "Following modifications with special gears and more propeller tuning, we had readings in the upper 170 mph on our radar." The official attempt took place on May 21st, 1986, at Parker, Arizona. Bob Hering was again in "the hot seat". His first two runs, with a prop speed of 8,800 rpm, were clocked by APBA at an average of 169.531 mph, a new OZ Class World Record. The prop was then changed and with rotation lowered to 8,600 a second two-way average of 165.338 mph was set up for the "Formula One" record. Sadly, Fred Jacoby who had raced so often with and against Davie did not live to hear the news of his buddy's new record, having passed on only the week before. As for Dean Draper of Detroit, who had prepared the Class X engine which enabled Davie to lift this same record to 78 mph back in 1937, he too died, but a month later. Pro-F1's initial plans for the season had been for five Grand Prix races in America and five in Europe with a stunning $150,000 prize purse per race, three times that of 1985. With such a lure, even FONDA drivers John Hill, Tony Williams, Jon Jones and Michael Werner were considering defecting to the 3.5-litre V-8 brigade. But as winter drew on, news filtered through that not only was Pro-F1 in financial difficulties, but that Charlie Strang, Chairman of the Board of OMC, was planning a drastic reduction of the number of races in Europe, and indeed, when the spring arrived, that number had dropped down to two, making the chances of sponsorship for teams such as Percival-Hodges Ltd virtually nil. In the end there were no European races at all. This however, did not affect those at Second Effort Performance Products who, with builder-driver John Nichols, had begun to build their own Formula One *SE* cats.

At first, Bedford Davie had intended to sponsor just one of these *SE* boats as a trial horse to test out and develop an engine for a faster record later in the year. Then team manager Ted Jones (no relation to the famous hydroplane designer)

Bob Hering lifts the world outboard to 169.5 mph in the 520 hp Evinrude-Karelsen Special.

told him that the way the prize money was distributed, Davie would come out better if he sponsored two boats. Then John Nichols offered him a third boat and additional sponsorship. Ultimately, Davie ended up as team owner of a four-boat squad with Ben Robertson, John Nichols, Art Kennedy and Gene Thibodaux. Never before had such glamorous prizes been presented for the outboard circus, once known as "the poor man's sport". Winning on both Saturday and Sunday races was drawing a cheque for $13,250 when getting first place at all seven race on both days made the prize some $592,750 plus a $10,000 bonus. Nor was an innovative approach entirely lacking. Cees van der Velden, seven-times World Champion and last of the old brigade, had developed a cat reminiscent of Bill Brown's aluminium Cosworth Carlsberg of two years before with bolt-on/bolt-off sponsons for smooth or choppy water conditions. Inside the central carbon-fibre safety cell hull, Velden had also engineered a hydraulic power steering system. As if taking on the entire Second Effort team was not enough, officials ruled that if the Dutch master's boat had qualified with one set of sponsons, it must race with the same set. Among those modifications tested out with Second Effort *SE* cats was an enclosed cockpit. There were also front sponsons of differing length to improve cornering; a sliding fuel tank which as it emptied moved in such a way as to maintain an optimum planing angle for the hull; a four-bladed propeller where two blades were shorter, which was particularly effective around choppy circuits. Without safety cell,s this could well have been a lethal season, but as it was, tens of thousands of spectators fully enjoyed themselves watching thrills and spills. At Beaumont, Texas, Gene Thibodaux won the Championship and grossed $62,000 in prize money. With two long straightaways and only two turns, the 1.5 mile course was exceptionally fast and Thibodaux averaged 122.29 mph for the 50-lap event. Team mate Ben Robertson of Charleston, South Carolina, set a new Formula One lap speed record of 141.33 mph, almost rivalling the turbine-powered *Miller American* and *Budweiser* hydroplanes. The final Grand Prix at Toledo, Ohio, was also memorable. Tom Henderson of Ontario, Canada, crashed first, but was unhurt. Then on lap 32 Barry Woods' *International Hobbies* cat hit a roller and nose-dived into the water at more than 130 mph. Wood's boat was completely destroyed on impact, but the Velden-type safety capsule and five-point harness saved the pilot, who suffered only minor cuts.

The arrival of the safety cell was certainly making an impact on outboard racing. During one race in Minneapolis, a boat took off at 135 mph, completed a loop in the air and re-entered the water backwards with such force that its remains became stuck in the bed of the Mississippi. The driver, safe in his capsule, escaped with a lump on the leg. 1986 was also the year that FONDA got wise to an innovation born in their rival camp, where some 25 drivers from nine nations went point-scoring in a series comprising Milan, Bristol, Augusta, Amsterdam, Hannover, Dramman, St. Louis, Casale, Paris, and even Singapore. The three heats had been replaced by time trials and one 30-minute Grand Prix. At first not every entry ran with a safety cell, but following Jorgen Askgaard's death at Bristol and Will Taylor's at Holme Pierrepont, FONDA boatbuilders Seebold, Molinari and Burgess announced their intention of bringing out their own version of the Hodges design. Indeed, by the Dramman Grand Prix in Norway, Molinari's safety cell had saved the life of one of his young drivers.

*Ben Robertson pioneers
the enclosed cockpit Formula
One cat. 1986. Despite lap
speeds of 141 mph, he had
far greater protection.*

Guido Cappellini, in his first FONDA season, spectacularly barrel-rolled at over 100 mph at the pit turn. Using a mercury-activated switch, his cell worked perfectly, automatically lifting the front of the boat and driver out of the water: Cappellini was unhurt.

Possibly the greatest achievement during the 1986 FONDA series was 29-year-old Mark Wilson's victory at Augusta, Georgia. Although Wilson sustained a superb driving technique, he was beaten to the FONDA Trophy by John Jones, with 55 points to his 34. As for the Harmsworth Trophy, heat one was held at the St Louis Grand Prix and in the 50-lap race around a 1.2-mile course in 90-degree temperatures. Mike Seebold fully lived up to the expectations of his thousands of local supporters by averaging a victorious 107.2 mph. When Mike Seebold won heat two at London's Royal Victoria Docks, the 86-year-old bronze plaque might once again have been shipped across the Atlantic Ocean, had not the most recent regulations forbidden the Seebolds from doing so. By December 1986, the safety cell approach originated by Chris Hodges and deliberately left unpatented had so far saved some 25 lives. Already given the 1985 "Bill Muncey Award", the 43-year-old co-founder of the now formidable Cougar concern was also presented with the "Silk Cut Nautical Award" for technical innovation in boat design. From now on it would be a question of refinement. The lethally "heroic" days appeared to be over.

For 1987, the FONDA series obtained sponsorship as the "Budweiser World Grand Prix Series" with races at Seville, Bristol, Augusta, Lignano, Dublin, London, Munich and Singapore. All of the total entrants were equipped with Mercury engines, all but one with safety cells, and some with wing mirrors. Guido Cappellini, 28-years old, from Lake Como, as Italian National Go-Karting Champion in 1982, had tackled his first race afloat, the 100 miles of

Lario, in 1983, following which he had graduated from Formula 3 to FONDA. During the next fifteen years, he was to equal the legendary Renato Molinari in his successes. But first he had to learn to win. At the Munich Grand Prix, Cappellini and Englishman Anthony Hiscock approached the put turn side-by-side, neither of them prepared to give way to the other. The inevitable happened and the boats collided. Hiscock somersaulted through the air over the top of Cappellini. Both were unhurt although out of the race.

The 1987 Championship hinged on the Singapore Grand Prix. Jon Jones was just 5 points behind veteran campaigner Bill Seebold. Seebold led the nineteen-strong field from start to finish, with Jones never more than 5 seconds behind. It would indeed be innaccurate to suggest that the French had not been enjoying the sport with their highly popular "Formula 3000", with its 850 cc limitation. Jeanneau was a yacht building factory at Les Herbiers, many kilometers from the nearest stretch of testwater. In 1985, Jeanneau employee and race driver Michel Rousse, persuaded his directors to start building build racing catamarans. A F3000 boat was built on the lines of the successful cats built by Cougar in England, but with a much higher tunnel. Its originality came from its 435 lbs hull weight achieved by construction in carbon and Kevlar, despite an initial ignorance of how it would resist during competition. At the start of the 1985 Rouen 24 Hours, Michel Rousse with French co-pilots Degus and Larue astonished the pack by establishing a 1 hour 30 min lead after only two hours' running. But then their Jeanneau composite, with its innovative integrated front headlights, suffered structural problems at its stern. Unable, through lack of knowhow, to make composite repairs in humid conditions, this potential victor had to be withdrawn. Once such pioneering structural problems had been solved, Michel Rousse became French Champion in 1985 and 1986. Having installed an airbag safety system to an already innovative hull, Rousse then

Four winners
of the FONDA Trophy:
John Hill,
Michael Werner,
Tony Williams
and Jon Jones.

teamed up with Englishman John Hill and Yves Degus to win the Rouen
marathon in 1987 and 1988. At the same time young Guido Cappellini went into
partnership with Attilio Donizelli to create the DAC boatyard at Comense
(Como), so filling the chair left vacant by the legendary Molinari brothers, who
were now branching off into offshore raceboat building and driving. The 1988
Budweiser World Grand Prix Series took place in Augusta, Bristol, Lignano,
Dublin, St Louis, Milan, Malaysia and Singapore. Two new builders were on the
scene for this season, Jeanneau and DAC but the well-tried triumvirate of
Burgess (UK), Seebold (USA) and Velden (Netherlands) continued to build for

November 1989: Bob Wartinger pilots Bud Davie's modified Karelsen, now powered by 600 horsepower, to a new world record of 176.556 mph at Parker, Arizona.

an ever-growing fleet of Mercury-engined hulls capable of lapping various 1.3 mile course at 88 mph, their four-blader "wheels" now turned at 9,600 rpm. For this year, the UIM rule that it was mandatory for all Formula One boats to be fitted with safety cells.

As Dave Burgess explained: "We no longer put in a safety cockpit as such with the exception of the running surfaces on the sponsons. The best part of a boat is built in Kevlar-carbonfiber composite so it is no longer a reinforced cockpit bolted to a wooden boat. Three-quarters of the boat is made of composite so the whole centre becomes a monocoque."

In 1988, Burgess built Jon Jones a circuit cat which was noticeably faster and Jones qualified on pole position every Grand Prix that year. Jones had to run propellers 1 inch bigger than normal. But this was before the mandatory weight limit of not less than 884 lbs was brought in. The 1988 championship winner was American, Chris Bush, a 28-year-old from St. Paul, Minnesota. Driving a Seebold rig, Bush also won the Duke of York's Trophy for the second time. For the 1989 FONDA series, David Parkinson of JBS Associates in London pushed wider and wider for venues including a Grand Prix at Minsk (USSR) and Budapest (Hungary), together with another nine races. The four Burgess cats of Kerton, Jones, Werner and Stoddard sported fully enclosed canopies, designed to initially deflect the shock-impact of water should the raceboat submarine at high speed. Jones explained: "I was involved in a horrendous accident in the Singapore Grand Prix when the boat did two somersaults in the air at high speed. The enclosed cockpit took the impact out of the water hitting my face. It definitely did its jobs and aids a little bit on the aerodynamic efficiency of the boat and it handles slightly better". Accident apart, the Welsh bank clerk won the '89 Championship ahead of Swedish driver, Peter Lindenberg. Seebold and his US compatriots did not turn up to Bristol as Budweiser announced their intention of concentrating their marketing in the States. More likely, Seebold, his son Mike, and Chris Bush wanted to take on the OMC-powered Formula One machines in their Mercury-supported craft.

Perhaps an example of a driver consistently saved by the "safety monocoque" cat was, again, 30-year-old Guido Cappellini. Known to be wreckless, pretty desperate to win for his DAC boatyard, he collided at Munich in 1987. In 1988 he crashed with Michael Werner at Bristol, then with Erkisson at Lignano. In 1989, his DAC hull ripped open after hitting debris at high speed on a qualifying heat at Bristol. Changing to boat n° 2, he had to leap for his life when that boat suddenly burst into flames while lying 2nd. At Minsk, Cappellini's boat exploded at a turn and ploughed into a barrel-roll, tearing off both sponsons. Without the safety monocoque, "Mr. Crashellini" would never have survived this sequence.

By 1990, OMC's Charlie Strang had decided to cancel the V-8 Formula One circuit. Instead, this veteran of the sport drew on his wealth of experience gained from setting up stock racing in previous decades, and put the money into developing and manufacturing stock racing versions of OMC's 2, 3 and 4 cylinder engines to grow "grassroots" tunnel boat racing in the US. This has turned out to be a very successful program. The "45 SS" Class, utilizing the aforementioned 2 cylinder engine is the largest class in APBA today. Even so, the "King Kong" outboard was not totally dead and buried. For three years, since setting the World speed record, financed by the irrepressible Bedford Davie, Gary Garbrecht's team had been working diligently to take their existing average up to the 200 mph. For their test pilot, they chose 44-years-old Bob Wartinger, a Boeing Aerospace and Electronics system engineer from Seattle. During a twenty-five year racing career with stock hydros, this quietly-spoken outboard veteran had been accumulating 100 outboard speed records - 47 of them UIM homologated. As for the boat, following aerodynamic and hydrodynamic studies made by Wartinger's colleagues at Boeing, Ed Karelsen modified Davie's boat with further streamlining and a cockpit canopy. Meanwhile, Second Effort

In the USA,
the Formula One
" Pro Tour" cats gave
American fans
and supporters all
the thrills and spills
they desired.

engineers Les Cahoon and Jack Romanovski had been searching out increased horsepower. The engine was fitted with twin injection, twin fuel ignition and by running on pure methanol with 8 % nitro-methane gave a phenomenal output of around 600 hp. As well as differing gear ratios and propellers, they had come up with a computer-controlled nitrous-oxide system which primed the engine for just 35 to 40 seconds without creating piston meltdown, and got the boat up to speed just before entering the time traps. A confident team arrived beside at Parker, Arizona, at the end of November 1989. But the weather was windy and unforgiving. On one trial, the boat had reached 140 mph when it rocked and bounced ripping off part of its transom and sinking. While its hull and engine were being reconditioned overnight, the level of the Colorado dropped an unannounced 2 ft. Next run out, Wartinger hit a pile of rocks, wrecking gearcase, best propeller and ripping the rudder off the transom. Despite further overnight repairs, an untested prop and side-winds saw six runs at a disappointing 170 mph. But on November 30th, Wartinger clocked 176.556 mph, a new world record.

As the sport entered the final decade of the 20th century, the outboard again became the wetnurse for an unusual boat design, hailing from Scandinavia and aimed to bring safer offshore racing. In 1990, Ocke Mannerfelt, a Swedish designer was faced with designing a boat to enable his fourteen-year son Ted to go racing. After testing a number of designs, Ocke came up with the ingenious idea of equipping his monohull bottom with "speed rails", longitudinal strips of aluminium which forced the spray downwards instead of allowing it to spurt outwards. Built in Kelvar and powered by a 25 hp Mercury, the prototype often reached 57 mph. But it proved dangerous on the turns. So Ocke next created two transverse steps in the hull, a design regularly used for flying boats half a century before. He also drew out swallow-like side-wings to improve lateral stability. In this guise, the 21 ft "B-22", built in Poland, not only won a Swedish Design Excellence Award, but with navigator Thomas Berglund, Ted drove a 90 hp Tohatsu engined B-22 to win the Swedish national championships in 1993 and then the world title in the

The Swedish alternative: Ocke Mannerfelt-designed Batboat B23 appeared to inject a new approach to outboard-engined offshore raceboats.

Following a boating escapade in the feature film *Batman Forever* that same year, the nickname "Batboat" seemed to catch on. Ted Mannerfelt, by now transport design student at Coventry University in the UK, next assisted his father in developing the overall design of a "B" hull of 28 ft. A "B-28", built by Båtbyggarna, a state-of-the-art boatyard on the Swedish west coast, and powered by two 200 hp Mercury outboards, enabled the British crew of Colin Stoneman, driver and navigator Mark Bridges to win the World Class III 4-litre Championship in Norway in 1995. In the hands of drivers from Sweden, Great Britain and other nationalities, "batboats" competing against catamarans, won five world championships in four years and fifteen national championships, their hullshapes under continual refinement by the Stockholm design team. During this period, Formula One racing had grown even more international. In 1990, through the efforts of David Parkinson, the series had been officially designated as "UIM Formula One World Powerboat Series" with races in Zolder, Bristol, Leningrad, Lignano, Budapest, Nottingham, Milan, Châlon, Penang and Singapore. Among 31 pilots representing 10 countries, Japan's Tadaaki Ishikawa and Akinori Konishi would race against Australia's Kay Marhsall and Craig Bailey. At the first race at Zolder, causing most interest in the pits was the Russian entry of hydroplane champion, Alexei Ichoutine. Created by a Leningrad design team, it had one sponson of a different design to the other and a further central undersurface. Sadly the Russian boat's deck holed at 100 mph forcing a huge fountain of water 30 ft into the air. Tragically, the Bristol Grand Prix, always a treacherous course, but usually attracting 200 to 250,000 spectators over two days, saw François Salabert of France crash with fatal injuries.

The composite boat hooked and veered off into the dock wall on the 4th lap. Salabert broke his neck before he ran into the other wall at the end of the dock, not the fault of the Jeanneau safety cell. Ironically during the same meeting,

François Salabert, France's most promising pilot for his generation, was killed at the 1990 Bristol Grand Prix.

Steve Kerton became the first driver to make a lap of the 1.8-mile circuit at 110.06 mph, beating the previous record of 98 mph set by Earl Bentz back in 1979. The 1990 series, on points, was won by veteran John Hill of England. The 1991 UIM Formula One series was scheduled at Como, Châlon, Dunaujvaros, Rotterdam, Milan, Penang and Singapore. Although two "classics" - Bristol and Paris - were no longer run, the pitch to which the circuit sport had developed was evidenced by presence of a staggering 500,000 spectators at the Dutch Grand Prix at Rotterdam, where Andrew Elliott, taking advantage of the lightweight Jeanneau composite hull, beat 29 drivers from 9 countries. The quality of performance was measured by the fact that during timed trials there were only 1.5 seconds between the first ten boats, for as one driver commented : "You only have to blink and you're halfway down the field." Contributing to such acceleration were the newly arrived 6 cylinder outboards, shipped over by Mercury. These were in fact 2.4-litre "bridgeport" units, sleeved down to the limit of 2-litre. Builders such as Burgess and Jeanneau had incorporated a water ballast tank up in the bows of their cat. Some of the courses were varying so much now that ballast was the only way to get the balance exactly right. Some were even considering the possibility of coming to each race with a roughwater and a smoothwater boat, depending on the finance available from their sponsor. In a Burgess hull originally built for the American Don Johnston, during the winter of 1990, Jon Jones had spent four to five days testing to prepare it for the 1991 season. At the Hungarian Grand Prix at Budapest, he showed what it could do by qualifying 15th and then pulling up from 15th to 3rd position in the first lap before he was "T-boned" by Cappellini on lap 2. Whilst Jones was rushed to hospital, "Crashellini" was unhurt. Having undergone a five-hour operation

where plates and pins were put in his leg, Jones was unable to race for three months. By late October, whilst undergoing hard physical training, the Welshman sent his new boat out to Penang. Some 21 boats with drivers from 10 countries, including the debut of Thai driver Sawasdee gathered along the pits with temperatures of 100°F. Timed practice sessions saw just 5 seconds separating the fastest and slowest drivers. A dislodged buoy and two lethal barrel-rolling boats meant two re-starts and with daylight running out, caused the cancellation of the Grand Prix with only 20 laps completed. Although Cappellini was declared the winner, Werner still led on points for the World Championship title. One week later, on November 10th, the circus had moved to Singapore. Great Britain's Steve Kerton led the 55 laps race from start to finish. Jon Jones came in 2nd and by gaining 6 points, beat Werner to the World Championship. Ironically, Jones had only competed in the first two races, won both and been out of action until the last race. Peter Lindenberg barrel-rolled at Penang, becoming trapped under a boat that would not right itself. He was rescued and taken to hospital. Hodges' original design was for a self-righting safety cell and not a "reinforced cork".

In 1992, with financial support from Castrol, the UIM F1 Powerboat Series began at Durban, South Africa - on Sunday March 15th, at a time of great political tension. Drivers from thirteen different countries validated Parkinson's concept of the show of 350 hp boats racing at 135 mph on tight courses, in city centres and resorts. At Durban, the 29-strong fleet included Jim Hauenstein's two-boat Arcadian Team from the USA and some 9 South African drivers including the irrepressible Peter Lindenberg. But victory went to Fabrizio Bocca in his DAC hull. With an itinerary marked out for Como, Châlon, Belgrade, Dunaujvaros, Stockholm, Rotterdam, Milan, Penang and Singapore, it was lucky that such venues as Berlin or Rio di Janeiro had not made it to the grid. The Como Grand Prix was won by Steve Kerton of England in a 140 mph Mercury-engined cat built by Mike Richards. Throughout the race he was hotly pursued by Tadaaki Ishikawa in his Mizuno-sponsored Seebold cat, although it was Jon Jones who came in 2nd. To the fury of the Italians fans, nine Italian drivers failed to make any impact on home waters. Newcomer Anders Anderson of Sweden won the French Grand Prix at Châlon-sur-Saone, perhaps because Kerton suffered a failed trim pump bracket, whilst Jones was stopped by a failed piston. Second came Fabrizio Bocca in his Mercury/DAC. Then, the Formula One event in Belgrade, Yugoslavia was cancelled due to the Serbo-Croatian conflict so the scene shifted to Dunaujvaros in Hungary, where Cappellini scored a victory. Englishman Phil Duggan's winning the Stockholm Grand Prix meant that a different driver had won every round of the 1992 Championship. Rotterdam was cancelled after practice due to high winds on the dockland circuit. Milan saw Kerton clinch his second victory, Bocca having retired with mechanical problems and Cappellini having flipped. Only 3 points now separated Bocca, Kerton and Hill from the Championship title. The Singapore Grand Prix at Penang was dominated by veteran builder-driver Bill Seebold. The Maestro appeared for the first time in the season and, in characteristic style led the 27-boat fleet from start to finish. By placing 2nd, Bocca was able to clinch the World Championship on points, just one point clear of Kerton. The F1 fleet then moved on immediately to Pattaya, Thailand for the first round of the 1993 World

Championship. This was held on December 13rd and won by Cappellini, who was to continue his winning ways through the whole season.

Taking a leaf out of the UIM Class I Offshore Championship, Parkinson was able to stage one of the 1993 races at Abu Dhabi, for the Middle East's first Formula One circuit race. There were 22 boats whose drivers represented 7 countries, gathering in the Emirate state to contest round 2 of the Championship. After a week of high winds, practice sessions placed Cappellini in pole position. Big local interest centred on the Puerto-Rican born US national and Dubai resident, Felix Serrales, one of the *Victory* team of offshore drivers. But Cappellini, who had brought with him his most technically sophisticated boat, featuring longitudinally mobile ballast, variable geometry hull configuration and telemetry, beat every team. Tragedy had marred the event with the death of 59-year-old British veteran John Hill. Michael Werner, who had lost Abu Dhabi by clipping a turn buoy, made up for it when he won on the Idroscalo in Milan, with Cappellini 2nd and Kerton 3rd. The race at Chalons, France, was won by Cappellini, then, Cardiff by Werner, Como by Werner again, Dunaujvaros by Cappellini, whilst the last race of the season was cancelled. Indeed Guido Cappellini became the 1993 World Champion against Werner, second.

Over in the USA, the American F1 championship was a walkover for the Seebold family : Bill coming first, with sons Mike and Tim finishing second and

The Anheuser-Busch brewery concern put its weight behind a variety of classes in powerboat racing, including circuit.

third in the series standings. Despite the truly global nature of circuit racing during the past five years, the main criticism of Parkinson's circus was that if was an all-Mercury show. Among those who disapproved of this was UIM President Ralph Fröhling, who believed that a return must be made to multi-brand racing.

After sixteen years devoted to the sport, David Parkinson was unable to sign again for 1994 with the UIM. The contract was awarded to Nicolo di San Germano's Lausanne-based Idea Marketing SA. He had been involved with OMC and Champion in F1 boat racing as far back as 1985. At first the FONDA drivers expressed their disquiet with the UIM's process of selection, complaining that the assessment of presentations was incomplete and the financial guarantees given by the successful bid were inadequate. In response, UIM President Fröhling convened a forum in Frankfurt in January where he proposed a Formula One Management Committee, in which he would have no personal role. The proposal was accepted. The only other issue was whether Malaysia, Thailand, Australia and New Zealand should break away to race Formula One for the Asia Pacific region. In the end, di San Germano made no major

Nicolo di San Germano took over management of the Formula One circuit series from David Parkinson.

*Guido Cappellini's DAC
factory workshop
near Como, Italy.*

changes, organizing race venues at Dunaujvaros, Porto Cervo, Chalon, Cardiff, Campione d'Italia, Sattahip in Thailand and Abu Dhabi. Perhaps through his hard experience, Guido Cappellini's DAC yard was advancing powerboat speed in its innovative catamarans. State of the art combination of wood, Kevlar and FRP composites, including the deformable sponsons and nose-cone, were manufactured from expanded polyurethane to absorb shock loading on impact.

The hull shapes had been modified for added speed, and extensive wind-tunnel testing resulted in a more air-cheating shape, aided by a fully enclosed cockpit with an aircraft-type canopy. Continuing problems of high interior temperatures and misting had been cured by the installation of lateral filtered air intakes and air conditioning. Cappellini and his partner, Attilio Donizelli, had built three new boats for the season. Guido took the Laserline Police Castrol livery, whilst the second went to Bocca under Rainbow Racing Colours and the third to the Japanese Sugihara with also Laserline colors. True to spectacular but safe form, Dunaujvaros saw twenty-five teams with only six boats finishing. At the Costa Smeralda race in Sardinia, with twenty-two boats, Cappellini performed a 360° barrel-roll, the boat landing the right way up and continuing

*Racing at Corfu in July
1996, Cappellini battles
with Werner
on the Mediterranean sea.*

to race on. Jon Jones beat the Italian. The French leg at Châlon saw a record thirty-one boats to contest for twenty places. It was again a demolition derby with three re-starts necessary and a staggering 10 out of 15 starters either damaged or destroyed. Again Jones beat Cappellini with Werner 3rd. It would have been fitting for Jones to win on home waters at Cardiff, but Werner won. Then, Cappellini won at Campione d'Italia on Lake Lugano. His victory pushed him ahead of Werner to lead the Championship points after five races. The race between Singapore and Malaysian peninsula welcomed 27 teams from 11 nations and witnessed the victory of intruder Mike Seebold. But it was still Cappellini who led Jones in the title-hunt with two races remaining. Indeed it was Guido from Como who clinched the 1994 World Championship with a points total of 108, followed by Jon Jones with 97 points and Michael Werner with 92 points. That experience counts was proven when "Maestro Bill" Seebold showed up in Thailand and walked away with victory. Felix Serrales, as might have been expected, climbed out of his Victory cockpit to win the race at Abu Dhabi, against 32 drivers from 10 nations. At the end of the season, di San Germano had proved that he might make a fitting successor to the Parkinson heritage. For the 1995 Championship, he had been assembled a hard core of 24 boats teams which raced and crashed in eight-venue worldwide circus, with the novelty of the Chinese Grand Prix in Hang Xhou, where China's first F1 driver, Peng Lin Woo came in at 13th place.

Maestro Cappellini at speed.

Time traps to better than 1/100th of a second and a red and yellow light system mounted on each and every steering wheel to warn drivers of hazards and stoppages were given extended trials. Whilst several drivers experimented with aerofoiling, there was universal condemnation of the regulation silencers. Michael Werner had wanted to win a final Championship before hanging up his helmet but Cappellini's ambition was to complete back-to-back titles. In this way the German and the Italian clocked up three wins each, so that the showdown was the Abu Dhabi race. Werner came 4th and even in 9th position, Guido fulfilled his ambition. Burgess won the Constructors Championship with a resounding 145 points. Over in the States, Gary Garbrecht, with associates Bill Seebold and Bob Gilman, purchased the North American F1 Championship known as the PROP Tour from Terry Phipps. Although at first there was a demand for 2-litre Mercurys, the V-6 2.5 unit gave better acceleration off the dock. Sponsored by Budweiser and Champion Spark Plugs among others, nine races were televised across the USA and Canada.

In Europe, the Monte-Carlo based UIM had been considering changing the Formula One 2-litre engine to bring back OMC with their 3-litre into the fray.

After Charlie Strang's retirement from OMC in January of 1990, one of his successors now made the decision to withdraw from racing. Strang was later

Being packed behind the leaders means a lot of wash.

instrumental in convincing him to at least keep racing going in Europe with Cees van der Velden building the 3 and 6 cylinder Evinrude/Johnson engines in Holland. The 1996's nine-race program took twelve competitive two-boat teams, representing 15 countries from Italy to Hungary, France, Greece, China and the United Arab Emirates. The use of a "pace-boat" and team uniforms further advanced di San Germano's choreographic philosophy close to top car racing. There was some fierce scrapping between Werner, Jones and Finland's Leppala, but for the 37-year-old Cappellini in the 16 ft *Laserline-Castrol/DAC*, 1996 season was almost a clean sweep, except ironically for the Italian G.P. on Lake Lugano where his Mercury suffered spark plug problems. The victory went to Jon Jones in a Burgess. To his four consecutive Championships, Guido also held the Formula One Class speed record of 138.13 mph. That season both Cappellini and Jones had benefitted from improved telemetric equipment on the circuits. Measurement of engine performance, prop performance, speed of acceleration and top speed meant that each boat could be "tailored" with greater precision for ever-changing water conditions over which it would be racing. Telemetry also revealed that coming into turn buoy at 135 mph, an F1 driver was subjected to forces up to 7.6 G. With the F1 flotilla muscling up for 1997, outsider Scott Gillman from Basalt, Colorado, arrived unexpectedly with an impressive record

Like car racing, team managers are in constant communication with both driver and pit crew.

Cappellini and team victorious yet again...

including US PROP Formula One Championships in 1990, 1995 and 1996. Gillman's yellow and black hull came from the Seebold yard. Although Jones, Roggiero and Werner had also changed from Burgess to Seebold hulls, Gillman's "secret weapon" was an Anderson-prepared Mercury engine. For some time, Ron Anderson, a high-tech engine tuner with workshops in Seattle and Melbourne, Australia, had progressively raised the horsepower of the 2-litre

Mercury from 270 to 360 hp by careful grinding of the ports. This meant top speeds of 135 mph and average speeds of 100 mph. "In the US, engines have an electronic chip limiting rotation speed, making the boats circuit within a few seconds of each other, whilst in Europe, there is a bigger variation in speeds and the lead boat can lap the last men eight or nine times in a race. This calls for a completely different driving technique which I am only beginning to learn" explained a quiet Gillman. But learn it he did. During the 1997 season, he clocked six consecutive pole positions at speeds above 113 mph, and by clinching five wins out of the nine starts took the Championship with 142 points, 34 points ahead of Finn Pertti Leppala, who finished a respectable runner-up via consistent placings. Cappellini and Jones had to content themselves with only two wins each, Jones was involved in four accidents, two of them in collision with Cappellini. The Championship was marred by the now rare event of a death. During the Mediterranean Grand Prix, South African driver Anton van Haarden performed double barrel-roll, his jammed canopy tragically preventing immediate extraction. Easy-access air supply valve system would then become mandatory.

The following year, sixteen two-boat teams having been whittled down to di San Germano's dozen were scheduled to compete in twelve rounds of the '98 Championship, taking in new circuits in Austria and Finland and bringing back Thailand. Whilst the winning Gillman and Bocca stayed together with *Rainbow Belco Avia*, Cappellini was joined by Massimo Roggiero for *Laserline* and Werner came back with Tadaaki Ishikawa's Mizuno backing. With John Player withdrawing sponsorship as quickly as they offered it, Jones found a teammate in UIM Formula 3 champion, the 37-year-old Hungarian Rudolf Mihaldinecz. By round 9, no driver an unapproachable advantage. Indeed it was by consistently clocking four seconds that Jones put up in second place. So yet again, the decider was the final Abu Dhabi Grand Prix. With engine failure forcing both Cappellini and Gillman to retire, Jon Jones nursed *Dragon* through to his first win of the season and the Championship in the bargain. Whilst the odd Japanese driver had competed in the UIM Formula, over in Japan, nationwide public gambling on the highly lucretive "Kyo-Tei" stock racing had continued to provide huge revenues for the state. Some 1,700 "jockeys", including 160 females, competed annually. The most victorious driver in 1998 was the 28-year-old Shigeru Matsui who won 209,310,000 yen in prize money.

But with only a 10 ft wooden hydroplane, powered by a stock 32 hp 400 cc Yamato outboard, speeds remain

The great rivals of the late 1990s, the American driver
Scott Gilman (Emirates Team) and Guido Cappellini (DAC Team)

To prepare for Kyo-Tei stock outboard racing in Japan, pilots must undergo fourteen months of training at Lake Motosu.

The cockpit of the new Belco Avia racing boat, like a fighter aircraft.

Kyo-Tei is run like horse racing with gambling. Winning drivers walk away with anything from 100-200 million yen.

in the 39 mph range, separating it from a sport where 300 hp composite cats were regularly clocking 120 mph. Where increased safety was concerned, following much experimental work with Cappellini and DAC yard, each 1999 cat must carry a UIM approved 200 lt. inflatable bag system positioned directly behind the cockpit for bringing an upturned hull back into an upright position within eleven seconds. Within five seconds of the upturning, a microswitch releases two hatch covers at the back of the boat which immediately fill with water and sink while at the same time an air bottle inflates the airbag to bring up the cockpit well clear of the water. Added to the safety cell, a Lexan reinforced screen, carbonfiber hull and collapsible picklefork, never has the outboard racing driver been so protected.

Jon Jones's fourth title now brought him level with Cappellini. With Burgess changing over from wood to composite boats for the final year of the millenium, a healthy duel seemed in the offing. In addition, di San Germano was projecting a 1999 season to include rounds in both Hong Kong and in the Malaysian capital of Kuala Lumpur. Among Cappellini's strategy for the new season was the laying-out on his test area of copies of the courses to be used in races. The first one, 50 laps in the tight confines of the Portimao harbour in Portugal, showed the runners and riders for the season. Of the ten competing boats, nine came from the DAC yard - the exception being Jon Jones in the all carbonfiber Burgess. Cappellini was now racing for Monaco, whilst American Scott Gillman was over again, racing for the Emirates UAE team. But not only did Cappellini win Portimao. The Italian continued his 20-point victories at Cagliari and Châlon where the French were even considering naming a street after him. But then Scott Gilman broke Cappellini's winning streak, perhaps because the Italian had brought along a shorter calmwater cat and race day at Istambul saw a

But for Kyo-Tei, with only a 3-metre wooden hydroplane, powered by a stock 32 hp 400 cc Yamato outboard, speeds remain in the 39 mph range (left) separating it from an international sport where 300 hp composite cats are regularly clocking 120 mph (above).

choppy and rainy Bosphorus Straits. With the Danube proving undrivable for the Vienna race and Hong Kong's Tai Po race already cancelled, Cappellini had done enough to take his fifth title but decided to notch up a fifth race victory in 1999 by winning the Emirates GP in Abu Dhabi, even though Frenchman Philippe Dessertenne had dominated for 35 laps before a gearbox failure robbed him of his maiden victory.

The year 2000 UIM series saw participation from no less then seventeen countries. With the capacity limitation increase, old rivals Mercury and OMC were back sparring together. Cappellini and his arch rival Scott Gillman used 2.5-litre Mercury units on their DAC hulls, whilst Jon Jones used a 3-litre OMC on his Burgess.

As it always had in the past, outboard powerboat racing coverage kept abreast with the latest technical developments. Nicolo di San Germano, UIM F1 promoter, signed an agreement with the California-based Loudeye.com to provide live web streaming for the races on the 2000 season via www.f1boat.com. The main technical challenge throughout the new season was to make a new fuel-injection system work reliably. Mercury had been testing with Cappellini pre-season, though the Italian kept some information to himself, so that by the Hungarian Grand Prix in mid-May, it looked as if the Italian

For the 1999 season, DAC introduced a new safety device – the airbag.

Gillman and Cappellini fight it out on the Neva at the 1999 Moscow Grand Prix.

Di San Germano in heated conversation with Jones, Mihaldinecz and Cappellini.

5-time World Champion was almost unstoppable, having led every lap of the first three races on his way to a perfect 60 points score. Then the rivalry resumed. Gillman won his first race of the year at the Grand Prix of Latvia. Cappellini won the French Grand Prix further increasing his lead to 80 points. But Gillman hit back by leading all the way on the 40-lap Grand Prix of the Mediterranean GP at Cagliari, Sardinia. Then to the surprise of all, Italy's new rising star, 25-year-old Francesco Cantando, won his first career victory at the Grand Prix of Poland. It looked as if Cappellini was heading for a sixth Championship, but at the Bulgarian Grand Prix, he lost his cool. The season had been blighted with some problems in timing the boats, too much for "Capo" to handle and even though there was no race in Bulgaria, the irate Italian put a hammer through the timing key pad, after disputing the time that gave him 2nd on the grid. Not even the invincible are untouchable. The UIM suspended him for 2 races, fined him $10,000 and forced him to reimburse the costs of the timing equipment. This now laid open the points opportunity to Gillman and to

Almost ready to hang up the old helmet. 58-year-old veteran Bill Seebold's last Championship was the 1997 "Prop Tour".

a lesser extent to the young Cantando. But despite being unable to race at Vienna and at the Emirates, Cappellini only re-emphasised his supremacy by producing the best DAC hull in memory, winning both the Turkish and the Italian races. Then, at the Emirates Grand Prix, Francesco Cantando won his second victory of the season. So on points the whole championship hinged on the outcome of the final race, held in mid-November in Abu Dhabi. Gillman had 130 points, the young Cantando 121 points and Cappellini 120 points. Although Capellini secured pole position with a lap of 99.32 mph around the 5-turn, 1.2 mile course and came second behind Cantando in the race, Gillman merely placing 3rd gave him 143 points, sufficient to clinch his second World Championship in 2000.

Over in the States, Bill Seebold had retired after the 1997 season, in which he had won his PROP Tour F1 championship which included a seventh St. Louis Grand Prix, so preventing '95 and '96 winner Scott Gillman from clinching a hat-trick. Seebold, 58 years old, had won more than 900 races and 69 world and national titles in a career spanning 46 years. This made him arguably the most successful outboard race driver of all time. The 1998 PROP Tour, as organized by Garbrecht's children Bart and Amy, with some paternal help, was won by Bill's younger son Tim Seebold, after some close racing against his older son, Mike-very much a family affair. For the 1999 PROP F1 Tour, sponsored by the Laughlin Visitors' Bureau of Las Vegas, Nevada, boats built by DAC, Seebold,

Hoffman, Grand Prix, Lee, and Kaniffs competed in eight US cities and received national weekend television coverage on ESPN2. The 1999 series was not won by a DAC-hulled boat, but by a Seebold. Tim Seebold's brilliant driving gave giving him back-to-back Formula One World Championships for 1998 and 1999.

For the following season, in 2000, the US series also had its own website named www.formulaoneprop.com. The series was closely fought between the Seebold brothers. Before the final race of the year, the Miracle Toyota Formula One Shootout, held in mid-October on Lake Eloise, Cypress Gardens, both Seebolds had won two race victories in the US Tour. Despite a hairy 130 mph crash, necessitating the use of duct tape to repair his boat, Mike won at an average 119 mph, placing just seven points ahead of his kid brother Tim, Todd Beckman of St. Louis, Missouri, coming third.

As the century of outboard racing came to a close, the sport seemed to be going in two opposite directions. Although those traditional sparring partners, Mercury in Formula 1 and OMC in Formula 3 having been kept safely apart for over a decade, the UIM announced that as of the year 2000, the Formula One limit would be increased to 3-litre. The reason was to revive multi-brand racing. Cees van der Velden who, since OMC had pulled out of factory support in 1995 had been the exclusive supplier of 850 cc OMC engines to the Formula3 fleet, had spent the winter of 1998/1999 testing three 360 hp V-6 3-litre engines. Although the power/weight ratio would be thrown out of balance, Velden considered the power increase justifiable as this would then "soup up" the 2.5-litre Mercury, currently in use for the American PROP Tour and maybe encourage Yamaha of Japan to enter the Formula 1 circus with their 2.99-litre engine, also destined for the PROP Tour. At the same time, it was becoming obvious that two-stroke engines of any capacity would have increasingly stricter environmental restrictions imposed on them. Reduced emission would become a vital requirement if the sport were to survive.

Back in 1997, at the gruelling Rouen 24 Hours marathon, Mercury Racing first introduced their "green" 3-litre 200 hp V-6 OptiMax unit. Working with the Australian firm Orbital, they had produced an engine with extremely low emission levels : hydrocarbons reduced by over 80 % and carbon monoxide by over 60 %. This was well below US Environmental Protection Agency requirements for the year 2006. This was done by directly forcing a precisely timed and measured more-air-than-fuel mix into each cylinder just before emission.

OptiMax was virtually smoke free at any speed because oil was not part of the air/fuel mixture. The OptiMax cats placed 4th and 5th, one came as co-driven by France's Didier Jousseaume, Britain's Andy Elliott and America's world outboard speed record holder Bob Wartinger, whilst the other as driven by Australia's Kay Marshall, the world's top Formula 1 women driver. By 1999, Mercury was presenting a range of four new OptiMax outboards from 135 to 225 hp. At the Rouen race, a 2.5-litre OptiMax 200XS powering a DAC hull placed 3rd as co-driven by Australian Kay Marshall, American Richard Hearn and Frenchman Amaury Jousseaume.

Again at the 2000 edition of the Rouen marathon, the factories' favorite test ground, first and second places were taken by entries with S2000 Mercury experimental engines on the sterns of DAC hulls. Inevitably, as Mercury now offers lowered-emission racing units, OMC and the Japanese manufacturers are also testing new concepts, leading to a multi-brand "greener" competition. But, perhaps, this will not be the only route for outboard racing in the next century.

A cleaner way ahead? The Mercury V-6 OptiMax outboard with its reduced emission levels.

Miss Nickel Eagle was the first electric boat to break a record officially recognised by a federation.
Her speed of 45.76 mph was homologated by the APBA in 1978.

A New Connection

At the very beginning, the world's first outboard was electric. Since then, first with the sparking plug, then with electric and then electronic ignition, the outboard has always needed some vital spark. But with increasing concerns for the environment a small and eccentric number of people have thought the impossible - that one future solution for the outboard sport would be to run again battery-electric motors. This initiative began with an inboard. In December 1988, Fiona, the 70-year-old Countess of Arran was persuaded by the author to make an attempt on the World electric water speed record. The original record of 45.76 mph for the Measured Kilometre had been set back in 1978 by the 14 ft *Miss Nickel Eagle*, powered by Eagler-Picher nickel-zinc batteries driving a 94 hp General Electric motor. Since this record had only been homologated by the APBA and not by the UIM, for the Arran attempt, a new record class was created but still retaining the requirement that the time elapsing between the two runs (including battery recharging) must not exceed 30 minutes.

Once again, her Ladyship's friend, designer Lorne Campbell, came up with a 15 ft three-point hydroplane, built in Kevlar and plywood and weighing only 210 lbs. The four, radial armature permanent neodymium magnet motors, designed, built and tested by Cedric Lynch, self-taught 33-year-old engineer would give a total 60 hp, whilst 12 swift-yield energy lead-acid jet aircraft starter batteries were provided by Hawker Energy Products.

Following 47 mph trials on the Welsh Harp lake, North London, Lady Arran towed *An Stradag* (Gaelic for "the spark") up to the Holme Pierrpont Watersports Centre, near Nottingham and on 22ⁿᵈ November, 1989, with a 30-knot wind gusting down the rowing course. Her Ladyship set up a two-way average of 50.825 mph. Between the two runs, a Benning Belatron traction charger replenished 80 % battery energy in just 12 minutes. With improved motors, additional batteries, finer-tuned propellers and streamlined cowling *An Stradag* could well have increased its own record to between 60 to 70 mph. But lack of sponsorship for this pioneer boat relegated it first to the National Motorboat

Piloted by the Countess of Arran, An Stradag broke the electric world record in 1989 with an average 50.825 mph.

A Prestolite forklift unit mounted on a Mercury "Speedmaster" outboard racing lower unit. Power output: 150 hp 144 volts/800 amps and 6,500 rpm.

Museum in Essex and then to the Lakeland Motor Museum in Cumbria. There were however many spin-offs. In particular, UIM Article 592 from the Sporting Commission proposed to accept electrically propelled boats as an International Series divided into two classes: battery-powered and solar-powered.

This proposal was voted in at the UIM General Assembly on March 17th, 1991, with 22 votes for and 5 abstentions. In July a contest was held on the River Po, Italy, to further establish rules for racing. In October 1991, Lady Arran challenged both Fabio Buzzi of Italy and Bob Nordskog of America to build powerboats that would break her two-year-old record. To-date these gentlemen appear to have been too busy to respond yet. The electric power boat challenge was however taken up in Washington state, USA. The original idea was to get the electric speed record back for the US. Led by veteran driver John Paramore, a small group of home-built electric car enthusiasts with Burton Gabriel, Fred Saxby, Don Crabtree and Dave Cloud joined forces with another longtime powerboat speedster, Norm Boddy. To get things going, Paramore obtained APBA permission to race electric boats head-to-head as an exhibition event at scheduled outboard races around their home state of Washington. For 1994, they chose five races sites and ran 8 two-mile sprint races from June to September. Even after running at speeds between 30 to 40 mph, the electric raceboats had power surplus at the end of each race. By the end of the series, they had publicly proved that electric powerboats could plane, corner buoys and tramp up to speeds of 50 mph. Finally, in the Kilometre Trials held on October 8th, 1994, at Lincoln City, Oregon, Norm Boddy of Edmonds, Washington, capped the season by setting a new world record, driving his runabout *Hardly Normal* to a speed of 55.913 mph. His motor was a 48-volt Prestolite forklift unit mounted on a Mercury "Speedmaster" outboard racing lower unit. His runs both ways were made without re-charging, though Boddy lost a little speed because he

came off the plane on the turnaround and was too close to the trap entrance to be at top speed on re-entry. The 1995 six-race season in Washington saw Norm Boddy competing in a 14 ft Blackwell hydro, the first powerboat custom-built for electric racing. Although Boddy easily won the National Drivers' Championship with speeds of 60 to 70 mph, it was Dave Mischke who lifted the World record. On October 14th, again at Devil's Lake, Mischke piloted the 144 volt 14 ft hydro designed and built by David Cloud of Seattle to a new 70.597 mph average. Energy came from twelve 12-volt Optima lead-acid batteries powering an outboard Prestolite 48-volt DC pump motor developing around

500 amps or 96.5 hp. For 1996, electric boat racing saw Steve Cloud duelling regularly with Brad Boddy in race after race, regularly achieving over 70 mph on the straights. Unfortunately during the past four years at the annual speed trials on Devil's Lake, none of the "boys from Washington" have been able to reach the elusive 80 mph. At the time of going to press (January 2001) there are two new attempts underway to lift the electric water speed record to 100 mph, one on each side of the Atlantic. After all, the electric Land Speed Record stands at 245.523 mph.

If we keep the idea of removable electric motors in mind, there are other options developing. For the past decade, solar-powered boat contests have been

Norm Boddy's 14ft carbon fibre hull was fitted with a wooden deck.

An electric raceboat photographed at full speed in 1997 on Capitol Lake, Washington State.

taking place on select lakes around the world. One such contest has been on Lake Hamana in the Shizuoka prefecture of Japan. In 1997 sixteen boats took part and in the 200m sprint contest, the winning boat, a solar-powered hydrofoil was clocked at 19.95 seconds, equivalent to 22.4 mph.

In Milwaukee, Wisconsin, some 18 American university teams have come together to vie for the fastest time over the 300-metres sprint during the Solar Splash event. The fastest speed so far – 25.4 mph - was established by the University of Michigan entry *Vee-N-Verse II.*

These are, of course, very modest speeds – rather like those obtained by gas outboards back in the mid 1920s. But from small acorns greater oaks can grow. The regular appearance of growing fleets of electric outboard raceboats – 2nd or 3rd generation developments of these Japanese and American hydrofoils but with the addition of easily removable fuel cell motors - would certainly be welcomed by a world becoming increasingly disenchanted by noise and pollution and ever more concerned about the environment. After all, the sport of the detachable marine motor must go on.

Transformation of an 8ft Karelsen hydro into an electric raceboat. This boat holds the speed record in the 48 volt Class at 30.96 mph.

*The Japanese solar-electric
hydrofoil GoldenEagle II
was developed by a team
lead by Hirofumi Wada
at the Kanazawa Institute
of Technology
in Ishikawa, Japan.*

*Golden Eagle II's control
cockpit and energy-yielding
solar panels moulded
to the deck curvature.*

*One of the American
entries enjoying top sprint
speed during the Solar
Splash contest
at Milwaukee, Wisconsin.*

*Sponsored by the Roland
Company, Soland silently
foils at sprint speed across
Lake Hamana.*

227

Appendix

WORLD OUTBOARD SPEED RECORDS

Date	km/h	mph	Driver
29/09/1928	67.19	41.75	Eldon Travis
xx/xx/1929	76.19	47.32	H.G.Ferguson
xx/xx/1929	77.30	48.00	Passarin
xx/xx/1929	77.89	48.37	H.G.Ferguson
xx/xx/1929	79.63	49.45	H.G.Ferguson
28/07/1930	80.01	49.72	Ray Pregenzer
19/10/1930	81.61	50.77	Aldo Dacco
xx/xx/1930	83.12	51.60	Ray Pregenzer
20/12/1930	83.65	51.98	C.H.Harrison
05/04/1931	84.66	52.64	Aldo Dacco
xx/xx/1931	85.31	52.98	Dick Neal
17/06/1931	87.20	54.00	Aldo Dacc
03/10/1931	89.16	55.37	Dick Neal
19/12/1931	89.42	55.56	C.H.Harrison
17/10/1931	91.23	56.71	Tom Estlick
16/07/1932	95.69	59.47	Soriano
18/10/1934	104.95	65.21	Jean Dupuy
11/07/1936	119.71	74.39	Jean Dupuy
16/10/1936	125.11	77.75	E.T.B.Davie
17/10/1937	125.69	78.12	E.T.B.Davie
20/05/1939	127.18	79.04	Jean Dupuy
26/09/1953	134.34	83.47	Leto di Priolo
07/06/1958	173.64	107.82	Hu Entrop
03/05/1960	184.51	114.65	Hu Entrop
05/05/1960	185.92	115.54	Burt Ross
06/09/1960	197.92	122.98	Hu Entrop
07/03/1966	210.90	131.05	Gerry E Walin
08/08/1973	219.48	136.38	James F Merten
14/10/1981	222.02	137.96	Tony Williams
11/10/1982	224.71	139.66	Bob Spalding
10/10/1983	232.00	144.16	Rick Frost
21/05/1986	272.78	69.53	Bob Hering
30/11/1989	284.10	176.56	Bob Wartinger

OUTBOARD (UNLIMITED)

Boat	Engine	Country	Location
Spirit of Peoria	Elto Quad	USA	Peoria
Blue Streak	Johnson	USA	
	Laros	Italy	
Blue Streak	Johnson	USA	
Spirit of Peoria	Johnson	USA	Peoria
	Elto	USA	
Mariella IV	Laros	Italy	Lac de Garde
	Elto	USA	
Non Sequitur III	Elto	GB	River Medina
	Laros	Italy	Lac de Garde
	Johnson	USA	
Folgore 'F39'	Laros	Italie	Lac de Garde
	Johnson	USA	
Non Sequitur X	Elto	GB	River Medina
	Johnson	USA	California
'F-54'	Soriano	France	Maisons Laffitte
	Dupuy	France	La Seine
'Y'	Dupuy	France	La Seine
Jacoby	Draper	USA	Green Pond, NJ
Jacoby	Draper	USA	Green Pond, NJ
Jacoby	Dupuy-Soriano	France	La Seine
Massimo	Soriano/Lesco	Italy	Idroscalo (Milano)
'RX-3'	Mercury	USA	Lake Washington
Starflite Too	Evinrude	USA	Lake Havasu
RX17X	Mercury	USA	Lake Washington
Starflite III	Evinrude	USA	Lake Havasu
Starflite IV	Evinrude	USA	Lake Havasu
Twistercraft II	Mercury	USA	Fox River, Wisconsin
	Mercury	GB	Lake Windermere
JPS Special	Johnson	GB	Lake Windermere
	Johnson	GB	Lake Windermere
Karelson/SE	Evinrude	USA	Parker Dam
Bud	Evinrude	USA	Parker Dam

229

SHORT CHRONOLOGY OF OUTBOARD DEVELOPMENT

1896	American motor company	1st production petrol single cylinder	1-2 hp
1899	« Lautonautile »	1st inboard-outboard	1,75 hp
1907	Trouché - Motogodille	1st alternate-firing twin	8 hp
1912	Archimedes BS" (Sweden)	1st opposed firing twin	2.5 hp
1913	Lutetia (France)	1st underwater exhaust	
1914	Evinrude	1st flywheel magneto	5 hp
1915	Caille	1st self-winding starter rope	
1921	Elto	1st overall alloy housing	2.5 hp
1922	Johnson « Light Twin »	1st lightweight motor	
1922	Johnson « Light Twin »	1st anti-cavitation plate	
1925	Johnson « Big Twin »	1st use of die castings	6 hp
1927	Johnson/Evinrude	1st use of roller and anti-friction bearings	
1928	Elto « Quad »	1st four-cylinder motor	17 hp<50hp+
1928	Cross	1st radial 5-cylinder motor	30 hp
1929	Johnson Sea Horse	1st rotary valve	32 hp
1930	Evinrude/Elto/Johnson	1st electric starting with generator	
1930	Evinrude-Elto Speedibee	1st rotary valve (crankshaft)	25 hp
1937	Dupuy-Soriano (France)	1st 6-cylinder (opposed banks of three) supercharged 4-cycle	80<110 hp
1957	Mercury Mark 75	1st 6-cylinder in line	60 hp
1958	Evinrude/Johnson	1st V-4	75 hp
1961	Mercury (white livery)		80 hp
1964	Mercury Black Widow	1st 100 hp production outboard	100 hp
1965	Evinrude Starflite		100 hp
1967	Evinrude/Mercury/Johnson	1st all electronic-type ignition	110 hp
1968	Mercury		125 hp
1971	Mercury Twister		140 hp
1972	Johnson Stinger		125 hp
1973	OMC	1st Wankel rotary turbo	300 hp
1975	Mercury Black Max	V-6 cylinder, loop-charged	230 hp
1977	Johnson	V-6 cylinder motor	235 hp
1978	Johnson	V-6 cylinder motor	240 hp
1979	Mercury Twister T4		370 hp
1980	Mercury Twister T4		400 hp
1980	OMC King Kong	1st 3.5-litre V-8	400 hp
1995	Prestolite	electric racing outboard engine	96,5 hp
1997	Mercury OptiMax	reduced-emission V-6 racing outboard	200 hp

World champions
Formula 1, 1999

WORLD CHAMPIONS

CLASS OZ-Unlimited		
1969	Cesare Scotti	Italy
1970	Bill Sirois	USA
1971	Bill Sirois	USA
1972	Johnny Sanders	USA
1973		
1974	Bob Hering	USA
1975	Billy Seebold	USA
1976	Reggie Fountain	USA
1977	Earl Bentz	USA
1978	Tom Percival	Great Britain
1979	Bob Spalding	Great Britain
1980	Bob Spalding	Great Britain

FONDA (2-litre)		
1981	Tony Williams	Great Britain
1982	Michael Werner	Germany

FORMULA GP		
1983	Michael Werner	Germany
1984	John Hill	Great Britain
1985	John Hill	Great Britain
1986	Jon Jones	Great Britain
1987	Bill Seebold	USA
1988	Chris Bush	USA
1989	Jon Jones	Great Britain

FORMULA 1		
1981	Renato Molinari	Italy
1982	Roger Jenkins	Great Britain
1983	Renato Molinari	Italy
1984	Renato Molinari	Italy
1985	Bob Spalding	Great Britain
1986	Gene Thibodaux	USA
1987		
1988		
1989		
1990	John Hill	Great Britain
1991	Jon Jones	Great Britain
1992	Fabrizio Bocca	Italy
1993	Guido Cappellini	Italy
1994	Guido Cappellini	Italy
1995	Guido Cappellini	Italy
1996	Guido Cappellini	Italy
1997	Scott Gillman	USA
1998	Jon Jones	Great Britain
1999	Guido Cappellini	Italy

CLASS ON/0.2000 (2-litre)		
1970	Renato Molinari	Italy
1971	Renato Molinari	Italy
1972	Cees Van de Velden	Holland
1973	Renato Molinari	Italy
1974	Cees Van de Velden	Holland
1975	Cees Van de Velden	Holland
1976	Renato Molinari	Italy
1977	Billy Seebold	USA
1978	Erwin Zimmerman	Germany
1979	Cees Van de Velden	Holland
1980	Renato Molinari	Italy
1981	Billy Seebold	USA
1982	Michael Werner	Germany
1983	Michael Werner	Germany

PARIS SIX HOURS : RESULTS

Date	Driver/co-driver	Nationality	Class	mph
1955	Guyard	France	585 sport	175.20
1956	Desfilles	France	585 util.	177.88
1957	Brunet	France	R.02 sport	227.49
1958	Caldéac/Bonnet	France	C1 util.	213.57
1959	Million, R.	France	R.02 sport	219.25
1960	Kirié/Viry	France	XU 1.200	245.42
1961	Colombé/Fauré	France	XU	244.00
1962	De Biasi/Prat	Morocco	XC	264.25
1963	Melly/Merryfield	Great britain	XT	276.71
1964	Melly/Merryfield	Great britain	XC	281.91
1965	Guyard/Monier	France	R.1	286.21
1966	Molinari/Scotti	Italy	ON	293.49
1967	Rasini/Rasini	Italy	ON	328.01
1968	Léonardi/Molinari	Italy	ON	381.50
1969	Molinari/Pellolio	Italy	ON	405.86
1970	Sanders/Posey	USA	ON	438.67
1971	Pellolio/Donard	Italy/USA	ON	464.24
1972	Molinari/Hering	Italy/USA	ON	523.02
1973	Sanders/Schumacher	USA	ON	455.15
1974	Van der Velden/Seebold	Holland/USA	ON	382.85
1975	Jouseaume/Jousseaume	France	ON	458.61
1976	Percival/Spalding	Great britain	OZ	513.98
1977	Percival/Spalding	Great britain	OZ	505.34
1978	Spalding/Seebold	GB/USA	OZ	546.24
1979	Van de Velden/Posey	Holland/USA	OZ	542.57
1980	Spalding/Stevenson	GB/USA	OZ	522.68
1981	Inward/Cripps	Great britain	..	
1982	Werner	Germany	ON	
1983	Hill/Williams	Great britain	..	501.55
1984	Hill/Williams	Great britain	..	524.55
1985	Wilson/Kerton	Great britain	..	

FORMULA 3 EUROPEAN CHAMPIONS

CLASS OZ-Unlimited		
1981	Lasse Strom	Sweden
1982	Rick Frost	Great Britain
1983	Fabrizio Bocca	Italy
1984	Andy Elliott	Great Britain
1985	Lennart Strom	Sweden
1986	Lennart Strom	Sweden
1987	Piergiorgio Chiappa	Italy
1988	Lennart Strom	Sweden
1989	Andy Elliott	Great Britain

1990	Lennart Strom	Sweden
1991	Danny Bertels	Belgium
1992	Danny Bertels	Belgium
1993	Danny Bertels	Belgium
1994	Rudolf Mihaldinecz	Hungary
1995	Ian Andrews	Great Britain
1996	Rudolf Mihaldinecz	Hungary
1997	Steve Hill	Great Britain
1998	Ken McCrorie	Great Britain
1999	Peter Sandor	Hungary

PARKER ENDURO RACE

From 1946, powerboat racing on Parker's Lake, Moovalya in Arizona had been dominated by V-8 auto-engined inboards. 1970 was the first time that outboards took 1st, 2nd and 3rd places. The following year, Paris Six Hour victors Sanders and Posey won Parker. Again in 1974, Paris winners Seebold and van der Velden won Parker. The only time when the outboard domination was broken was in 1985 by Mitch Lembke in a Jaguar ET hull. In 1982 the race was shortened from 9 hours to 7 hours in deference to the energy crisis. In 1991 in was further reduced to 3. Between 1994 and 1997, it was a 500 km race. In 1998 and 1999, there have been two two-hour races over one weekend.

WINNERS

1963	Tom Davis
1964	Mike Wallace
1965	Bob Nordskog
1966	Mike Wallace
1967	Lou Brummett
1968	Lou Brummett
1969	H McCormick
1970	Allan Stinson & Gerry Walin (OMC/deSilva rig)
1971	Johnnie Sanders/Tom Posey
1972	Jimbo McConnel/Ted May
1973	Denis and Duane Berghauer
1974	Bill Seebold Jr /Cees van de Velden
1975	Renato Molinari/Bob Hering
1976	Geoff Briggs/Bob Larson
1977	Renato Molinari/Bob Hering
1978	Ron Hill
1979	No Enduro
1980	Bob Spalding
1981	Johnnie Sanders

Year	Winner
1982	No Enduro
1983	No Enduro
1984	Jimbo McConnell
1985	Mitch Lembke
1986	Dick Sherrer
1987	Don Johnston/ Johnnie Sanders
1988	Don Johnston/Johnnie Saunders
1989	Scott Gillman
1990	Francois Salabert, Michel Rousse, Don Johnston
1991	No Enduro
1992	No Enduro
1993	No Enduro
1994	Greg Foster
1995	Jason Campbell
1996	Todd Bowden
1997	Todd Bowden
1998	Todd Bowden
1999	Todd Bowden/Tracy Hawkins/John Schubert

Index

Photo Credits